Pd 10¢ at garage sale at 824 S. McClelland, SLMA
17 March 1990

ONLY IN SAN FRANCISCO

ONLY
IN
SAN
FRANCISCO

BY HERB CAEN

Doubleday & Company, Inc., Garden City, N.Y.
1960

TYPOGRAPHY BY SUSAN SIEN

Library of Congress Catalog Card Number 60–15169
Copyright © 1960 by Herb Caen
All Rights Reserved
Printed in the United States of America
First Edition

CHAPTERS

6

PREFACE

"Only in San Francisco . . ."

In twenty-two years of writing a column about the city I have used that phrase perhaps more than any other.

"It could only happen in San Francisco." Is it pure conceit to think there is something so unique about the city that its day-to-day adventures could happen nowhere else?

I think not. Surely there is a special quality to the city, elusive as a streamer of fog lying lightly on Twin Peaks, romantic as the muffled moan of a foghorn somewhere in the misty Bay, insistent as the pounding of the waves under the windows of the Cliff House.

It is a quality built, as some insist, on legends and fables—and yet the incredible bridges are there for all to see. San Franciscans are no longer quite so sure where the magic can be found, other critics say—but there is still the patter of invisible feet along the dark alleys of Chinatown on a moonless midnight. The city of today is not The City That Was, complain the disenchanted—but Golden Gate Park still marches, green and unchecked, from yesterday's bay windows to the Pacific shores.

"Only in San Francisco . . ."

But, you protest, New York has skyscrapers, Pittsburgh has hills, Rio has a harbor, Sydney has bridges.

True. But where else do you find them all jumbled together with such artless charm: wooden shacks nestling against gleaming apartment houses, a financial district dissolving suddenly into Bohemia, freighters inching along at the bottom of your own private hill, so near you can hear the captain's commands. All this (and more) within a few square miles, in a city so small and personal you can almost cup it in your hands and hold it to your heart.

But the people, you say. Surely people are people everywhere —no different in Keokuk or Kankakee from those in San Francisco.

Perhaps, perhaps not. Walk a few blocks in any direction and see the San Franciscans in action, in action uniquely San Franciscan: the cable-car gripman pulling heroically on his lever, the Chinatown market owner chasing a squawking white duck along Grant Avenue, the old Italian gentlemen arguing under their wide-brimmed hats on their North Beach corners, the beatniks in their bearded trances, Harry Bridges' longshoremen cocky in their white caps, a banker's limousine rolling down an alley alongside the City Morgue and pulling up at an excellent restaurant across the way—all this (and more) in the space of a fifteen-minute stroll.

Oh, the cable cars, you shrug. Now the San Franciscan is pulling in a ringer—a bell ringer, as it were. All right, so nobody else around the country has cable cars, and who wants them: outmoded, dinky, slotted anachronisms. But there you are wrong, friend. The cable cars are part of life in San Francisco, woven to its core with steel strands.

Everybody rides them, if he can get a toehold, for much that is unique about the city happens aboard them. I recall a typical incident:

An elderly tourist couple boarded a Powell car, and the man became fascinated immediately. "Can I ring the bell?" he asked the gripman eagerly. The gripman nodded with a smile, whereupon the oldster grabbed the cord and rang the gong furiously for two blocks.

All the while, however, his frozen-faced wife was grabbing at his coattails, snapping: "George, sit down—George, you're making a scene—George, this is ridiculous—GEORGE!"

At last the gripman had had enough. Leaning over to her, he announced to the delight of the onlookers, "Madam, I don't know where you're from, but in San Francisco, it's against the law for a wife to bother her husband while he's ringing a cable-car bell!"

And another incident, likewise typical:

One morning the California Street line was shut down for the day so a new cable could be installed. Not all the customers knew what had happened, of course—and shortly after 8 A.M., they were standing as usual on the street corners, waiting watchfully for Old 8:02.

Old 8:02 didn't come along. But its gripman, Clarence E. Davis, did—in his own car. He drove along California, calling out to his passengers: "Pile in. Wouldn't want you to be late for work." The fare: nothing.

Only in San Francisco?

Where else, indeed.

Herb Caen
San Francisco
February 1960.

1. IN SEARCH OF A CITY

My assignment: To write about San Francisco and San Franciscans. My deadline: Now and tomorrow and all the tomorrows. My problem: To find the city and its people . . .

But there are so many San Franciscos, so many San Franciscans. So you walk and you talk, you look and listen, and the truth goes on dancing brightly—just beyond reach. Where does the pulse of the city beat most strongly? The clichés flood into your mind, making their familiar patterns: the Powell Street wooden merry-go-round (and the brass ring of the cable bell), Siciliano fishing boats bobbing like corks in the debris-laden waters of the Wharf, the sailboat (white and fluffy) against Alcatraz (dark and craggy), Coit Tower all golden and perfect at sunset, looking like the last time I saw Parrish (Maxfield). The picture-postcard San Francisco, dream city of a million tourists, and, strangely and wonderfully, of close to a million residents.

A million people, a million San Franciscans—where do you find the prototype? The well-worn shell-thin adjectives come to mind easily enough: sophisticated, urbane, worldly. The fashionably emaciated woman in the $500 Little Black Suit That Will Go Anywhere, with the slim legs and the even tan and

the corner booth at El Prado (and a laugh that sounds sus-
piciously neurotic). The Montgomery Street gentleman in the
Homburg, with a *pied-à-terre* on Nob Hill, a house down the
Peninsula, another at Tahoe, heading for lunch at Jack's (his
eyes are tired, and they sneer). Mr. and Mrs. San Francisco,
stepping right out of the four-color magazine ads, the real thing,
the genuine article. And they've been around—everywhere, except their own city.

You walk along Market Street and look at the San Franciscans on parade, piling into busses, bumping into each other,
crowding off the curbs, darting across the intersections like
water bugs on a pond. Stout, perspiring housewives, wispy of
hair and panting of breath, in cloth coats that are too short, too
long, too thin. Tough young boys, all leather jacket and grease,
slouching along, hands defiant in tight pockets. Schoolgirls four
abreast in a sweatery cloud of giggles, swimming like bait in
front of a pack of sailors. The lame, the halt, the blind, and the
man giving away Bible quotations, softly murmuring, "Bless
you" each time a passer-by shoulders him aside. These are San
Franciscans too busy to look up at Twin Peaks in all its green
glory and the Ferry Building in its Freeway-hidden shame, too
involved in their own struggles to have heard of El Prado (is
it a movie?) or Jack's (a bar, maybe?).

The city—everywhere and nowhere, to each his own, to each
his zone. The neon fable of Chinatown (clatter of chopsticks
and clink of glass), and down the dark alleys and up the dark
stairs, the tenements and the bare wooden floors, the communal
bathrooms and the sweatshops (but the children: fresh-faced as
flowers after a rain). The garlicky gregariousness of North
Beach (the pizza, the dago red, whaddya know-a Joe), and at
midnight the old men, gray under their wide-brimmed anonymous hats, alone in the corners of Mike's pool hall and the

old women looking down from the open windows in their tiny flats (but tomorrow they will meet in Washington Square to talk of the good days in Lucca). You don't get the picture, all you people. Why aren't you at Kan's and the Ricksha, at New Joe's and Vanessi's and Sorrento? Acting like real San Franciscans.

The San Franciscans—who are they, and where? The mayor nibbling on French bread at lunch, waving his expressive hands, talking about his boyhood struggles—he's one. So is the little Negro boy playing in the rubble of the razed Western Addition, looking around carefully, picking up a rock, heaving it through the window of a dead mansion. Assessor Russ Wolden and his handsome wife rolling along California Street at midnight in their sleek convertible—they're San Franciscans. So is the young Marina housewife pushing her baby carriage along Chestnut Street, looking for bargains in the neighborhood grocery (certainly she knows about the Junior League—when her little boy is old enough to play baseball, maybe he'll be in it). Commodore Dan London, dapper in his yachting outfit, bounding up the stone steps of his St. Francis Hotel—he's a San Franciscan. So is Monk Fowler, the ex-fighter who peddles papers at Fifth and Mission. So is Horace Stoneham, backing his Cadillac convertible out of his Telegraph Hill apartment. So is the newcomer washing his car (with the Texas license plates) in front of the house he just bought in the Sunset District; he never heard of Ben Swig or Louis Lurie, but he's a San Franciscan all the same.

San Francisco: all things to all people. Sunday brunch at the Lochinvar, or a hot dog at the beach. Standing in line for a midnight movie at the Fox, or standing in line for an elevator to Top o' the Mark. Irish coffee at the Buena Vista, a beer at

Laurel Lodge, or a sunbath on the Marina Green. A cold wind ruffling the wash on the line in the old back yards of Hayes Valley, a cold martini served by a butler in a Pacific Heights mansion, coffee getting cold on a mahogany desk in a Russ Building office. Pigeons in the square, squirrels in the park, queer ducks in the bushes, and a white swan to feed at the Palace of Fine Arts—little bits of a big city, impossible to glue together.

San Francisco, yours and mine, nobody's and everybody's— always moving away just as you reach out to touch it.

2. MR. SAN FRANCISCO

He is so sharply aware of his own city that he wonders, in constant flustration, whether it's true that "San Francisco isn't what it used to be," and if the old town was really as great as the historians would have him believe; and if it isn't as good now, is it HIS fault . . . ? Among his recurrent nightmares: he is driving up Powell behind a cable car and it starts to slide back on him; he is driving off the Bay Bridge on a down ramp, and a speeding car suddenly roars up the ramp; he is barred for life from Trader Vic's; he is walking across the Gate Bridge and is suddenly seized with an irresistible urge . . . He is given to bad jokes about the opera (but goes once, out of deference to the tails he bought fifteen years ago), he hates cocktail parties (but goes often, to keep his hate alive), and he is contemptuous of the beatniks (because in his era at the Black Cat and Izzy's all the bohemians were fired up about something every minute, and once in a drunken moment he even volunteered

for the Abraham Lincoln Brigade; sober, he changed his mind)
. . . A la Fred Allen he sometimes croaks, "There are more
bores around than when I was a boy"—and he even allows himself to concede that perhaps he's become one of them.

He still gets off his conditioned-reflex gripes about Los
Angeles, but when he's down there (which is quite often, oddly)
he dines surpassingly at Chasen's, Scandia, La Rue, and
Perionos's and admits, *sotto voce*, "They're coming along, coming along. Not bad at all" . . . He accepts without question
that his city is "the cultural capital of the West," but don't ask
him to name our leading artists, musicians, and writers; lemme
see now, there's—uh-hm, waitaminit now . . . And, as a matter
of fact, don't expect him to identify the eleven members of the
Board of Supervisors—or is it nine, or maybe thirteen? But he
knows every bar in the financial district where you can pick up
a pretty girl, and he is cozier with the bartenders than he is
with most of his wife's relatives.

Every time he drives through the teeming Sunset District
he sighs heavily to his wife: "Why, I remember when this was
nothing but sand dunes. Could've picked it up for nothing."
And he could've slugged her the time she retorted: "Well, why
didn't you then? You had plenty of nothin'!" . . . No matter
how many new garages are built downtown for his convenience,
he'll still drive around for fifteen minutes in search of a parking
space and finally park illegally; gambling on a two-dollar tag
seems somehow more dashing—and San Franciscan—than a
mundane, sheeplike, six-bit garage ticket . . . Being a man in
love with his city, he is keenly aware of its lore and its traditions;
when he has tourists in tow, he can point out the bedquarters
of almost every long-gone madam of the '20s and '30s, a
phenomenal feat of memory.

He's heard about racial prejudice in Baghdad-by-the-Bay, but
it must be something somebody else has, not he; doesn't he

go to Chinatown once a month and order chop suey—and
doesn't the Japanese waitress in the sukiyaki joint giggle at
his pidgin-English jokes? . . . Being a creature of habit and
habitat, he lunches in the same place almost every day—not
because the food appeals to him, particularly, but because it
has dice boxes; shaking for the drinks and tab is part of his picture of himself as a worldly citizen of a worldly city . . . He
probably went to Cal, in which case (even if he's eighty) he
still cackles, "But not for me!" when the Stanfords sing,
"'Stanford for you . . .'" If he went to Stanford, the fact
somehow comes out in the first five minutes of conversation.

He gets lost in the Ingleside and makes all the wrong turns
atop Twin Peaks—but he knows every rainy-day short cut
through the downtown skyscrapers and (which is more important) where the private washrooms are located upstairs . . .
The weatherman is one man he seldom trusts; that's why you
catch him on Postreet with a heavy overcoat on sunny days—
and without his umbrella in the rain . . . Golly, how he misses
those dear, quaint, sweet wonderful ferryboats; but when he
had to wait in line for an hour to board an auto ferry on weekends his was the loudest voice hollering, "Aren't they EVER
gonna get those bridges built?"

Our Mr. San Francisco, poor beastie he, has a stereotyped
picture of a Real San Franciscan that he tries to live up to,
and he's resentful of people who don't; hence his curled lip
when he sees women downtown in slacks and men in side-
burns and wild sport shirts (and a Southern drawl sounds much
more out of harmony to him than the singsong cadences of an
Oriental, or a darkly foreign accent) . . . More in what he
considers the tradition: chauffeured limousine waiting at the
curb on Montgomery Street at dusk, sprig of daphne on venerable furs at the Friday afternoon symphony concerts, picnics
with cold chicken and chilled white wine on the velvety greens

of Golden Gate Park (on a weekday afternoon), a white-haired rounder, deeply tanned, with his blond keptive (spindly legs, brassy voice, too ready laugh), buying drinks for the bar in a dark spot on Geary—late at night, with the Day People gone, the fog making a wet halo around the street lamps, from the post-midnight bay the farewell forlorn moan on a ship bound for Singapore.

Mr. San Francisco, with a personality as split as the tails on his conservative jacket—demanding changes and fighting progress, wanting only to grow old gracefully and peacefully, as his father did, in his best of all possible cities, and why can't they leave it (and him) ALONE?

3. TALES OF THE TOWN

These are the vignettes—or, at least, a few of them—that add their peculiar touches to the atmosphere of San Francisco, "the city where almost anything can happen." As anecdotes come and go, they are not particularly remarkable, but, in my own chauvinistic way, I cling to the illusion-delusion that they could not have happened anywhere else. Slices of life—some tender, some tough, some amusing. For example:

The town knows Lawyer Jake Ehrlich as a hard-boiled, gimlet-eyed mouthpiece who'll defend anybody or any charge —if The Price Is Right. But on the other hand . . .

Several years ago Jake was killing time in Women's Court, where a pretty fifteen-year-old "bad" girl was on trial. "Send her to a state home," ordered the judge. Jake, who'd been lounging among the spectators, leaped to his feet. "Your Honor," he called out, "don't do that to this girl. Why don't you send her home to her parents?" When it was explained that the state had no funds for such a service, Jake dug into his wallet and came up with the money to send her home—all the way to Montana.

Well, that was a long time ago. Seven years later Jake got a letter from the girl. "I don't remember your last name," the letter said, "but thanks to you, I got home to my folks. Then I met a wonderful boy and we got married, and I just became the mother of a son. I've named him Jacob, after you."

The town knows hard-boiled, gimlet-eyed Jake Ehrlich, all right. That letter from Montana was addressed simply to "Lawyer Jake, San Francisco."

Earl Plessman has been driving a Yellow Cab for more than twenty years, but he picked up his favorite fare one day at 11 A.M. in front of the Ferry Building. An old man, in patched but neat clothes and carrying a battered suitcase, signaled Earl and asked:

"Hey, how much wouldja charge to show me some tall buildings? I ain't never seen any."

Earl explained about meters and such, and as they drove off the old man leaned forward from the back seat and grinned. "I'm sixty-nine years old, I'm sheepherder from Montana, and I never seen no boats neither till I came over on the ferry."

They drove through the financial district and then down to Fisherman's Wharf, where Earl pointed out the crabs. "Golly, they EAT those things?" the sheepherder asked incredulously. "Yep," nodded Earl. "Why don't you try a crab cocktail?"

"No, SIR," answered the oldster. "I never was one for those fancy drinks."

Later, as they were driving along Market, Earl asked, "Have

you ever been to a movie?" When the visitor shook his head, the cabby suggested, "Care to see one?"

"Not unless you go too," said the old fellow. "Heck, without you I'd get lost."

After the movie the sheepherder said, "I think you better get me to the depot now. I'm goin' down to San Luis Obispo to visit my niece."

"Does she know you're coming?" asked Earl.

"Nope."

"Do you have her address?" wondered Earl.

"Nope."

"Well," ventured the cabby. "Why don't you call her and have her meet you at the station?"

"Shucks, that won't be necessary," said the man from Montana. "She's been there 'bout three years now. Everybody in town oughta know where she lives by THIS time!"

Tough Guy Frank Scappatura always boasted that he could beat any rap.

When he was arrested during the Nick de John murder case, he had only one thing to say. "I can beat it." And he did, at the last minute. And when the doctors told him he had cancer, he said the same thing. "A bum rap, I'll beat it."

A few days later Scappatura was driving to lunch at Fior d'Italia with his business partner, Mike Abati. Mike was serious. "Frank," he said, "I've found out some things about the kind of cancer you got. It's spreading all over. You can't stop it."

Tough Guy Scappatura wasn't impressed.

"I can beat it," he rasped. "I wantcha to advance me some money from our business. Buy me plane tickets. I'm flying to New York. I'll see Winchell. I'll get the best treatment there is. I'll beat it, I tell ya."

Abati shook his head. "I can't do it," he said. "The income tax people are after me. They've tied up everything. We've got no money at all."

All of a sudden the fight went out of the man who could beat any rap. He slumped down in the seat of the car. "Frank!" shouted Abati, but it was all over. Frank Scappatura was dead.

It happened during Christmas week, on hurly-burly Third Street between Mission and Market.

The uniformed cop was standing there, blowing on his hands to keep them warm, when a Skid Rowgue shuffled up.

"Hiya, Looie," said the cop. Looie nodded "Hi." There was a pause, and then the bum flicked one of the cop's brass buttons playfully and said, "Hey, you got a cigarette?"

"Yeah, yeah, I got one," sighed the officer, shaking his head slightly. He groped inside his uniform and produced one. "Here."

"Thanks," said Looie, lighting it. Then he looked up at the cop and said quizzically, "Y'know, I kinda hate to bum 'em from PEOPLE."

Looie turned to go, took a deep drag, and smiled. "Thanks again for the smoke. Just for that, I'm gonna work the other side of the street today."

The cop grinned for the first time. "You're a pal, Looie," he said. "Merry Christmas." "Same to you, copper," said Looie, jaywalking briskly across Third Street.

Tony Compagno is a jitney driver. Pretty tough guy. Has to be. Tough job.

One day during the rush hours he picked up an old lady on Mission Street. She handed him a Municipal Railway transfer.

"Hey," growled Tony, "this is no good on a jitney."

"It must be," she stammered. "The conductor gave it to me."

Tony glanced at her over his shoulder. He noticed her crinkled eyes, her gnarled hands, her heavy packages. Then he reached back and snatched the transfer.

"Sorry, lady, yer right," he mumbled. "I guess I was thinkin' of some other kinda transfer."

The late Jack Manion, the great police officer, whose iron fist smashed tong warfare in Chinatown, had a wonderful trick. Every day he'd stand for a few minutes in front of the Chinese newspapers posted on walls and pretend to read them—although he didn't understand a word. But his Chinatown enemies were never SURE.

One of his methods of scaring the tongmen: He'd stride into their meetings, listen silently, and then, waiting for the key moment, suddenly whip out his handcuffs and slam them on the conference table. Manion had little truck with psychology, but that's what he was using.

He had a temper, too, and it reached fever pitch one day when a tong chieftain sent him a fabulous gold-plated dinner set, each cup and bowl stuffed with greenbacks. Jack carted it back, flung it at the donor, and kicked him out of Chinatown—"and STAY out!"

But despite his occasional harshness Jack Manion was beloved. My fondest memory: the grizzled old officer walking slowly along Grant Avenue through an army of Chinese youngsters, all of them greeting him warmly with the same phrase: "Hello, Daddy!"

Is it too trite to say that they don't make 'em like Jack Manion any more? Trite, but true.

Amelio J. Maionchi, co-owner of the Liquor Mart on Post Street, got himself a crew haircut one morning—and when he returned to the store, everybody began calling him "Fuzz-head." This is not the end of the item. This is the beginning of the item.

A guy browsing through a Daily Racing Form in the corner mumbled, "Fuzzhead, Fuzzhead"—and then let out a shout. "Hey," he yelled at Amelio and his cronies. "A hoss named Fuzzhead is running in the seventh today at Del Mar!"

He had no more to say. He didn't have to. He merely whipped off his hat, plunked a pile of greenbacks into it, and passed it around among the dozen others in the place. Everybody contributed his all to the hunch bet of the season. Total: slightly over $1500.

But alas, San Francisco is now a "closed" town. They phoned every bookie they'd ever heard of, but nobody was answering the phone. And time was trotting on.

"Somebody'll have to get to the track," panted Amelio. "We'll draw straws." The short one was drawn by Dario de Martini, Amelio's partner. "So long," he yelled, stuffing the $1500 into his pocket. Then he leaped into his car, raced to the airport, and grabbed the next plane to Los Angeles.

Dario did well. He made connections all along the line, and got to the window at Del Mar just in time to bet the $1500 on Fuzzhead to win in the seventh.

There's only one thing wrong with this tale of dedicated men in action. Fuzzhead came in sixth.

The three men were sitting around in Skipper Kent's, discussing one of man's favorite topics: receding hairlines. "Yep," said Retired Banker Wilbur Scrubby, rubbing a hand reflectively over his bald pate, "it's worries that do it. And a banker has plenty." "I agree," nodded Vic Klinker, also a retired banker, stroking his thinning locks gingerly. "We should've been in the Navy, like Wiley here. Look at that thick head of hair, will ya?"

Admiral H. V. Wiley (Ret.) of Berkeley smiled demurely under his luxuriant mane. "I guess I had it pretty soft, all right," he murmured. Then he stared away into space. Back to April 1933, perhaps, when he was executive officer aboard the dirigible *Akron*, which went down off the East Coast with only three survivors. Or back to February 1935, maybe, when he was commander of the dirigible *Macon*, which fell into the sea off Point Sur with eighty-one survivors. Or back to three Navy sinkings in which he was the lone survivor.

Yes, Admiral Wiley has his hair. Lots of it. And all white.

Dr. Mortimer Adler, director of the Institute for Philosophical Research and one of the world's most noted philosophers, called a Yellow Cab to his Jackson Street home one morning. As he settled into the back seat, the driver, a thin, bespectacled man, said over his shoulder:

"Good morning, Dr. Adler. I heard your lecture at Marina Junior High, and I'd like to say that you're wrong, wrong, WRONG. Your contention that *'de gustibus non est disputandum'* is false. Just doesn't check out."

Recovering from the initial shock, Dr. Adler piped up weakly, "Well, would you say that a man who likes Edgar Guest has as good taste as a man who likes Shakespeare?"

"Oh, absolutely," said the cabby over the clicking of the meter. "Each one to his own taste, I always say."

"Uh—how about good?" asked Dr. Adler, rising to the battle. "Is THAT to everyone's taste?"

"Not at all, not at all," went on the cabby. "Good is a utilitarian thing, after all. Anyone can tell what's good or bad, or should be able to. But your lecture was on 'Beauty'—and that's according to a man's inner feelings."

The cab arrived at the institute, and, with some relief, Dr. Adler got out. "That'll be eighty cents," said the driver. "Here," said Dr. Adler, handing over a dollar, "keep the change."

"Oh, I couldn't do that, Dr. Adler," the cabby smiled. "No tipping among friends." And he left the doctor standing there with twenty cents in his hand, watching his fellow philosopher rattle away.

You think cops are tough now? Listen to this true tale of Old San Francisco:

Back in the '90s one of the most notorious shanghai artists along the Barbary Coast was a South American named Calico Jim. His specialty was serving well-drugged drinks to unsuspecting patrons, and turning them over as crew members to the skippers of "hell ships."

But one night Calico Jim made a fatal mistake. He shanghaied six men—all of whom turned out to have been police officers in plain clothes. When he learned the awful truth, Jim fled to his native Chile.

Eventually the cops got back to San Francisco, vowing revenge. Their fellow officers passed the hat to raise enough money for a trip to South America—and the six victims of Calico Jim drew straws to see who'd settle the score.

The winner tracked down Calico Jim in Chile, and killed him with six shots—one for each officer he'd shanghaied.

"I dunno—I'm always lousing things up" was young Bill B——'s favorite phrase.

The son of a millionaire, he got into so much trouble as a kid that his father sent him to several sanitariums. He loused up one job after another. And he didn't handle his father any better than his other problems. He was disinherited.

A few years ago Bill B—— got a job at a night club called

the Beige Room. As a waiter. But he was still lousing up—dropping dishes, mixing up his orders, spilling drinks. But just so the son of a millionaire shouldn't starve to death, the Beige Room bosses created a job for him. Backstage manager. Big title, small salary, but better than nothing.

Bill loused that up, too. Giving cues at the wrong time, opening the curtain when it should've been closed, forgetting the spotlights. "I'm sorry," he apologized to his employers. "But I don't feel so good. Terrible cold." Take a couple of days off, he was told.

The following day thirty-five-year-old Bill B—— attempted suicide in his room by swallowing sleeping pills. And he even loused that up. The autopsy disclosed that he'd died of pneumonia.

George Hilmer, a San Francisco hat salesman, was a student at Stanford, where, one day, he borrowed a book from the library and lost it. After buying a new one to replace it, he found the lost book and sent it to the library—only to get it back with a nice letter saying keep it, and thanks for contributing the new edition. That letter, neatly framed, now hangs on Hilmer's wall. But not his diploma. "The letter makes me a philanthropist," he explains. "The diploma merely made me a hat salesman."

Jack "Friday" Webb, star of TV's *Dragnet*, was invited one day by Police Inspector Ed Van Dervort to visit Cookie Picetti's noted Star Buffet on Kearny Street, favorite hangout for thirsty judges, lawyers, and coppers.

Webb loved the place. He also loved Cookie. "Cookie," he said warmly when he left, "I'm going to mention you and the Star on *Dragnet* two weeks from now. Don't miss it."

Don't miss it? Hah. The night of the program Cookie had

his wife, his relatives, and his friends jammed into the Star, all
staring eagerly at the TV set. On came *Dragnet*. Webb and his
partner, Ben Alexander, were talking about a suspect.

"He used to hang out in Cookie's Star bar on Kearny," said
Webb.

"Has this Cookie got a record?" asked Alexander.

"Not locally," said Webb.

"Think Cookie might have seen him in there lately?" asked
Alexander.

"Doubt it," said Webb. "He's too busy watering the drinks."

That was all. That was enough. By the time Webb and
Alexander got to the end of their "plug," Cookie was tearing
frantically at his necktie and shouting, "Get me a lawyer—I'll
sue that guy for a million bucks!"

Bill Edison, an Amherst graduate and heir to a shoe fortune,
became fascinated with the saloon business after reading
William Saroyan's tender fable of life in a bar, *The Time of
Your Life*. In fact, he got so fascinated that he turned down
a soft job with his father to work in Barnaby Conrad's bistro,
El Matador.

Well, one night, who should wander into the Matador but
Saroyan himself. As he sat down, Edison confronted him
angrily and said, "The saloon business isn't at all the way you
said it would be. It's nothing but work, hard work, that's all."

"Sit down, kid," invited Saroyan amiably. "Tell me all about
it."

For the next two hours, they sat together and talked of
saloons and many other things. And all the while Saroyan kept
buying drinks for the kid who'd believed *The Time of Your
Life*.

At 2 A.M., as Saroyan was leaving, young Edison pumped
his hand and said happily if fuzzily, "Thanks, Mr. Saroyan.

Tonight, for the first time, the saloon business was JUST the way you said it would be."

It always is—when Saroyan is around.

This is the city. A million souls and a few thousand heels. I am a columnist. One of the few thousand heels. My assignment: Get a story.

The time: 4:19 P.M. Muni Railway Inspector Philip Weinberg was on duty at Union and Van Ness, where the No. 45 bus stops. A young man, about twenty-eight, ran after the bus and missed it. As it rattled down Union Street, he walked over to Inspector Weinberg. He was trembling and there were tears in his eyes. Overacting, obviously.

"Hey," he panted to Weinberg. "Is the 45 bus the one that takes you near the bridge approach?"

Weinberg nodded yes, looked closely at the young man, and decided to take a shot in the dark. "You aren't by any chance thinking of jumping off, are you?"

"Well," said the young man, hesitating, "I am, frankly. Got plenty of domestic troubles. And no job. Why shouldn't I jump off?"

Inspector Weinberg reached into his pocket and fished up some small change. "Here," he said. "Go to the restaurant down the block and buy yourself a good meal. Make you feel better."

The guy shook his head. "Don't want a meal," he said. "Want a bus."

4:34 P.M. Another 45 bus came along. The young man jumped into it. Inspector Weinberg flagged down a passing police car and told the officers the story. They followed the bus into the Presidio terminal and spotted the young man without difficulty. He was sitting alone on a bench and crying. Still overacting.

4:53 P.M. The officers picked him up. He said that he was Clyde E. Schmidt and that he lived at 286 Second Street. The officers took him to Central Emergency, where he was examined by Dr. Oscar Rappaport. "I'll be all right now," he told the doctor. Then the officers took him to Mission Emergency, where he was examined again and released again. "I'll be all right now," he said again. Again. He is all right now.

This is the city. I am a columnist. My assignment: Get a story. You get a story and you check it out, that's all you can do, check it out. Sometimes it's a story, sometimes it isn't. You never know.

There's nothing timely about this story. The only excuse I can possibly make is that it's never been printed before. So:

Fortunato Auguiano was a friendless Mexican dishwasher who worked in an Embarcadero restaurant. He was unremarkable except for the fact that he seemed constantly depressed —and had an obsession about even numbers: would live only at even-numbered addresses, insisted on being paid to the even number, even if it meant losing a few pennies, and was forever telling the customers that odd numbers were bad luck.

Well, after the ninety-ninth victim leaped off the Golden Gate Bridge, the patrons began needling him. "Hey, Fortunato," they'd yell at him, "you gonna be the hundredth? Here's your big chance to be an even number forever!"

It was only a waterfront rib. Nobody thought twice about it except Fortunato Auguiano, who, on June 28, 1948—ah, those nice even numbers—became the hundredth suicide off the Golden Gate Bridge.

4. A TIME TO REMEMBER

To me San Francisco seems different, somehow, during the slow, cold days between Christmas and New Year's. I find it a time for introspection, for staring out a high window over the gray city, for recounting the fables and legends that are as important to San Francisco as the story of Christmas is to mankind.

Jumbled thoughts in the lull between the Great Holidays. The city sprawling fat and full on its hills, its windows agleam with Christmas lights, and time standing still to catch its breath. In the hush, memories stir restlessly—and the city's yesterdays come to life and steal quietly along the empty streets.

The city that was. The elegance of South Park, the most fashionable faubourg in town, and nearby, the substantial homes on Rincon Hill, where the ruling class lived. Surely this was the real San Francisco, the city that would live forever. But now South Park is a forlorn, forgotten plot of land South o' Market, and Rincon Hill lies buried beneath the approaches to the Bay Bridge. Gone, the fine homes, the delicate young ladies in the long dresses ("Her feet beneath her petticoat, like little mice stole in and out"), gone the old gentlemen dozing in the sun on the benches of South Park.

The memories that bless and burn. Fabulous parties at the great Flood mansion on Broadway. Artist Toby Rosenthal making his reputation with lush canvases titled *Love's Last Offering, The Exile's Return*, and his self-styled masterpiece, *Elaine* (the model for this one, according to wide-eyed legend,

was the corpse of a young girl). Iodoform Kate ruling over
the notorious cribs in Morton Street, now Maiden Lane. And
Ambrose "Bitter" Bierce delighting newspaper readers with
such squibs as "A morning paper says three unclaimed gold
watches are in the hands of the police, and that it is not
definitely known who stole them. It is definitely known who
will steal them."

The panorama of the past—flashing through your mind in a
jumble. Alcatraz a bare rock in the Bay, populated only by
thousands of pelicans. The first San Franciscans, discovered by
the Spanish explorers—a few Indians living miserably at what
is now the corner of Bay and Hyde. William Ralston planning
his Palace Hotel—and W. & J. Sloane opening a branch store
here, merely to supply the carpets. The What Cheer House on
Sacramento Street, famed far and wide because it featured
"Delousing Rooms for Miners." And Joaquin Miller writing
enthusiastically of the Bay: "Such room of sea! Such room of
sky! Such room to draw a soul-full breath! Such room to live!
Such room to die! Such room to roam in after death."

The city at ease, and a curtain drops over the present. You
look back, the bridges are gone, and a great sailing vessel is
throbbing through the Gate, home at last from its long voyage
around Cape Horn (or "Cape Stiff," as the mariners called it).
On Market Street, Colonel Kowalski, Lucky Baldwin's pal,
lounges against a building, fast asleep (awaken him, and
he'll explain, "Sleeping sickness, y'know. Caught it in the Bel-
gian Congo, on a secret mission for King Leopold"). The saloons of the Barbary Coast—the Dew-Drop Inn, the Rosebud,
the Tulip—featuring "waiter-girls," the forerunner of today's
B-girls, cajoling the men into buying champagne ("Please, sir,
only five dollars, and I get a percentage"). The city changes;
the people stay pretty much the same.

Only yesterday. The Bay alive with ferries, and if you missed the last one to Oakland, you could always take the tiny cockleshell "paper boat" delivering the morning newspapers to the East Bay at 4 A.M. Telegraph Hill, still uncrowned by Lillie Hitchcock Coit, a rocky home with goats and solid Italian citizens (the artists were yet to come). The Silver Dollar saloon at Sansome and Halleck, with real silver dollars inbedded in the marble square of the floor—and only a few missing near the entrance, where the temptation was too strong. And at Sutro Baths, wealthy dandies tossing five- and ten-dollar gold pieces into the pool, and kids diving frantically for them off the springboards.

That was San Francisco. Gelett Burgess writing his classic poem, *Ballad of the Hyde Street Grip*, little dreaming that one day his beloved cable line would be forever threatened. America's first overseas troops—California's First Infantry—sailing out to the Spanish-American War on the *City of Peking*, while all of San Francisco, it seemed, stood beside the Bay to wave farewell. There was a dog track at Ocean and Phelan, and the Market Street Railway had a black streetcar for funerals (the coffin was placed aboard it, and the mourners rode with it to the cemetery). And if you were daring, aviator Roy Francis would fly you from Fleishhacker Pool to the Cliff House for only five dollars.

The storied yesterdays—how quickly they come to mind when you've time to look back. Jack London, George Sterling, Jack Densham, Idwal Jones, and Maynard Dixon, whiling away the hours in Bigin's Bologna Cafe on Columbus—the first authentically bohemian hangout. Studio Seven, the upstairs rendezvous at California and Polk, where Frank Norris, Theodore Dreiser, H. L. Mencken, Blasco Ibáñez, and Hugh Walpole gathered on occasion—and burned their names into the walls, so the world would know forever that they'd been there (their names live on, but Studio Seven, burned walls and all, is long gone). Lillie Coit's tower rose straight and spare on Telegraph Hill, the goats vanished, and down on Market, Lotta Crabtree demonstrated her love for the city by donating an ornate fountain. Which the jolly Irish women of the Mission promptly dubbed "Lottie's Pump."

San Francisco, with its "citied hills," as Robert Louis Stevenson put it. A city that was never a town, but always a city —with fables and legends, glory and heroes. When the Christmas lights glow from the windows and the streets are quiet, the harbor seems alive again with a forest of masts, the gaily colored cable cars fan out along Market, and the candles flicker late into the night at the Maison Dorée and the Poodle Dog. For it is in the pause between the Great Holidays—when the memories wait to be summoned—that the city's endless yesterdays come to life.

5. McSHEEHY THE GREAT

For most of what follows I am indebted to my good friend, Virgil Elliott, a City Hall executive and former newspaperman whose hobby is collecting notable quotes from former city supervisors for inclusion in a publication called the *City-County Record*.

As you read them, you will see that our present supervisors, while honest, forthright, and God-fearing, are indeed a bunch of dull clods. Their predecessors, most of whom have passed out, as it were, to their reward, were men of style, wit, and gift for mixed metaphor unmatched even by Samuel Goldwyn.

There are, of course, the usual well-remembered ones—such as Cornelius Deasy's during an argument over how many gondolas, if any, should be installed in Golden Gate Park's Stow Lake. "Gentlemen," suggested Deasy, "why don't we just buy two and let nature take its course?" And the ineffable James McSheehy, who looked at the plans for a public building and said balefully, "It has all the earmarks of an eyesore." Again, McSheehy, thundering forth on another issue: "The handwriting on the wall is as clear as a bell." And finally, his ultimate triumph: "Gentlemen, let's grab the bull by the tail and look the facts squarely in the face."

However, McSheehy was not alone in exhibiting this remarkable flair for picturesque speech.

His contemporary, Adolph Uhl, trumpeted wildly in the midst of a critical discussion of a city official, "We are slapping him on the wrist with a compliment in an effort to nail him to the mast." And on another occasion he told his fellow supervisors that their delay in settling the rapid-transit question reminded him of "watching water run off a duck's back—it goes in one ear and comes out the other."

Supervisor Alfred Roncovieri had moments of greatness, too, as when he raised a finger and intoned, "The increase of a reduction is very important." This was good, indeed, but the economy-minded Roncovieri managed to top himself later by shouting angrily, "This thing is not on the up and up, and now I'm going to give you the berries in the coconut." The whirring sound that accompanied this statement came from Luther Burbank's grave.

Even Dan Gallagher, a man of notably sober mien, was

affected at times. An all-night session on the budget reached
its high point at 4 A.M. with a long argument over whether to
reduce the budget for maintaining the Police Department's
mounted patrol in Golden Gate Park. "Gentlemen," said
Gallagher wearily, "I make a motion we cut the horses in half."
Supervisor John Ratto hastily moved that "we defray action."

Still and all, there was nobody like McSheehy. Who can
forget his shining moment of gallantry when an indignant
citizen in the audience hollered at the Board: "How can you
fellows be so cocksure of what you're saying?" Outraged,
McSheehy barked back, "You, sir, can't use language like that
before this board!" And when one supervisor referred to
McSheehy as "the incumbent," our Jim was equal to the
challenge. "I may have been ill and unable to attend meetings,"
he said, a fine edge to his voice, "but no one has the right to
say I've been incumbent." And once when he had been in-
terrupted by Arthur M. Brown, he declared indignantly, "I
am going to continue, sir, and when I am finished you can
interrupt me."

The list of vintage, authenticated McSheehyisms is long—
and as you read his words you can see that we had a reggela
Ralph Greenleaf Emerson in our midst. To wit, and this ain't
the half of it:

"These people are in loggerheads together" . . . "The Government has pruned every man and woman on the list" . . .
"This defecation of character must cease" . . . "Since the beginning of this discussion we have had three movements in
this chamber" . . . "Let us call a shovel a shovel, no matter
who we hit."

To say nothing of: "I am the presiding officer of this de-
liberate body" . . . "Don't think I won't rule on this, because I won't" . . . "I am going to make a motion which I am

not going to make" . . . "Let us all get in and hurdle together"
. . . "I am going to have my legal attorney there."

And then he said, "I am a candidate for mayor, but I haven't
yet decided whether to run" . . . "The boys are indulging in a
little repertoire" . . . "We don't want to have Van Ness
Avenue used for an artillery" . . . "They don't need that much
money for the next physical year" . . . "Ladies, I have here
some figures which you can carry in your heads, which I know
are concrete" . . . "Gentlemen, this comes within a few cents
of being a vast and fabulous sum."

Who among us can forget James McSheehy for: "If anyone
wants to condone themselves, why do so?" . . . "Yes, I agree
that it is all water over a wheel, but now it has come back to
haunt us" . . . "You good people should not make all this
pantomime and tumult" . . . "You can't straddle the fence
and still keep your ear to the ground" . . . "Gentlemen, you
are putting the horse before the cart" . . . "This is crouched in
language which is perfectly oblivious" . . . "I try to organize
my mind in order to destroy it."

As you can see, the late great McSheehy made Sam Goldwyn
look like a bum—even the apocryphal Sam Goldwyn, who,
upon being invited to a party in the home of Sir Samuel Hoare
in pre-World War II London, was warned, "Try to avoid using
Sir Samuel's last name. He is very sensitive about it." Sam
nodded wisely. And when he was leaving the party, he shook
the host's hand and smiled. "If you ever come to Hollywood,
Sir Samuel, let me give YOU a party." Then he added confidentially, "And that, of course, goes for Lady W., too."

6. THE THINGS YOU SEE

The weather-beaten wooden cottages huddled together (like old people waiting to die) on the edge of the Pacific, the frustrated hot-rodders gunning their cars with a defiant roar through the Broadway Tunnel (and jamming on the brakes as they emerge meekly, frightened by their own daring), the Masonic Temple's great white marble pile (warring aesthetically with the gray Gothic glory of Grace Cathedral)—and a Muni bus weeping beep-beep-beep as it noses its bewildered way through the Geary traffic, a lost baby elephant searching for its mother.

The Christmas sounds (the rattle of a tin cup, a Bach chorale, the hard cling of a cash register) on Postreet, Lafayette Square with its smug green complacency and its protective ring of yesterday's mansions (an old nurse pushing a pram, a chauffeur dusting an old car), at noontime on Sansome Street the office workers emerging to perch on cold hard ledges and turn their faces to the thin sun (lunch in a paper bag, life in a hollow shell)—and the illuminated nighttime majesty of the City Hall, its dimensions geared to giants, its marble halls echoing to the patter of micelike feet.

Two scavengers, swinging a huge bundle back and forth on Grant and then heaving it with perfect rhythm to the top of their truck (these are the athletes of a metropolis), recorded music piped, canned, and labeled like tomato soup filtering through the loudspeakers of Maiden Lane (this is the big city humming to itself), the cops the whistles the signs the horns the white lines the cars winding round and round behind anxious chrome noses looking for a place to nuzzle in (this is musical chairs on wheels)—and the acrid smoke rising from the Powell slot as an overloaded cable groans up the hill, an old lady carrying too many bundles but gallant, gallant.

The dark ugly blob on the Bay that is Treasure Island (on gray days it looks more dismal somehow than Alcatraz—for this was an island created for pleasure), a shabby-fronted old saloon peering across Sansome at the pillared pile of the Federal Reserve Bank (in San Francisco, good neighbors of equal importance), the midweek merry-go-round at Playland-at-the-Beach spinning around with empty saddles and swinging stirrups (but the ghosts of a million children shriek above the tinny music)—and the old brick fort brooding away under the sweep of the Gate Bridge, guarding nothing but the past.

Corps of crop-headed students trudging up Chestnut toward the School of Fine Arts (but the finest art in the school is the building itself, a frozen chunk of Spain), the best show in town: the downtown Christmas windows and the mechanical toys that move up and down back and forth (and the child in all of us stands and stares, eyes in unison), the street-corner newsboys (the lamed, the blind, the dwarfed, the hunched) shouting the headlines of tragedies much less than theirs— and the night lights of Sausalito, now spreading up and over the hills, for reality has come to the enchanted village and it sleeps no longer in innocence.

The regimented gray-flannel'd skyscraper-trodden army of Montgomery marching along with eyes on each other's heels (but escape is always near: at the end of the street Coit Tower stands white and serene on its magic mountain), the traffic plunging in its laughable pell-mellodrama up Market (but at the end Twin Peaks throws up a cold shoulder and looks the other way), here and there old restaurants and theaters coming down to make space for parking lots (and soon there'll be more places to park than places to go)—and at 3 A.M. a taxi cruising along Columbus, looking lonely in a city that is forced to call it a day at 2 A.M.

The clatter of noontime dice in the Palace's Pied Piper as the men (in this last outpost of manliness) shake for lunches they never intend to eat, the high-pitched waves of female cat-chatter rolling back and forth across El Prado (lunch and din and the counting of calories in dry whetting martinis), the dark coeducational little restaurants where the girls perch at the bar and the men stand nudging alongside (for some there is nourishment in a push in a squeeze in a pinch)—and on California the workmen retiring from the cable-scarred tracks to sit in the sidewalked shadow of tall buildings, munching thick homemade sandwiches and silently watching the trim ankles twinkle past.

The Nikes (cold intruders on our peace of mind) sticking their snouts out of the Marin hills where once we hiked, a barge dragging reluctant heels across the Bay (a boy on his way to school) at the tail of a puff-chested tug, the light-footed crowd swishing happily through the Opera House lobby for the ballet (this is THEIR opera season), off Yacht Harbor a pelican diving into the water followed by a cloud of sea gulls (even a big mouth can't swallow everything), the twelve-o'clock sirens and horns along the Embarcadero, making the ghosts stir rest-lessly in the dust-musty corners of the Ferry Building—this is San Francisco, this and the hills where time stands still, this and the streets where traffic stands still, this and the yesterdays that stand in the shadows and still watch over the city.

7. I CAME, I SAW—AÏDA?

Let me tell you about a madly San Francisco day.

It started out with a divorce (not mine), went on to a snail derby, continued with a champagne supper in a museum, hit a truly Wagnerian climax with a Verdi opera, and ended, some fifteen hours later, with your insipid correspondent face down on the dance floor of the Mark Hopkins' Peacock Court. Not drunk, mind you. But the dance floor was slippery, my Paris pumps were new, and you know how it is. Don't you?

The divorce that wasn't mine happened to be Emmagail Lewton's. Emmagail, a bewitching brunette with blue eyes, had disposed of her husband, Lawyer Michael Lewton, that morning in Superior Court—and then, with her mother and Attorney James Martin MacInnis, repaired to the Clift's Redwood Room for a post-operative drink. It was Emmagail's fourth divorce, but her eyes were bright, her mouth firm, her chin determined—and her attractive mother was equally dauntless. "Well, Emmagail," she said, lifting her glass, "here we go again!"

Now then, about the snail derby. It was staged at darkest noon at Le Trianon, the excellent French restaurant on the Rue O'Farrell, and the room was positively swash with champagne and celebrities: Lisa Kirk, Barnaby Conrad, a girl who said she was once married to Don Sherwood, several TV cameramen, and Mr. Patsy D'Amore, a Hollywood restaurateur who flew up with his own racing snail.

With excitement and garlic in the air the crowd gathered around the Snailodrome, a large box with parallel wooden strips for the snails to race on. The snails, numbered and pulling tiny plastic chariots, were lined up amid loud cries of "Go, escargots, go!" And do you know how you make a snail go? You spread a few drops of champagne in its path, and those snails positively zip along.

"How do you know they like champagne?" I asked Monsieur Jean Lapuyade, one of Le Trianon's owners. "They're French, aren't they?" he answered stuffily. "*Où est le lapin?*" asked Lawyer MacInnis, a bilingual habitué of dog tracks. "*Olé!*" cried Mr. Conrad. The snails thundered on, gulping champagne hungrily. At the halfway mark one snail fell off the track, drunk. Another died (*Où êtes-vous, Société de la Prévention de Cruauté aux Animaux?*). The winner shot off the end of the track and kept right on going, looking for more wine, and a band struck up "La Marseillaise."

Meanwhile, we sat nearby, eating a few dozen snails that had been adjudged not brave enough for the competition. They were excellent, but still, it was an eerie sensation. Like watching a horse race while eating filet de filly.

Reeking to high heaven of garlic, I raced home, liberated my tails from the moths and silverfish, and prepared for the next cultural event on the agenda, the moment supreme for the town's dressmakers and beauticians, triumphant hour of bliss, night of delirious enchantment . . . Is he talking about the opera opening? Yeah, sure is.

I tore out to my waiting Cadillac limousine (if you gotta go, go first cabin) and fell inside, spewing collar buttons and studs in all directions. "Onward," I shouted to my driver, Honest Ben Droney. "Same place?" he inquired. "True," I answered, and he drove me straight to the Ready Room, a bar at Van Ness and McAllister, where I fortifried myself for the champagne supper in the Museum of Art across the street. Did it ever dawn on you that this town is absolutely foundering in champagne? Well, it is.

The evening started early—about 5:45 P.M., in fact—when John Parks Davis, the barrister's barrister, was seen walking down Van Ness Avenue in impeccable full dress, plus top hat. Homeward-bound workers and sidewalk loungers surveyed him curiously, as though they expected his starched shirt front to light up and say "Cremo—the Five-Cent Cigar."

It didn't. For Mr. Davis, plus seven hundred other members of San Francisco's four hundred, was en route to the annual preopera ritual—the Champagne Supper in the Museum of Art. People fight and claw for tickets to this because it's so handy to the Opera House. You can eat there, and, at the sound of a warning bell that frightens firemen for blocks around, run across the courtyard just in time to miss the first curtain. You can eat elsewhere—the St. Francis, Vic's, or the Palace, for example— and also miss the first curtain, but not so narrowly. Pour le sport, I always say.

Ah, the Museum supper. Partially nude young men standing around, making décor. Partially nude young ladies standing around, making small talk and mentally fingering each other's silks and brocades. Food by Trader Vic, champagne by Almadén: "Slightly better than last year's," decided Louis Petri, a rival. "Did you ever stop to think," sighed Stephen Zellerbach, running a finger around his tight collar, "that we'll be doing this every year for the rest of our LIVES?"

Thus sobered, we trooped over to the Opera House, where all was controlled chaos. A veritable *fin de siècle* (trans.: "Five dollars for the bicycle"). Everybody was trying to squeeze through the carriage entrance at once—"Let's try to act like little ladies and gentlemen, shall we?" suggested a cop, sweetly —and in the process, trains were ripped, pedicured toes were trampled, and a flask was dropped and broken. There was a moment's silence for the dead soldier.

James Ludwig arrived in a collar two sizes too large. "I couldn't find mine," he complained, "and all my friends have thick necks." Snapped the aforementioned John Parks Davis to Mrs. Herbert Richards: "Will you kindly move on?" "I will," she retorted spiritedly, "as soon as you get off my dress." Mr. Davis debarked from her train with a bow so gallant it buckled his shirt front, and his clip-on tie described a gentle arc through the air.

A heady aroma of moth balls, perfume (French), and champagne (domestic) arose in the Grand Foyer, where the women appraised each other and the men considered a vital question: "How do you keep your tie from turning yellow between seasons?" Herbert Richards took a pair of opera glasses from the attendant and looked distressed when he was asked for a five-dollar deposit. "I don't have five," he confessed, "but I'll leave you my driver's license."

Mr. Richards peered through the glasses. "Pretty weak, aren't they?" he ventured. "They should be," said the attendant. "Your driver's license expired two months ago."

The opera happened to be *Aïda*, made magnificent by Leontyne Price. Tenor Jon Vickers sang well in what looked like a suit of blue winter underwear, against a backdrop of a Sphinx that resembled Nasser. John Rosekrans, Jr., slept and Attorney J. Francis Carroll remained awake, even though he'd thought to bring a sleep shade. "I can't hear a thing," grumbled Jimmy French. "Too much steel in this building." What he meant was, he couldn't hear the Giants' baseball game on his transistor. "I," announced David Hulburd, echoing the immortal words of Toots Shor, "am the only slob who doesn't know how *Aïda* ends." It ended, all right, with pauvre Aïda and pauvre

Radamès, still in his winter underwear, entombed alive—a finale that always struck me as rather cryptic.

These tragic events behind us, we all jumped back into our little limousines and sped to the Mark Hopkins, where Mrs. Spencer Wood was the first to kick off her shoes and dance barefoot, free-free-free. At 3 A.M. the long day and night of glory slipped into eternity, filled with sweet bitterness. Aïda had lost, the Giants had lost, and quite a few snails had lost, too. All in all, quite something. Madly San Francisco, you might say.

8. THE TOURISTS, BLESS'M

Tourists, tourists everywhere—a new record number in San Francisco each summer, sitting in station wagons, munching bananas, consulting road maps, stopping dead in intersections to question traffic cops, stopping you at Post and Powell to ask the way to Powell and Post, thumbing through phone books in hotel lobbies to find people with their own last names, walking, talking, frozen, squozen, gawking, squawking, spending, spending and—spending.

A loverly bunch of tourists, gazing blankly at one another in the St. Francis lobby, stepping gingerly among the pigeons in Union Square, measuring the distance across Market and wondering if they can make it, giving up their cable-car seats to women (another sure sign of the tourist), walking into I. Magnin in slacks and wedgies, staying at slightly off-sounding hotels like the "Hopkins," the "Sir Francis," and the "Sheraton."

From the four square corners of the globe they come, to eat

in restaurants San Franciscans never heard of, peer at Alcatraz through the telescopes on Telegraph Hill ("I saw somebody move!"), press their noses against the blue windows of the Cliff House to see the sea lions that aren't there, walk backwards up the hills (because it's easier and you get a better view), giggle over the discovery that "snails" for breakfast are merely sweet rolls, and never jaywalk across Stockton between Geary and O'Farrell—another sure sign of the tourist.

They arrive by land, sea, and air, impressed with the airport, enthralled by the ride across the Bay Bridge, sniffish about the Third and Townsend railroad station ("THIS is San Francisco?"), failing to make the badly marked turnoffs on the Bayshore Skyway and winding up in Oakland (furious), halting their cars aghast at the crest of the Filbert hill, screaming their way down the Lombard curlicue, toiling breath-batedly up the Taylor Street hill in low and stopping dutifully at the arterial sign (while horns honk behind them), parking innocently in towaway zones—and dashing off letters to the editor signed, "Indignant Visitor."

The tourists, touching, touched, tough, tormented, tickled, tackled, waiting in long lines at Tarantino's and Grison's, discovering that you have to wear a necktie at Trader Vic's, puzzling over the French menu at Fleur de Lys, struggling manfully through the mammoth sandwiches at David's Delicatessen, asking for "beetle juice" in Chinese restaurants, bravely sampling the hottest curry at India House (water, water!), bringing their ladies into the Palace's Pied Piper (sorry, no ladies), sitting their ladies at the bar in the St. F.'s English Grill (sorry, no ladies at the bar), asking for local cracked crab at Amelio's (sorry, out of season), ordering chop suey at Kan's (sorry, we don't serve it), going up to the Top o' the Mark for dinner (sorry, no food, just booze and views).

Up and down and around they go, squeezed five in a cab,

grazed by signal-shooting busses on Market, wandering lost in
Golden Gate Park (Signs? What signs?), staring entranced at
the fabulous windows of Gump's (and half afraid to go inside),
looking askance at the decayed gingerbread of the Western
Addition, revolted by Skid Row ("We wouldn't ALLOW this
in OUR home town"), impressed with Pacific Heights, agog at
the clinging houses of Russian Hill, disappointed over their
failure to find a Bonanza King's silver palace on Nob Hill ("Is
the Pacific Union Club open to the public?").

Beloved strangers, white shoes turning brown, straw hats
wilting in the dampness, linen dresses covering goose pimples,
cameras aimed at cable cars, guidebooks open to landmarks that
have since disappeared, walking through North Beach and trad-
ing giggle for giggle, goggle for goggle with the natives in their
strange costumes of slacks, sandals, and soiled shirts that exude
the exotic, untrammeled perfume of dirt ("Wouldja believe it,
those square tourists walked into Miss Smith's Tea Room and
actually ordered TEA!").

Dogged, determined, dedicated to their duty, devoting their
precious days to buying back-scratchers on Grant Avenue,
examining the vandalized murals in Coit Tower, tramping
through the de Young Museum, enraptured in the Morrison
Planetarium, feeding the Zoo-hungry animals (Mommy, what's
a fleishhacker?), snickering at the entrance to Finocchio's ("Oh
c'mon, so what can it hurtcha?"), looking in vain for the ghosts
of the Barbary Coast, standing at 2:15 A.M. outside the Papagayo Room and sneering, "NO place to get a drink now?
Some wild wild city!"

The tourists—bless 'em all, the long and the short and the
tall. They pays their money, they takes their chances, they ride
the cables, they dance their dances. Shivering, shaking, griping,
groping, footsore, weary, broke but oke: once they've been to
San Francisco, they'll never be the same. Back in their snow,

their slush, their heat, their flatness, someday they'll dream of
the cool gray city with its head in the sky and the salt spray in
its face—and they'll long to return. And they will, bless'm.

9. OUT OF MY MIND

(Or, they're MY opinions, and I'll thank Mr. Voltaire to keep his to himself.)

Bronzed baby shoes don't look touching or sentimental to me.
They merely look slightly grisly.

I realize the Navy isn't in the exterior-decorating business,
but does Treasure Island really have to be that drab and
drizmal?

Truer words were never spoken than Milton Kreis's: "The
only time it rains enough in San Francisco is when it rains too
much."

I'll bet no San Francisco law is broken more often than the
one that states that when a public clock isn't running, its hands
must be set at 12.

The City Hall hasn't had an authentically fascinating character since Controller Harold Boyd died; a man of warmth,
taste, talent—AND humor.

Every time I read the stories (including my own) about what
a great joint Izzy Gomez ran on Pacific Street, I wonder if
they're authentic—or if nostalgia is clouding the backward look.

Old-timer: One who recalls that it was Pacific STREET until
Van Ness, after which it became Pacific Avenue.

I never see those ads for quarter-horse racing at Bay Meadows

without wondering, "Quarter horse and three quarters what?"
Like those funny dogs. Afghan and 'alf what?

Newly engaged young couples, pictured on society pages,
all look alike to me.

Add TV heroes who have no—repeat NO—verisimilitude
with their real life counterpart: private detectives. If you've
seen a real private eye, you know what I mean.

Height of condescension: The habit (exclusive with women,
I think) of referring to the men who wait on them as "little."
You've heard them: "The little man behind the counter . . ."
"So the little man in the service station . . ." "And then the
little man in the grocery . . ." Little minds at work.

I've tried, you have no idea how I've tried, to like the new,
white square Masonic Temple on Nob Hill, but I still think it
looks out of place across the street from the Gothic stateliness
of Grace Cathedral. The critics who call it "Disgrace Cathedral"
are going a bit too far, though.

Whenever I see two empty seats in the front row of a crowded
theater, I begin wondering what happened to the ticket holders.
They had an accident? A fight? They thought it was another
night? Death in the family? Or maybe they just forgot.

My idea of good public relations: Union Oil's, in painting
its storage tanks those wild and whimsical colors (even purple
and pink) in the hills near Highway 40 north of Richmond.

Nominated for oblivion: Muni bus drivers who pull away
while you're beating on the door. I'll bet they're wretches at
home, too.

Since I can't even tie a granny knot myself, I could stand all
day at the gift-wrapping counter in Macy's, watching those
flying-fingered females wrap impossible items in a matter of
seconds. Makes me feel even more helpless than usual.

If you measure wealth in terms of automobiles (oh, some of
those ghastly nouveaux still do, you know), I suppose John

Miller of Crestlake Street must be considered a Millernaire, at least. He owns a Jaguar, a Cadillac, a Lotus sports car, an MG, a Crosley Special, and a GMC pickup. Nice stable.

I wonder if the proponents of an "open town" remember when practically every other address along downtown Geary, O'Farrell, Jones, etc., was a house of prostitution? This was the "open town," but was it good?

Used to be you could spot a model a block away because of her hatbox, but now that the dolls have taken to carrying those huge zipper bags, they look more like underfed bowlers.

Aside from a half-dozen notable exceptions, all the restaurants in town seem to serve the same entrees. Matter of fact, they could switch their menus and you'd never know the difference.

The town of Richmond smells so strongly of gas that I'm afraid to light a match there. Whoooom!

Pianist Erroll Garner keeps winning all the jazz polls, but is he really a jazz pianist? Pretty, yes. Commercial, undoubtedly. Widely imitated, yep. Jazz? No.

Every time I start sifting old jokes with friends I recall my favorite from World War II. About the GI who's dancing with his girl on Saturday night, nuzzling her cheek, kissing her neck, and finally whispering desperately, "Baby, I'm being shipped overseas Monday, you know what I mean?" "Well, JEEPers," she replies, "I'm dancing as fast as I can!"

Every time I see a blind man walking across Market, armed with nothing but faith and a white cane, I try to imagine what a terrifying experience it must be.

Headwaiters seem so unreal it's hard to believe they have a home life just like anyone else.

Group pictures taken in night clubs always look like they'll wind up on the front page of a newspaper, captioned "In Happier Days," or "Before Tragedy Struck."

Dr. Scholl's Footpads always sound to me like an organization of private eyes headed by an evil German medic.

If you want to impress a visitor with the elegance of San Francisco, drive him past the Spreckels mansion on Washington; that never fails.

I like the motto of the San Francisco Senior Center at Aquatic Park: "To Add Life to Your Years, Not Years to Your Life."

The WAbash phone exchange in Marin seems out of place by a couple of thousand miles—and I wish they'd change it to something more indigenous, like WAter, or WArm, or even WAnderful. Besides, I'm still sore at the phone company for taking the old CHina exchange away from us. That had the proper San Francisco ring to it.

People in show business, especially the unsuccessful ones, are the most clannish I've ever met; mediocrity loves company.

Every time a psychiatrist uses the word "catatonic" I think of a medicine for neurotic felines.

Being incurably naïve, I'm still shocked by the discovery that there are square-jawed, clean-cut people who can look you right in the eye—while lying in their gleaming white teeth; give me the shifty, furtive ones every time.

How about attaching flutes, Chinese-style, to the Union Square pigeons so you could hear them coming? Jim Howe, the Walnut Creek rancher, attaches flutes to HIS pigeons, and the musical effect, as they whirl through the air, is quite electrifying. Like the Stukas of World War II.

Nothing makes me feel more grossly Caucasian and clumsy than the delicately graceful waitresses at Yamato Sukiyaki, kneeling at your side to pour hot sake in your ear. All right, I mean cup.

If you'd care to write a book about a philandering husband (or wife), I've got a title for you: "Slippery When Wed."

The Bay Bridge is more overwhelming, but the Golden Gate Bridge seems friendlier—thanks to the toll collectors who greet their regular customers by name, lend them quarters out of their own pocket, and trade all the latest Marin gossip.

Could anything be neater than the fact that Sherman, Clay & Co., is run by a man named Clay Sherman?

I suffer real guilt feelings when a motorist lets me into line (as I drive out of a garage) and is then trapped by the next red light, while I get across.

Even the late Steve Hannagan couldn't do a better job of public relations than the hot-rod clubs whose members help motorists in distress—asking no thanks in return except a little understanding. Impressive.

If we had any brains, friend, we'd go into the bowling-alley business—or haven't you tried to get into one lately? Jammed. My father opened Sacramento's first fancy bowling alley years ago—and then lost it, just before the big boom started. Sort of like Victor Borge's pop, who tried to invent a new soft drink called 4-Up, which failed. Then he tried 5-Up and 6-Up, which flopped, too, and then he died. "Poor Father," Victor sighs. "He never knew how close he came."

Only the restaurants that aren't advertise themselves as "Famous."

Add phrases that annoy me, perhaps unduly: "Checking it out." Something wrong with just plain "Checking?"

Great luck, to a male San Franciscan, is when he wears an overcoat downtown in the morning—and it stays cold all day.

You're wrong when you call them koala bears. They're koalas, period, and aren't related to the bear family. End of lesson. And is there anybody more insufferable than a columnist who just discovered something you've known all along?

I look my blankest when a visitor demands, "Show me San Francisco night life."

Would you spend almost $200,000 to gamble on getting a $26,400-a-year job? That's what candidates for mayor do.

Waiter: Mysterious man who becomes invisible when you want him but reappears in a puff of smoke (and a huff of questions) just as you reach the punchline of your favorite joke.

Plane trips are every bit as routine as bus trips these days, but every time I land safely at my destination I feel as though another major miracle has occurred.

Dyed-in-the-fog San Franciscan's idea of a perfect trip: driving across the Gate Bridge to Vista Point—for a look at San Francisco.

How come your pink and blue shirts fade to exactly the right shade in the same washing that finally wears them out?

I'm always surprised when a man who has a Jr. after his name turns out to be old.

A man who says he's wearing a "tux" always take out a girl who wears a "formal."

A good bootblack is one who reddens your face by staring critically at your shoes as you walk past his stand.

Army titles are confusing. A major outranks a lieutenant—so why is it that a lieutenant general outranks a major general?

"Women aren't geniuses because they don't have wives," unquote. I don't know who said that, but it must've been a woman. Of course, you could also say that women don't have heart attacks because they don't have wives—but why start a fight?

Some of my former best friends were people who kept on saying, "Some of my best friends are . . ."

Add once-stylish words that have disappeared from the language: nonchalant. However, Murads that made you nonchalant when you lit 'em are still around.

Best way I know to start the day is to walk through Chinatown, swept along by a fresh-faced flood of shiny Chinese

children on their hopping, skipping, giggling way to school—
each child a thing of scrubbed beauty. The mothers, their most
important job completed, then troop off slowly to work in the
sweatshops.

One of the few spots that has the old-time San Francisco
feel to it is Jake's Place at Powell and Union—where the food is
good, plentiful, and inexpensive, and the air of camaraderie
around the bar (among the newspaper and City Hall types)
seems genuine.

People who pronounce "larynx" as though it were spelled
"larnyx" also refer to "realtors" as "reelators."

If you're as addicted to puns as I am, you'll be pleased with
Larry Adler, who saw a peculiar-looking drum and asked its
owner what it was. "Spanish," came the answer. "I see," saw
Larry. "You mean it's a snare Andalusian?"

Venerable clichés rewritten: San Francisco is a great place
to visit but I wouldn't want to leave there.

In answer to queries: Yes, I coined the word "beatnik," but
I'm even sicker of it than you are.

When the term "a real pro" pops up in a conversation, one
name immediately flashes into my mind: Bob Hope. Followed
by Jack Benny.

450 Sutter: Where you wait too long in line for an elevator
that takes you in a hurry to a place you didn't want to go to in
the first place and where you have to wait some more besides.

Wondering muse: Whom does the phone company phone to
make sure they're giving the right time at the right time?

Real, 200-per-cent San Franciscan: guy who boards a cable
car with a transfer, thinks things over for a few seconds—then
tears up the transfer and digs down for the fare.

The trouble with telling a good joke is that it always reminds
the other fellow of a dull one.

The average San Franciscan likes a little vice to be available here—but only to impress his out-of-town friends who crush him every time they sneer, "Boy, is THIS town dead."

Don't believe all the malarkey about the weather changing due to radiation, shifts in the Japanese current, and whatnot. The most truly unusual day in San Francisco's history occurred 'way back on September 16, 1913—when the temperature hit 101.2. I wonder what the guessperts of the era blamed THAT on? Kaiser Wilhelm's saber-rattling?

It's strange but true that parks are never the same, once they've been excavated for garages and then replaced. Union Square and St. Mary's for example, don't seem half as soft and inviting as they were in their virginal state.

Whenever I see a motor scooter in a meter zone, I think of a bald man in a barbershop: both paying for more than they're getting.

One of the delicious things about being a San Franciscan is the feeling that you're a perennial tourist in your own home town, forever stumbling across something new—even if it's a strange old house you suddenly noticed for the first time yesterday after passing it for years.

Can you believe that Treasure Island originally was intended to be used as an airport after the '39-'40 fair? Boy, what a mess THAT would've been! If it had been tried, I don't imagine the Bay Bridge would be intact today.

If women are so smart, how come they sit down in a theater and THEN try to take their coats off?

Suggested title for a book to be written by Trader Vic's bartenders: *The Rumpots We Watch.*

Wouldn't that octagonal house on Green Street make an ideal honeymoon cottage for two squares?

Would you call a lopsided doughnut an ugly dunkling? I suppose not.

When I have nothing better to do, which is almost always, I

think about inventing a hollow chopstick, so you can use it for the soup, too. I can't understand why the Chinese didn't think of this several thousand years ago, when they were inventing gunpowder, kreplach, and spaghetti.

Every time you see a Readymix concrete truck in operation, don't you expect biscuits to come popping out? Shake.

San Francisco is a city of bells—but none seems as fascinating as St. Patrick's on Mission; deep and rich, sonorous and reverberating dramatically through the neighborhood's drab buildings.

Whatever happened to restaurants with curtained booths for romantic couples? With a buzzer on the wall, to keep the waiter from popping in on you unexpectedly.

Another reason why San Franciscans are the luckiest creatures on earth: they not only get a vacation with pay, they have San Francisco to come home to.

Old-timer: one who can remember when "fallout" was a word he thought about only in connection with his teeth and hair.

Every time I look at a freeway I'm sorry I didn't listen longer and harder to the experts who insisted (rightly) that San Francisco is a subway kind of city.

After all these years I still can't figure out what the late Gertrude Stein meant when she said, about her birthplace, "The trouble with Oakland is that there's no there THERE." Or maybe the inflection was "THERE there." Either way it's more baffling than her immortal "rose is a rose is a rose" line.

Add people who make me feel inferior: Those who chuckle wisely at the untranslated dialogue in foreign films.

Bullfight jargon is almost as wearisome as that of psychiatry—especially the phrase "Moment of Truth." As H. Allen Smith once asked in a very amusing essay, is there some definition of truth we don't know about?

As long as it's legal to bet at race tracks, I will find it impossible to think of a bookie as a criminal.

Whatever happened to those "experts" who said that San Francisco would never go for (1) motels—"this is strictly a hotel town"; (2) drive-in restaurants—"weather's not right for it"; (3) small foreign cars—"never make the hills, won't stand up." I guess they disappeared along with an earlier crowd of know-it-alls who said the Sunset District wasn't good for anything except location shots for Foreign Legion films.

Wondering muse: After posing as a customer in order to trap a prostitute, can a police officer look at himself in the mirror the next day?

Visitors who complain they're "disappointed" in Market Street merely demonstrate that they don't know much about cities. The allure and beauty of a metropolis is seldom, if ever, to be found on its main street—and that goes, in spades, for New York's Broadway.

10. THIS IS SAN FRANCISCO, MR. K.

(On the visit of Nikita Khrushchev to San Francisco, September 20–22, 1959)

No matter how far and wide you travel, Big Red, you won't find another city quite like ours: forty-five square miles (most of them vertical), over 800,000 people (most of them with vertigo), more telephones per capita than any city west of Washington (The Party Line is a big thing here, too), a fantastic cost of living (and a fantastic life to go with it), the world's greatest ocean at our shores, the world's greatest bridges spanning our world's greatest Bay, the world's greatest disc jockey on our air, too many cars, too many bars, and too many high livers (a record number of them with cirrhosis of same). But then, you understand about things like that.

A crazy, mixed-up town, Comrade Nikita. Our biggest building is called the Russ—but not in honor of your motherland. Our most capitalistic gathering place, the Stock Exchange Club, features a mural painted by a Mexican communist, Diego Rivera—who chose as his central figure not a downtrodden worker but a downtrodding tennis star, Helen Wills Moody. Our most radical labor leader, Harry Bridges, who has been accused of being a communist more often than you have, is a registered Republican. From your Mark Hopkins suite you can see only one building higher than yours: the Clay-Jones Apartments, once owned by a millionaire lawyer, Vincent Hallinan, who defended Mr. Bridges and has been called a Red, too. You can also see Russian Hill. If there's a communist living there, he's so far underground the only thing he could overthrow is the Hyde Street cable.

Like you, Mr. K., we dig culture. We have an Opera House, an Opera Bar and an Opera Alley—but the busiest bar is in the Opera House, especially during performances. We pay fifty dollars a seat to see your Bolshois and Moiseyevs, but rarely support our own Ballet Company, which does sellout business in Cairo and Buenos Aires. We have bars that feature operatic singers, bartenders who can sing *Pagliacci*, cabdrivers who write books, authors who run saloons, a Symphony conducted by a Spaniard whose name nobody pronounces correctly, wealthy art partrons who collect French impressionists, and starving artists who have a bad impression of art patrons.

Ours is an international city, Nikky. We have a Russia Avenue and a Moscow Avenue out in the Mission District, which is predominantly Irish. We have a Mr. Stalin living on Delano Avenue, and a liquor store named, not in your honor, "Mr. K." We have Italian markets in Chinatown, Chinese laundries in North Beach, Japanese restaurants at Fisherman's Wharf, Chinese chefs in French restaurants, night clubs run by Negroes in "Little Osaka," a White House that flies the French flag, and a Powell Street hotel named after a British pirate and topped by a big red star that does not signify Russia, the Texas Embassy, or the possibility that the owner has a son in the service. It marks a saloon.

It's a religious city, Mr. Khrushchev, even though, from your window, you can see that mighty Grace Cathedral is still unfinished. You'll find that the church bells are always chiming, from Grace to St. Patrick's to SS. Peter and Paul to St. Ignatius to St. Mary's Cathedral—which shares a block with a used-car lot and Mr. Tommy Harris' Joynt and overlooks another Great American Symbol: the Cadillac showroom. Just down the hill from you read the inscription on old St. Mary's ("Son, Observe the Time and Fly from Evil") and then gaze across the street at the stainless steel statue of a Chinese revolutionary who successfully plotted the overthrow of China in a San Francisco building that has since been torn down for a parking lot. Our patron saint is St. Francis of Assisi, who loved birds. The statue of St. Francis, in the garden behind Fred Maxwell's Art Gallery, is covered by a canopy—to protect it from the pigeons.

Some of our ways are strange, even to us, Nikita. We build freeways and then want to tear them down. We build the longest bridges in the world that turn out to be, alas, not wide enough. We lop off our beautiful mountaintops and uproot our precious trees to provide sites for boxlike houses, and we tear down the Victorian mansions that symbolize the past we are so inordinately fond of. We curse the busses and tear up the streetcar tracks, we fight to preserve the cable cars and blast them for obstructing traffic, and we build tremendous garages to house the autos we advise people not to drive to work.

It doesn't matter what you call us, Mr. K.—we have been called everything under the rocket-proof sun: "the most pleasure-loving city of the Western world," "the city that knows how," "the city that was never a town," the city that never sleeps, and even the city that never thinks. We have been called worldly and provincial, international and insular, tourist-loving and stranger-hating, stuffy and abandoned—the city with a flower in her buttonhole, the city with her nose in the air, the city with her mind in the gutter: you name it, we've been tagged with it. But, like your Stalingrad, we have survived disaster, and always will: for "her gaze is ever West in the dream of her young unrest."

I have a feeling, Excellency, that when you are back in the Kremlin, you will remember San Francisco, with its cluttered hills and streets, its soaring skyscrapers and spirit, its views of the past freshened always by the winds of the future. And, like all visitors, you will want to return to the cool gray city of love —and peace.

11. LITTLE OLD LADIES

Every columnist has his pet gimmick. Some wave the American flag as though they own every little star. Some quote their children at unconscionable length, in the apparent belief that their utterances (largely mythical) are of a wit and sparkle unsurpassed since Shaw. Some invent a colorful neighbor (generally fat, foreign, and female) with whom they discuss the events of the day, and others write of their pet dogs with a truly frightening anthropomorphism.

My gimmick is Little Old Ladies—but, not being as imaginative as some of my brethren, I regret to say I stumbled across them by accident, not design. I just didn't know what I was getting into, but I'm glad all the same. Little Old Ladies, hereinafter to be referred to occasionally as LOLs, seem to exist everywhere, and I find them a rather beguiling lot.

I heard my first Little Old Lady story years ago from actor Edward Everett Horton. After a particularly dismal matinee performance of a comedy at the Alcazar Theater—only an occasional titter had broken the silence—he was moping in his dressing room when two LOLs entered in a cloud of lavender toilet water.

"What is it?" asked Horton a little ungraciously.

"Oh, Mr. Horton," gushed one, "we just wanted to tell you how MARvelous you were this afternoon. Why, it was all we could do to keep from laughing!"

The first Little Old Lady I saw with my very own eyes was riding down Montgomery Street in the back seat of an ancient limousine driven by an equally ancient chauffeur. She wore all the regalia of the authentic LOL: a tricorn hat surmounted by an evil-looking bird of prey, a high whaleboned collar adorned with an heirloom brooch, a somewhat ratty chinchilla coat, black net gloves.

Two facets of her appearance made her meat for anybody's column. She had her legs comfortably crossed. And through a silver lorgnette she was reading a *Daily Racing Form*.

After I had chronicled the above, Little Old Ladies began turning up all over the place.

There was the LOL, prim and dainty in black, who was about to drop a dime in a newspaper box on Union Street. "Hold it, LOL," said Alan Shearer, standing nearby. "I just tried it and the box won't open."

"Well," answered she, fingering her pearls speculatively, "I'm a gambler. So here goes—and if it doesn't work, let's you and me kick the hell out of it."

Sometimes the Little Old Ladies have LOLs of their own. For example, Bill Remak, who owns the Glen five-and-dime store on Polk Street, has a dear little white-haired customer of eighty-five who keeps returning for electric cords, to the point where he advised her one day, "If you'll pull the cord by the plug instead of yanking it, it'll last a lot longer."

"Oh, I know, I KNOW," said the lady, wringing her hands, "but my mother is a hundred and five, and you can't tell her ANYthing!"

The Main Post Office, at Seventh and Mission, is a rewarding place to hunt for LOLs. Nick Geracimos found himself standing behind one who was told by the clerk, "Lady, you've got 'way too many stamps on this package," whereupon she said with great concern, "Odearodear, I hope it doesn't go too far." And another of our LOL Operatives, Fred Oberlander, was on hand when his Target for the Day started to leave a window, only to have the clerk call her back. "Hey, lady," he said, "you need another airmail stamp on this letter—it's too heavy." But she just laughed and laughed. "Silly boy," she said, wagging a bony finger. "If I put another stamp on it, it'll be even heavier, won't it?"

Some Little Old Ladies are nearsighted:

This one walked into Joseph Magnin's and squinted at Mrs. Dulce Finn's white poodle, curled up on a chair. As she leaned closer for a better look, the poodle suddenly licked her nose. "Perfectly amazing!" she said enthusiastically to a bemused salesgirl. "How much for this marvelous toy?"

Some LOLs are uncomfortably fast on the draw:

In the Golden Gate Fields' Turf Club one ordered a straight shot of bourbon and said to the bartender: "You must get all kinds of good tips, son. Please pick me a winner in the next race." "Lady," shrugged the bartender, "I couldn't pick my brother out of a carload of pigs." The Little Old Lady downed her shot at one gulp and glared at him. "Well," she snapped, "you know your brother better than I do."

And some are a bit thick:

In cabby Martin Dunlap's taxi one night an LOL piped up chattily, "Y'know, out where I live, I'm almost afraid to go home at night." "Dark and gloomy?" asked Martin. "No, Eighteenth and Guerrero," she replied. And Mervyn Green, supervising building appraiser for Assessor Russell Wolden, calling on an elderly woman to appraise her apartment house, stuck out his hand and announced, "I'm Green from the assessor's office." Concern and understanding appeared in her bright old eyes. "I know how it is," she said with a sympathetic sigh. "*I'M* allergic to wool rugs."

John Mills, another of our LOL Spotters, was aboard a Market Street bus that was loaded—but not quite as loaded as a big Marine sergeant who stumbled back and forth along the aisle, making jokes and conversation. At Fourth Street he bellowed at a white-haired lady who was preparing to get off, "Honey, if you were twenty-five years younger or I was twenty-five years older, you'd never get off this bus alone!" Whereupon she whirled around, grabbed the surprised Marine, and gave him the longest kiss in the history of the Municipal Railway.

Not to be outdone, he took off his marksmanship medal and, to the laughter and applause of the other passengers, pinned it on her brave old chest.

At times, however, our girls are merely delightfully confused. At Post Street and Grant Avenue, one day, a traffic officer bellowed at an LOL who didn't seem to know which way to turn her car, "Use your noodle, lady, use your noodle!" "Oh gracious yes," she fluttered back. "Now let me see—which button is it?"

The Peninsula edition of the species stepped briskly into the San Mateo County mobile chest X-ray unit in Redwood City, filled out her application, and waited impatiently for her turn. "You know," she smiled to Mrs. Martin Field, in charge of the unit, "this is the third one I've taken this month, and I feel better already!"

When the Equitable Life Assurance people installed a big temperature indicator on the roof of their new skyscraper, our LOLs were right there to discuss the addition to the skyline. "What do you suppose it is?" asked the first. And her friend replied, "I think it's to tell you how Equitable's stock is doing." "Then we should buy some," announced the first, firmly. "Do you realize it went up from 56 to 59 in an hour?"

I'll admit that Little Old Ladies can be irascible. On Post Street one afternoon a police officer in a loudspeaker-equipped patrol car called out to a woman who was jaywalking, "Hey, you there in the camel's-hair coat——" But he got no farther. "Peasant!" she shrilled back, continuing to the other side. "It's vicuña!"

And they can be impossibly sly. Ellis Tietze, a Yellow Cab driver, delivered one to the Fairmont Hotel, and as they got out of the cab, they noticed two pennies shining on the floor in the passenger compartment.

"Oh how wonderful," beamed the LOL. "It's good luck to find a penny, you know. You take one and I'll take one."

Then she asked how much she owed for the ride. "One dollar," said Ellis, at which she handed him a dollar bill—and, with a flourish, her lucky penny as a tip.

"See?" she cooed coquettishly as she swept into the hotel. "Your lucky penny has brought you more luck already!"

However, the Little Old Ladies don't win 'em all, I'm happy to say. Two of them boarded a Powell Street cable and asked conductor Charlie Ware, "Do we have to change to go to the Top o' the Mark?" "Nnnno," murmured Charlie, looking them over elaborately. "You can go just as you are."

And after a Democratic meeting in the Canterbury Hotel, Adlai Stevenson was assaulted by one of the more emotional types, who threw her arms around him and cried out, "Oh, Mr. Stevenson, I love you so much I could vote for you twice!" Wriggling free, Adlai asked wryly, "Didn't you?"

Of the lot, I have two all-time favorites:

When Robert Briscoe, then lord mayor of Dublin, came to San Francisco, he was given an enthusiastic parade down Montgomery Street, to the obvious bafflement of a Little Old Lady who had just stepped out of her broker's office.

She turned to a bystander and demanded, "What's it all about?"

"It's a parade for the mayor of Dublin," explained the Montgomery Streeter. "He's Jewish, you know."

At this her back straightened and her eyes got all bright and shiny.

"How wonderful," she said softly. "It could only happen in America!"

Novelist Kathleen Norris will probably, and properly, resent being included in this chapter—at eighty she's the brightest lady in San Francisco—but I don't know where else to put this anecdote, and I insist on telling it.

An old friend was describing to her the recent death of a San Francisco dowager: "Happened on a Wednesday. She got up early and spent the morning with her nieces and nephews. Then she had lunch at the St. Francis, went to a matinee, had tea with her family at home, took a little nap before dinner—and never woke up."

"Gosh," sighed Mrs. Norris. "Doesn't it just make your mouth water?"

12. MEMORIAL DAY WEEKEND

HEADLINE: "Highways Jammed by Holiday Crowds" . . .

Holidays. Sometimes it's hard to remember what you're celebrating—or observing. The rush to get away, the guilty glee at the bonus of an extra day—and all the time your mind blocking out the memories of the wars nobody wanted (but got) and the fear of The Big One (the final one) to come. This is the holiday to death, the holiday whose theme song is "Taps" and whose stage setting is the flag lowered to half-staff.

HEADLINE: "Resorts Report Record Throngs" . . .
The throngs, the mobs, the generations—every one gets its war, and the next one will get everybody, the slackers, the 4-F's, the black marketeers, even the politicians. Ah yes, the politicians: Their words will finally come true. There WILL be a war to end all wars and everything else—and while the world won't be made safe for democracy, it won't be safe for anybody else, either. Massive retaliation will do the job, and the rest will be silence. "Forevermore?" croaked the craven. Forevermore.

HEADLINE: "Memorial Day Observance at Presidio" . . .
Presidio. How quaint. As archaic as my war, World War II, the last "sensible" war. How sensible can a war get: merely shot and shell, all quite understandable and reasonable, for a war. Even the gay panoply: Great warships firing at each other over the horizon, the skirted "Ladies from Hell" skirling away on their bagpipes as they marched across the Libyan sands. And the planes: museum pieces, slow, obsolete, with propellers, mind you, and dropping peanut bombs that only killed hundreds. If they were lucky and aimed well.

HEADLINE: "Traffic Experts Plead for Safety" . . .
Safety. We all marched off looking for it, for safety under a tin hat, magically immune. It was the classic war: The Good Guys would live and the Bad Guys would die, and if a Good Guy should happen to get killed, it would be the other Good Guy. Off we marched into the wild goo yonder, off to faraway places with strange-sounding names (Sheppard Field, Chanute Field, Seymour Johnson, GI, CQ, BOQ, POE) and then even stranger-sounding names (Kasserine, Bizerte, Anzio,

Omaha, and Utah), and it didn't seem right that so many of
the Good Guys should get killed. But we would remember
them, even on Memorial Day.

HEADLINE: "Five Drown off Ocean Beaches" ...
Dead. Nobody should get killed on Memorial Day. You
should sit around, safe and sane, high and dry, and think about
the other people who got killed on beaches, their blood vivid
in the tropical water, their bodies slowly inflating like grotesque
balloons. But they died so many ways. In the hedgerows of
Normandy, with surprised looks on their young faces, as if to
say, "Not ME!" In the snows of the Ardennes, kept neat
and whole by the weather (the guys from 90th Division Graves
and Registration liked that—easy as cordwood). In a summery
field on the outskirts of Paris, very dejected, their faces buried
in the soft earth like disappointed children: So close to the
city their fathers had always talked about—Mamzelle Zig-Zig—
and now they'd never get there. You could almost imagine that
their last word was the GI's favorite four-letter one.

HEADLINE: "'Must Have Peace,' Says Ike" ...
Peace. I'll never forget the guy from the Deep Mission, who
called himself "a 4-F in uniform" and snaffled himself a cushy
job in London, driving a general. "I'm no hero," he'd say,
squinting through his thick glasses. "Hero today, gone tomorrow." One dark night near Piccadilly a buzz-bomb brought him
peace infernal and everlasting. Zim, from the Richmond: Now
HE had problems—a British girl friend in Chiswick (or Melton
Mowbray or Wigan, I forget) and a wife and three kids back
home in the Avenues. "If she ever finds out," he'd always say,
"I'm dead." German flak at Brest solved all his problems.
Mike, who lived on Union in North Beach: All he could talk
about was Joe's Specials and minestrone and everything alla

Milanese, if not Parmigiana. So happy to get out of England —"jugged hare, pfew"—and into France—"say what you want about the Frogs, they can cook." He could say all he wanted till St. Lô, where a sniper killed his appetite.

HEADLINE: "Holiday Double-Headers, Complete Scores" . . .

Games. And on and on they go, playing their most dangerous games: lifemanship, deathmanship, brinkmanship, no win or lose, just winner-loser. And the toys—magnificent and brilliant, miles ahead of World War II, with its burp guns and pop guns and bubble guns. Bombs alive with sunfire, rockets and pinwheels to celebrate the end of the world, and enough fallout for everybody. The greatest show on earth, with no encore.

HEADLINE: "Highways Flooded with Homecoming Traffic" . . .

Home. A pretty word, one of the very nicest, the guys in the campaign hats sailing through the Gate to Manila, the boys in the funny wrap leggings and flat helmets singing "Over There," the GIs with their Eisenhower jackets and pinups, the kids who'd never heard about Inchon or the Yalu, but were about to.

All fighting to get home for the kind of weekend we are celebrating because they didn't make it.

13. DAY BEFORE YESTERDAY

Bay and sky fusing in leaden monotony. An ugly tanker, riding low, inching sluggishly past the piers. In the secret gardens of the city, the first spring blossoms grinning with foolish unreality under the pall of winter. As you look out your window over the eternal hills, the outlines of today blur and fade in the gray hush—and the city's many yesterdays come slowly to life . . .

The city that was. Kids, clothed in nothing but screams, swimming in the cove off Marina Boulevard—warmed by hot water spewing from the pipes of the P.G. & E.'s old red brickstream plant. A sunny Sunday in Golden Gate Park, with knicker-clad young fops, bearing such stylish names as Tevis and Spreckels, whirling past on their bicycles. Market Street lined with double-decker billboards hiding the gaping holes left by the firequake. And the streetcars prancing along in fours, creating the unholy din that made Market "the noisiest main street in the world." To us who were very young, it seemed like something to be proud of.

Only day before yesterday. In the Sunset, the sand dunes marched in waves from Seventh Avenue to the sea, Sea Cliff was a windswept rock and the solid old-timers clustered together in the Paige-Haight-Masonic sector (the Keils, the Zellerbachs, the O'Douls, the Magnins). A pair of struggling young writers named Charles G. and Kathleen Norris lived in the Montgomery Block—and Polk Street saw a lot of strong-jawed Frank Norris, walking back and forth for the color that went into *McTeague.* It was hard for an artist to starve in those days: Bologna's on Columbus Avenue always had a long table reserved for them—and they could have all the soup and bread and chianti they wanted, free. They could, and did, repay the boss by doing a small mural on the wall. Murals that were hideous, but sincere.

Nostalgia on a gray day. A Ford tri-motor seaplane, with corrugated skin, flying a ferry service between Oakland and the Ferry Building. On Union Street, strange little close-coupled streetcars with doors in the middle—and on the Fillmore hill, mighty steel monsters that were half cable car, half trolley. On Sunday, the Sausalito ferry was jammed with hikers, humpbacked under their rucksacks—and there was always somebody with a concertina to accompany the songs that floated across the Bay to clash with the scream of the wheeling gulls. Tamalpais gleamed in the distance, and we stood at the rail and studied it solemnly, like Hillary gazing at Everest.

The past that is always present. Gentleman Jim Corbett, everybody's hero, having his shoes shined on Market between Kearny and Dupont by Cornelius Lyons, who wore a wide leather belt studded with tiny stars that proclaimed him "Champion Bootblack of the World." "Uncle Sam," the candy man, walking along Geary in his top hat, his star-covered coat, and his striped pants—and the character known as Iodoform Kate, who bummed the heady stuff from druggists, whiffing herself to dreamland in the downtown alleys. The rich people spread tanbark over the cobblestones in front of their homes, to deaden the clatter of the passing hoofs. And in the soft light of the gas lamps, the children scampered to the corner to buy hot tamales that cost only a nickel, and no wonder. The "chicken" inside was sea-gull meat.

The nights of old. Gambling at the Cafe Royal at Fourth and Market, and dancing to the then unbearably hot rhythms of Art Hickman at the St. Francis (a New York newspaper sent a reporter out to observe "the people writhing like savages to the beat of jungle drums"). A young man named Dave Falk won every Charleston contest at the Cabiria Cafe on Broadway, and at the Arcadia Ballroom at Jones and Eddy, band-leader Paul Ash was such an idol he spent most of his time signing autographs. Helen Morgan sang her sad songs from atop a piano in Joe Merello's Club Moderne, and we cried along with her, for we were all very young and sentimental and ready to weep over an era that was dying before our eyes.

The dear dead city, never quite beyond recall—a city that was small and knew itself intimately. Mayor Adolph Sutro inviting "everybody" to stroll through his Sutro Heights estate on Sunday, and indeed everybody came to sprawl on his lawns and listen to the music he provided. The invincible Seals of Recreation Park—Bert Ellison, Ping Bodie, Paul Waner—all nine feet tall and golden with immortality. A. P. Giannini seated at his desk in the middle of the main floor of his bank, talking to anybody who dropped in—and Jim Rolph rolling along in his Pierce-Arrow touring car, waving to the right and left, his every trip a one-man parade. And millionaire Gus Oliva trotting like a perspiring child across the meadows of Golden Gate Park on Easter Sunday, hiding eggs that contained hundred-dollar bills for his annual hunt that was generally a riot.

A gray day in Baghdad-by-the-Bay. Shadows of the past flitting along the dark streets, and your memory stirring back to the endless days under skies that were always blue and bright. Or so they seemed in the laughing city that was.

14. THE HORRIBLE FORTIETH

April 3, 1956:

This morning I got up, stumbled into the bathroom, and peered into the mirror at the face of a man forty years old.

"Happy birthday," I croaked, holding onto the washbasin to steady myself. It has always been a dreadful experience, meeting myself head-on in the morning. But this time it was worse.

I was forty. Unshaven but washed-up. A has-been who had never arrived.

I studied the ravages of four decades of clean living, hard work, and bum scotch. Under the heartless glare of the fluorescents, I counted the laugh lines with tears in my eyes. They are there to stay, even when I cry. I examined the vertical crease between my eyes. It looked like Yosemite Valley from the air.

I spent a few minutes trying various hair arrangements, but it was no use. The point on the top of my head still shone through, shiny as Fujiyama in the moonlight. With a sigh that rattled the windows, I brushed my teeth with Jack Daniel and prepared to face the few remaining dismal years.

Forty. It has a mournful sound, like a lost foghorn looking for its mother. Twenty sounds as joyous as springtime, and even thirty has a certain perky lilt to it. But forty . . .

A succession of miserable ads flashed through my mind. "Men Over Forty: Do you have backaches, dizzy spells, hot flashes?" (Yes, yes—how do they know these things?) "Have you faced up to your responsibilities? Will you leave your family safely provided for?" (No.) "Save your loved ones needless heartbreak. Investigate our layaway plan NOW!" (Stop!)

Over the hill, that's what. "Life Begins at Forty"—but whose? An elephant's, perhaps? From now on it's a matter of displaying extreme caution, merely to survive. See your dentist twice a day, brush your teeth twice a year. Every time you see a mysterious swelling, run to your doctor. If the swelling is in your wallet, he'll remove it almost immediately. Look both ways while crossing one-way streets. And keep your ears peeled. The next sound you hear may be that of your arteries hardening.

Mopping the perspiration, I put these thoughts to one side

and looked at myself in the mirror with a fresh perspective. From a distance of ten feet. I flexed my muscle with no visible effort and no visible muscle. I threw out my chest, followed closely by my sacroiliac. "I'll show 'em," I vowed—and put on the suit I'd graduated from high school in.

It fit perfectly. I was the fattest kid in school.

Forty. Time to be philosophical and put away, forever, my Mitty-like dreams of glory.

Too late now for *Time* magazine to describe me as "young (39), slim, boy-wonderish," etc. From this point on, it will have to be "balding, middle-aging (40), paunching." Of course, *Time* has shown no inclination to write about me in either vein, but it was nice to think about before the curtain dropped on my youth.

I will have to hang up my mental baseball spikes, too. No longer, with the bases loaded in the ninth with two outs and the home team at bat, three runs behind, will the manager look up into the stands, point a finger and shout, "All right, Caen, I'd hoped we wouldn't have to bother you—but come on, grab a bat." Followed, naturally, by the longest home run in the history of the ball park and a great future in baseball.

A thirty-nine-year-old rookie sensation is barely possible. But forty? Never.

Too late, too, for the 49ers to summon me to kick a game-winning field goal with less than a minute to play. And the chances seem slim that I'll ever be the tennis unknown who saved the Davis Cup for the United States—to be hailed by sportscribes as "that 39-year-old phenom with legs of steel and a will of iron who broke the backs of the opposition with his cannonball volleys and sledgehammer drives."

It's just as well. It might have been bad for my heart,

which is pounding away right now, sound as a dollar watch. And skipping just as many beats.

Forty. The nowhere age. Too old for the Junior Chamber's "Young Man of the Year" award and too young for the Senior Chamber's "Fifty Years of Achievement" accolade. Too old for sports cars and too young for a chauffeur-driven limousine. I don't feel like driving anybody's limousine anyway.

But then, I suppose age has its compensations, too. For one thing, people will no longer exchange amused glances when I swim side-stroke across the pool. It's a very serviceable stroke, and much superior to the Australian crawl, I've discovered. Whenever I try the crawl, my water wings slip off.

And for another thing, being several minutes into my forty-first year, I am now entitled to reminisce endlessly, observe at regular intervals that "I don't know what to make of the younger generation," and interrupt all conversations with "Well, in the good old days . . ."

And brother, they certainly were.

15. MIRACLE IN OCTOBER

This particular Saturday awoke like a day that had a good night's sleep.

The skies were a clear-eyed blue, and the Bay was as calm and unruffled as a pond. Even harsh Alcatraz softened under the warm sun; with a few white sailboats frolicking nearby, it looked like an island resort—the Alcatraz-Hilton?—and by screwing your mind's eye to a telescope, you could see prisoners stretched out for a sunbath.

Slowly, the city yawned, stretched, and came to life. Then it looked out at the day through its many windows and emerged to revel in the soft, dreamy magic of it all.

In late October, midsummer had come at last to Baghdad-by-the-Bay.

By noon, the city was working hard at the job of enjoying Saturday's warm miracle. The streets were full of convertibles that had blown their tops. The girls were dressed in sheerest joy. Small boys shed their mothers and their complexes and became just small boys again, heading Huckfinnishly toward the nearest shores, to dangle their toes and fishing poles.

Downtown, delighted tourists in aloha shirts pointed fingers and cameras in all directions. Old men and pigeons squinted at each other on the grass of Union Square. In the stores, the salespeople agreed every fifteen minutes that "it's much too nice a day to be working," and went on shirking. Cabdrivers took off their coats and the city followed suit, suitless.

On Montgomery Street, even Jake Ehrlich, a midwintery sort of fellow, walked to lunch at Jack's with his hat in his hand. The sun beamed down to see such fun, and the cow jumped over the moon, including, presumably, Lunik II.

Midsummer October in Chinatown. The smell of fish and poultry hanging powerfully in the heavy air. Girls in dark glasses and Bermuda shorts wandering along Grant Avenue, wrinkling their noses and staring through a dirty window at a huge dangling octopus that stared back with all its tentacles.

Chinatown was in a festive mood. A mighty politician had died, and his funeral was satisfyingly vast, tying up traffic for blocks and making the motorcycle cops sweat rings in their

black shirts. After the procession had broken up, the musicians
sauntered through the streets, still carrying their instruments
and now and then tootling a loud blast for no reason at all
except that the funeral was over and it was good to be alive on
a summer day in October.

The Ferry Building shining like all the golden yesterdays
at the foot of Commercial Street. Teak, jade, and junk in the
windows. In the Italian Market, which is Chinese, a young
man inserting an air hose into the necks of very dead ducks
and blowing them up like footballs, which makes them easier
to glaze for barbecued and Peking duck.

Three fire engines raced down Washington toward North
Beach, the firemen hatless. Children screamed for joy as the
hook'n' ladder raced past, and the tillerman, a blond hero with
crew-cut hair, waved a hero's greetings to his admirers. Through
an open window, you could hear a Chinese record, its voice
echoing the fading sirens. Old Chinese ladies, their once-
bound feet still tiny and misshapen, went on talking in the sunshine.

It was that kind of day, when firemen wave at children and
a funeral calls for a celebration. The sun hung high over Hang
Far Low, and Chinatown was full of life after death.

The day darkened, the Bay glowed in luminous beauty, but
the mercury stayed up, refusing to let go of the sudden summer.
Near midnight, the downtown streets of the city were still in
their shirt sleeves. A Powell cable cranked its way down Nob
Hill, cradled in the warm grip of passengers clinging to its
sides. A few were drunk. At each stop, they hopped off, let
the cable get a start down the hill, and then ran shouting after
it to leap back on. The conductor grinned foolishly at them.
It was a foolish night.

The big hotel lobbies were alive with cool young girls in their ball gowns, escorted by hot young men with damp foreheads. At the Roger Laphams' fiftieth wedding anniversary party in the St. Francis, the band played on and on, and the champagne swirled and bubbled like the Bay around a piling. Roger danced every dance with the pretty young girls and easily achieved the impossible: he enjoyed himself at his own party.

At 3 A.M., summer still ruled the night skies, and the lady in the window of Tiny's Waffle Shop was still making waffles.

Sunday got up late and gray-eyed, with a slight hangover. It groaned slightly in the voice of many foghorns and made a rustling sound, as though leafing through the Sunday papers. Sixty thousand jammed their way into Kezar Stadium—miles and miles of Park, and not a place to park—and yelled through the Grownups' Big Game. The sun, which had given of itself so lavishly the day before, made a few tired attempts to get up, pulled the pillows back over its head, and said, "Aw, the heck with it."

But it didn't matter. It had been a weekend to remember —a miniature season crammed with life and death, joy and tragedy—in the city that knows no seasons.

16. TIPS FOR TOURISTS

Nobody, I gather, likes to be mistaken for a tourist, especially if he is one. Therefore, for the guidance of the thousands of visitors who insist on visiting our town, I offer the following hasty guide, which, if followed carefully, will allow the newest newcomer to pass as a bona fide, old-time San Franciscan:

Never walk through Union Square. Walk around it. If you MUST see the Dewey Monument (but only to point out that Alma Spreckels posed for the statue) kick either two pigeons or one old man feeding same.

Fill conversational gaps with such inside remarks as "Never thought I'd live to see the day when women were working at Shreve's and men at I. Magnin's."

Never park in a meter zone if a fireplug is vacant. It's considered more dashingly San Franciscan to gamble on a tag than, cravenly, to feed the meter.

At the ball park, always boo Willie Mays. He's getting $80,000-plus a year and should hit a home run every time he's at bat.

No matter how overloaded a cable car seems to be, squeeze yourself aboard with an ingratiating remark, such as "Always room for one more on a good old cable car." Don't pay the fare.

At the San Francisco Museum, look at the abstractions and observe, "My kid could do better." At the de Young Museum, groan, "I've got better junk in my attic." At Legion of Honor, shrug, "Well, it's got a nice view of the Golden Gate."

While dining at Trader Vic's, be sure to tell the captains, the waiters, and the people at the next table that you remember Vic when he ran Hinky-Dink's in Oakland—"just a little corner beer parlor." At Amelio's, let it be known that you remember when it was a speak-easy. At the Blue Fox, the key line is: "How quaint—across from the morgue. Cancel my steak."

If Mayor Christopher's name comes up, buff your nails and yawn: "Good enough mayor, I guess. Too bad he can't learn to control his temper."

At the Matador, you prove that you're IN by inquiring, "Anybody seen Manolete lately?" Or: "It's my opinion that

Dolly Fritz just isn't the marrying kind." Or even: "Ran into Gorham and Behrens on their way to Stuyvie's at Pebble last weekend. Good chaps, all."

As you approach the "QUIET THROUGH TUNNEL" sign on the Stockton Tunnel, blow your horn.

When the fog starts to blot out the sun, take a deep, manly sniff and ahhh, "Ahhhh, for a while there I thought it was going to be a lousy day."

In all cultural interchanges, remember that the Symphony was better under Monteux, the Opera doesn't do enough (or too much) Wagner, and the Ballet should receive better support, especially from people who hate ballet.

Never drive all the way through Golden Gate Park. Use it only as a short cut from the Sunset to the Richmond.

If your cab fare is eighty cents, give the driver a dollar. If the fare is a dollar, tip him a quarter. If it's more than a dollar, give him a dirty look and a speech about New York cab fares.

No matter what the Southern Pacific does, it's wrong.

If you want to ruin a San Franciscan's reputation, spread the rumor that he has been known to CUT an English muffin.

Cross at an intersection only if the sign has changed to "Wait." It should be pointed out, however, that the really chic San Franciscan jaywalks exclusively.

Never give up your seat on a bus, even if Whistler's mother is standing alongside, whining piteously. Five extra points for taking an aisle seat and successfully blocking the empty window seat through ten stops.

When you see an empty pier along the Embarcadero, only two words are necessary, spoken in a hollow tone: "Harry Bridges."

No matter what fish is served to you at Fisherman's Wharf, mutter to your companion, "Frozen, probably."

Never admit you've been to Los Angeles for any reason except urgent business.

When another tourist says "The Skid Row here is the most disgraceful district I've ever seen, worse than Port Said, worse than Marseilles, worse than the Casbah," nod in quick agreement and look pleased.

If you go to the Top o' the Mark, pretend you are merely trying to find a friend from out of town.

At any intersection along Market, stand off the curb and dare the busses to hit you.

If the car ahead of you doesn't get going a second BEFORE the light turns green, toot your horn vigorously. Three extra points if the car has an out-of-state license.

At Coit Tower, you are permitted to use the coin-operated telescopes, but not to look at the view—only to peek into nearby windows.

When you are asked, "Are you a native San Franciscan?" answer, "No, but my father was." This effectively stops further discussion.

Follow the above tips, more or less faithfully, and you will find that they provide adequate protective coloration. In one or two cases, in fact, they might even give you a slight discoloration. But you'll pass, and that's what counts.

17. PEOPLE IN LOVE

San Francisco, to its critics, appears self-satisfied to the point of smugness—but how could it be otherwise? No handsome child could be more spoiled by extravagant praise than this

young-old city that has been described variously as "The Pearl
of the Pacific," "Queen City of the West," "Baghdad-by-the-
Bay," and even, in an outburst from Gelett Burgess, "San
Francisco the Impossible, the City of Miracles!"

Even so presumably hard-bitten a crew as the members of
the WPA Writers Project was swept away: "When the other
cities of the Coast were still hamlets in forest clearings or
desert cow-towns, San Francisco was 'The City.' It is 'The City'
still." Will Rogers put it more succinctly: "The city that was
never a town." O. Henry said grandiloquently: "East is East
—and West is San Francisco." Willie Britt insisted he'd rather
be "a busted lamp-post" on Battery Street than the Waldorf-
Astoria (a choice that was never offered him), and Franklin
Roosevelt decided, in the accents of Groton, that "when San
Franciscans start out to do something, I think they do it better
than the people of any other city."

Everybody seems to have said it since, but apparently
Katharine Fullerton Gerould wrote it first: "There are only two
real cities in the United States. One is New York and one is
San Francisco. The rest are just towns—very nice ones, some
of them, but not cities at all." (Novelist Frank Norris was a
bit more generous; he included New Orleans.) Even San Francisco's rubble seems to have been better than anyone else's:
after the 1906 disaster, Larry Harris wrote a rhapsody to "The
Damndest Finest Ruins!", a poem that toastmasters feel
called upon to recite at least once a year.

And in any restaurant on almost any evening, you are likely
to see an old-timer raise his glass in a long, ancient, and much-
favored toast in which San Francisco is compared to Naples,
Rome, Paris, London, Heaven, Paradise, and Valhalla—more
than favorably, I might add.

Do San Franciscans react to all this by digging their toes

into the pavement, murmuring "Aw, shucks," and hurriedly changing the subject? Not on your stereotype. They eat it up and come back for seconds. And although, in the eyes of some, the city isn't what it used to be ("And never was," in the cynical words of Will Irwin), the praise is still being ladled out in reasonably satisfying portions. Which is as it should be. "The worst San Francisco can get," the late Chester "Tiny" Armstrong once said, "is still better than any place else."

It is well-established practice by now for all visiting celebrities to tell the press, at the outset of every interview, that "San Francisco is my favorite city. You people who live here don't know how lucky you are." (Yes we do, thanks all the same.) The only star of any magnitude who went against this credo was Marie McDonald who, upon opening an engagement at the Fairmont Hotel, announced, "What's so hot about this town? Give me Beverly Hills every time." (Dogs bit her, children threw rocks at her, and her engagement was, in the show-business phrase, a bomb.) I have listened patiently while such luminaries as Frank Sinatra, Kirk Douglas, and Walter Pidgeon have said, at various times, "I love this town. I'm going to get an apartment here and come up every weekend." (They never do, but it's a nice thought.)

The protestations of undying love come from all quarters.

Horace Sutton, the excellent travel writer, tours the restaurants and calls San Francisco "the playing fields of eatin'." He watches the tourists at Top o' the Mark "filing past the view as if it were a bier." Billy Graham, prior to his arrival for a notable crusade, intones in Chicago, "San Francisco is a city that has lost its soul." The same Reverend Mr. Graham, after three weeks in town: "The Bay Area is so beautiful I hesitate to preach about Heaven while I'm here." The chorus is joined by Dr. George Harris Collingwood, Episcopal minister at Junction City, Kansas: "If I should receive a call to San Francisco, I would have a hard time deciding whether it was a genuine call of the Lord—or a dictate of my own desires."

One Herbert Mye of Tonawanda, N.Y., visits the city for the first time and expresses his wonderment: "It's a good thing the early settlers landed on the East coast. If they'd landed in San Francisco first, the rest of the country would still be uninhabited." Alathea Siddons of London looks at what Robert Louis Stevenson called "the citied hills" and sighs, "I feel sorry for children born here. How disappointing to grow up and find out the whole world isn't like this." William Hewitt accurately sums up the San Franciscan's private delight in his compact surroundings: "San Francisco is just small enough so you think you know everybody—and just big enough so you don't."

The citizens have the knack of twisting any comment about their city into a compliment. If a crusader thunders against "San Francisco's wickedness," the native is not at all discomfited; after all, the city was born in a brawl. If sociologists shake their heads over the rate of alcoholism—highest in the land— well, that, too, is in the tradition of The Champagne City, the Paris of the West.

There is even a certain amount of gratification to be found in the monumental suicide rate off the Golden Gate Bridge. Most of the leapers choose the east side, for an obvious reason: They want their last sight to be that of heaven on earth—San Francisco, the siren city, sprawled out languorously on her hills.

And if nobody else will say anything good about San Francisco, meanwhile denigrating her only rival, the San Franciscan will. It was during a miserable downpour that Larry Geraldi was heard to say, in answer to nobody's challenge: "I still prefer a wet San Francisco to a dry Manhattan!"

Being hopelessly addicted to San Francisco myself, I know

that all the foregoing statements were made in utter sincerity. I am so confident of the city's unparalleled attractions that my hackles no longer rise when a newcomer fails to respond to its charms. It's just a matter of time. Sooner or later, San Francisco gets 'em all.

A case in point is humorist Corey Ford, the kind of dyed-in-the-East New Yorker who thinks the sun rises out of the East River and sinks in the Hudson. San Francisco he once dismissed as "nothing but a kind of vertical Chicago" whose architecture was "Chinatown Victorian." But after spending a week in the Belvedere home of his friends, the Merritt Kirk Ruddocks, gazing at the golden flanks of the city across the Bay, he became a raving convert. He was last seen shopping for a summer place in the area, and showing the predictable change of attitude.

"It's a lot like Hong Kong," he decided, "but I like it even better. After all—Hong Kong doesn't have a Chinatown!"

The San Franciscan loves every part of his city—a generality we'll illustrate by a sort of guessing game. Freeman Pepper, who held the same job for twenty-one years, retired and moved his family to Palm Springs to fight an attack of arthritis. We'll tell you what Mrs. Pepper had to say as they moved away—and you try to guess where they lived in San Francisco:

"We hate to leave our place. The climate is wonderful—very little fog—and beautiful plants and flowers grow nearly everywhere. There are lots of little night-singing birds, and sea gulls, cormorants and a few pelicans. But the best thing is our million-dollar view. From our windows, we can see from the Gate Bridge to the Bay Bridge, and the sunsets are spectacular. And at night, with all the lights aglow, San Francisco is indeed a glamorous city. We shall miss our lovely home very much."

For twenty-one years, Mr. and Mrs. Pepper lived on Alcatraz, where he was a guard.

The true San Franciscan feels a pang every time a landmark disappears—a sentiment perhaps best summed up by Mrs. Stan Golding: "When the hills are leveled and the fog is a homeless waif; when the cable slots are silent and the clock on the Ferry Building tolls the hour of zero—where then shall we go to find a place called home?"

And the San Franciscan, bless his sturdy soul, still rises manfully to the challenge of those who would call it "Frisco." Some of us are inclined to retort harshly and rudely to those who use the dirty word, but there's another approach. Cyril Wright's, for instance, in a letter to an Eastern friend who said he couldn't understand the objections. Wrote Wright:

"San Francisco is a city set to music, and the words 'San Francisco' are part of the melody. Speak them, my friend. Speak them softly, as San Franciscans do. The padres, the missions, the haciendados, the '49ers; the gentle fog, the bright sun, the sea; the past, the present, and the future of this warm and friendly city—all are in those words. Speak those gentle syllables, good friend—San Francisco. Now say 'Frisco.' Do you see what we mean?"

Poet George Sterling called it "the cool grey city of love," and the love lives on—the love of a people for their place.

18. MADAM TO MADAM

Polly Adler, author of the best-selling *A House Is Not a Home*, and Sally Stanford, also a retired madam but with no literary rating as yet, met for the first time in San Francisco across a luncheon table in the Lochinvar Room of the Mark Hopkins Hotel, so we sent Our Man Jerome up to have a look and listen at the historic encounter. He came back rather confused, but this seems to be what transpired:

Lochinvar Room jammed with curiosity-seekers. Biggest Friday crowd in its history. Polly walked in, said, "Sally Stanford, I presume," and sat down. Miss Adler, who's about fifty and black-haired, very quietly dressed in gray knit dress, pearl and gold earrings, and eight-carat marquise-shaped diamond ring that once belonged to opera star Rosa Ponselle. Miss Stanford all mink and diamonds.

Girls very demure, talking small talk and trying to act like they weren't being stared at. Sally ordered martini. Polly shuddered and asked for "tall, slow glass of scotch and water," then went into a spiel about how glad she was to be out of The Business.

"You know the madam's lament," she sighed to Sally. Sally shook her head. "Everybody goes upstairs but us," said Polly. After Sally stopped shaking, Polly went on: "Yeah, it's quite a relief to open the front door and not have to look at the man's feet first." Nobody said anything, so Polly explained: "You know, big feet. Cops."

Toying with her scrambled eggs, Polly, who's short and rather dumpy, launched into a discussion of her book. "I wrote it in longhand," she said. "I understand Hemingway writes that way too. It's selling great. Number Two in the country. I can't seem to pass Dr. Peale's *Power of Positive Thinking* but I finally got ahead of *A Man Named Peter*."

The name of Dr. Kinsey crept into the conversation, and Polly said, "I wrote and asked him to write the foreword to my book. He said no—but what a gentleman. In my letter I misspelled foreword 'forward,' and in his letter he misspelled it the same way. So I sent him a copy of my book, inscribed, 'From one researcher to another.'"

A free-lance photographer named Barney Vogel came over to the table and took a picture of Polly and Sally. "We don't want any publicity," said Polly sharply, while Sally looked distressed.

Polly pulled out a piece of paper and said to Vogel, "Write on that, 'I promise not to use this in my newspaper,' and sign it." Vogel complied. "I'm tired of people looking at us like curiosities," she went on. "I've had enough of that." Sally went on eating her Hangtown Fry.

Henry De Gorog, who works for Miss Stanford, walked in with Sally's pet parrot, Loretta. "Isn't this wonderful?" said Sally delightedly. "Polly and polly. Polly, meet Polly." Loretta nuzzled Sally's mink, then rolled on the table and played dead.

"Hey," said Mr. De Gorog from out of nowhere, "did you know I was born in Buckingham Palace? Well, I was. My father worked on the kitchen staff there, and I was born in the palace." Nobody said anything and Mr. De Gorog subsided. He took the parrot away, much to Miss Adler's obvious relief.

Polly, who now lives in Burbank—"I love it there because I'm just a Russian peasant and I like to run around in my bare feet"—is attending U.C.L.A. First she studied Abnormal Psychology, and then switched to Great Literature. "I hated Nietzsche," she said, "but I'm having fun piddling around with Voltaire. Incidentally, know how respectable I am now? I live across the street from a church and a police sergeant. But rumors keep getting printed that I'm running a place in Coldwater Canyon. Ridiculous."

The ladies got up to go, with all eyes in the Lochinvar Room following them. "I'll probably do my next book about my patients," she said. That's what she calls her former girls. "I'm sure glad to be out of the business. The men. 'Press my tie, shine my shoes, drive me home, call my office.' Honest, it was worse than being married."

That night, Polly and Sally were to attend the opening of "The House," a restaurant in Miss Stanford's former establishment at 1144 Pine. "It's got a beautiful iron gate at the entrance," Sally said as they walked out of the Lochinvar. "I want to buy it for my mausoleum. Nobody ever got past that door unless I wanted them to."

They walked into the Mark lobby past a row of elderly ladies who studied them intently. "Why do people always stare at us?" asked Polly irritably. "Are we such curiosities?"

Robert de Roos, a free-lance magazine writer, stopped Polly to ask her how her book was selling. "The royalties are rolling in," she enthused. "It's just selling and selling and selling."

Writer de Roos sighed one of the world's oldest sighs.

"You amateurs," he said, "are ruining the business."

19. SOUTH SEAS INTERLUDE

I am writing this at what may very well be the end of the world—in an unknown hotel on the outskirts of a town whose name I only recently learned, at the western tip of an island familiar only to the more dedicated readers of Rand-McNally.

The hotel is the Mocambo. The town is Nadi—pronounced Nandi. And the island is Viti Levu, in the Fiji group.

What am I doing here? The answer is a saga in the classic tradition of Captain Cook and Captain Bligh, embracing in its heroic sweep San Francisco, Tahiti, Aitutaki, Western Samoa, and now Viti Levu—where, in a few hours, I was to have caught a Qantas 707 jet airliner out of Sydney for the long, swift voyage home. But fate, the slattern, has fickly fingered me. The word has just been received: Hurricane in Hawaii, twenty-four-hour delay.

And that is why I am at the Mocambo Hotel on the out-skirts of Nadi—pronounced Nandi—sitting at a typewriter and perspiring. Pronounced sweating.

My odd odyssey—or ill Iliad, if you prefer—began unevent-fully enough on a foggy morning in July when I boarded Matson's luxurious *Monterey* at Pier 35, ready to set sail for the coral-ringed isles of the far Pacific. I was tastefully and appropriately attired for the occasion: Sherlock Holmes deer-stalker cap, courtesy of Fred Martinez; large bass horn with bulb, courtesy of George Gutekunst, and a do-it-yourself Bloody Mary kit, courtesy of Enrico Banducci. Plus a bagful of beads for the natives. Little did I know then—but how soon I was to learn—that it's the natives who sell beads to the tour-ists.

"That brass horn," said the *Monterey*'s dashing skipper, Captain M. C. Stone. "What's it for?"

"It's an elephant's mating call," I explained, squeezing the bulb and producing a weird, prolonged oooooo-wahhhhh. The captain looked nervously up and down the deck.

"I'm glad it doesn't work," he said. "We have little enough trunk space as it is." I could tell that Captain Stone and I were going to get along.

A ship's departure is leisurely, even anticlimactic. You stand at the rail and wave down at your friends on the dock. Then you wave some more, smiling all the while. The arm becomes tired, the smile becomes fixed, but still you are rooted. You can't turn away from the rail, because that would be rude. They can't leave the dock for the same reason. Then, just short of wit's end, the liner slowly inches away, the band plays furiously, the smiles become cackles of relief, and the strands of serpentine break one by one (something quite significant there for you amateur psychiatrists). The ship, umbilically free at last, moves out. But it takes three days for the fixed smile to wear off.

After a brief stop at Wilmington, a little-known port on the outskirts of Los Something-or-other, the *Monterey* took a deep breath and headed for the open ocean. Next stop: Tahiti, isle of love everlasting.

The *Monterey* is indeed America afloat. Superb air-conditioning keeps her cool and dry, every hair in place, no beads of perspiration on her upper lip. She is tastefully decorated from stem to stern in whites and pastels. My stateroom had windows rather than portholes, and shoji screens to conceal the sea. Except for the traditional, immemorial slight creakings and rollings of a liner, you would think you were in a luxury hotel—and even the motion is reduced to a minimum by great fins below the water line.

The long, lazy days slipped past into the foaming wake. The weather grew steadily warmer, the sea bluer and calmer, the passengers more and more languid. We danced in the Polynesian Room, we drank at the Outrigger Bar, we flirted on the poop deck, we swam, played paddle tennis, and ping-pong, got into bridge and shuffleboard contests, fashioned funny hats for a party, and cracked eggs over each other's heads to celebrate the crossing of the equator.

And we ate. And ate. And ate. We ate 6 A.M. hot doughnuts and icy fruit at the pool, four-course breakfasts in the dining salon, five-course lunches, afternoon teas, seven-course dinners, and, for a final caloric flourish, midnight snacks in the Outrigger Bar. If you're hollow-cheeked and run down, Walter Titz, the *Monterey*'s executive chef, guarantees to add a pound a day to your weight—and I think he's being conservative.

Nine days, 4000 miles, and 37,000 calories out of San Francisco, the exciting cry of "Tahiti!" rang along the *Monterey's* decks at dawn. We crowded to the rails to stare at the fabled, mountainous isle of Gauguin, Loti, Bligh, and beauty. Golden-skinned Tahitian girls swarmed aboard to drape tiare leis around our fat American necks and kiss our fat American cheeks—and three Frenchmen, straight out of the film *Casablanca*, approached me. They were wearing rain-soaked trench coats, and cigarettes dangled from their lips.

Motioning me aside, one whispered, "M'sieu Caen?" I nodded guardedly. How had they found out I was carrying the Maltese Falcon in my luggage? Or perhaps they wanted me to smuggle money ashore, or even opium.

After glancing around nervously, the spokesman went on: "I am M'sieu Quelque Chose. I have the honor to invite you to speak Monday night—at the meeting of our Rotary Club."

I agreed enthusiastically. I was in Tahiti—and prepared to live exactly as the natives do, right to the hilt.

Papeete, Tahiti: The prototype, the original, of all South Seas ports. Red tin roofs steaming in the damp sunlight, acrid smell of copra along the waterfront, ships from the seven seas tugging at their lines: the great white *Monterey*, the *Tahitien*, the *Mélanésien*, a sleek Japanese training ship. In the distance the fantastic, jagged upthrust mountains climbing to six thousand feet, straight out of the sea, the shining sea. And, twelve miles offshore, the enchanted isle of Moorea—the original Bali H'ai—outlined against the setting sun, looking like a cathedral smashed by a giant.

Tahiti. Lush green world living a charmed and charming life far out of this world—four thousand miles from the American mainland, two thousand miles from the main airline routes, hard to get to, harder to leave. Shaped roughly like the figure eight, a tiny blob in the Pacific, a tinier spot on the map, and yet the most famous, the most fabled, the most dreamed-of, written-about, and sighed-over island in the world.

Pearl of Polynesia. Ever since Paul Gauguin, the vision of Tahiti has lurked in the back of men's minds, like a grain of sand in an oyster, irritating, troubling, always present, always growing, taking shape finally as a symbol of escape, the last place on earth to run away to, a volcanic retreat from reality to real values: love and laughter, peace and plenty. And so it is, even today. As the world grows harder, as the strontium 90 falls faster, Tahiti remains soft and warm and welcomes you with a kiss on both cheeks.

Paradise Isle. If you're a luxury-loving, efficiency-minded Westerner, its allure is hard to see at first. There is a certain tackiness, even a sloppiness, about Papeete. The traffic is a fierce and endless putt-puttpourri of tiny French cars, sputtering motor scooters and whizzing bicycles. The night clubs are bare, wooden, and primitive, and the beaches are sparse—either black sand or coral-encrusted. The girls are straight-backed, straight-limbed, and golden brown, but they don't really look like Dorothy Lamour in her prime—and even the best hotel doesn't have hot water. And the rains come and go and come again: hot, drenching tropical downpours that seem to evaporate into steam almost before the drops hit the ground. And yet, in a few days, all these things seem unimportant, as they should. The nerves relax, the tensions ease in a warm welter of laughter, and the ever-present scent of tiare Tahiti, the true gardenia. And at last you understand the truth of the old saying: "Three weeks in Tahiti is too much—and three months is not enough."

Tahiti: The island is never quiet. The roosters crow day

and night, as though in utter confusion. Thousands of myna birds chatter, discuss, argue, and fight—every now and then holding one of their fantastic "courts": gathering in a circle around an offending bird, deciding its fate and then all leaping on it with a flurry of pecks and wings (the victim usually escapes). Rats scuttle through the pandanus roofs, giant moths flutter against the lights, and large, hairy spiders (non-poisonous) lie in wait for the buzzing mosquitoes. And always, somewhere, the sound of guitar and ukulele, the click-clack-click of sticks beating rhythmically on bamboo blocks under the velvety night sky—where Venus shines bright as the moon, casting a wake over the black waters.

The Tahitians: By the hundreds they squat along the one road around the island, giggling and gossiping, waiting for "*le truck*"—the makeshift busses that carry more squeezed-in passengers than a Powell Street cable, plus pigs on the roof, and shiny tuna and bonita dangling from the rear. "*Le truck*," moving slowly from village to village to and from Papeete. If you want it to stop for you, you lay a palm frond on the road, retreat to a coconut tree and take a nap; the driver will awaken you, help you carry your packages, deliver your fish to a friend, back up to wait for your girl. The Tahitians, working very little, laughing very much, living happily off the land: the coffee bean grows outside the window, the bread fruit (delicious) hangs close at hand, the grapefruit is huge and sweet, the bananas, yams, and coconuts are everywhere, and there is always fish in the lagoon. And a quart of Hinano— the island beer—costs very little.

Tahiti. Contrast piling upon contrast, like the waves that break in slow-motion grandeur over the great reef. Island where perfume, pleasure, and sex are always in the air, island of church after church after church (some of them abandoned and slowly being reclaimed by the jungle). Island of primitive

shacks, where the symbol of success is a huge, shiny brass bed
that is never slept in; the people sleep alongside it on the floor,
but cook their food on an American-made barbecue that stands
just outside the door. Island where the girls read fashion magazines, employ Chinese dressmakers to copy Paris styles, still
believe that the tiki gods have the power to cast evil spells,
and go to doctors who cure their ills by jabbing them with nee-
dles. Tahiti: A fat native woman walking down the road in bare
feet, carrying a package of Tide.

Island of Love, of grown-up children playing in an eternal
park. But the outside world is jealous, and closing in on all
sides. The innocent days and languorous nights of Tahiti are
going, going . . .

All day and far into the night, the great trucks rumble along
Tahiti's one main road. The French watch them hopefully, the
natives watch them hopelessly, and any lover of Tahiti's
blessed inaccessibility can only look on in dismay.

For the trucks are embarked on a project that will do as
much to change the Pearl of Polynesia, as the visits of Captain
Cook and Captain Bligh who, two centuries ago, brought the
white man's burden of disease and almost decimated the population.

The trucks are carrying fill from the valley to the reef-filled
waters near Papeete and, slowly, inexorably, an airstrip is being
built. When it is finished, it will be the longest airstrip in the
Pacific: over eleven thousand feet, big enough for the largest
jet, big enough to let the whole world fly in, and big enough to
bury the tiny island under a tidal wave of tourists.

Considering the difficulties, the airstrip is a miracle of con-
struction. And a tragedy.

"It is progress," shrugged the high French official, handsome
in his spotless whites, as he relaxed behind his desk in the

governor's mansion. "Tahiti needs tourists for the economy. The coconut trees are getting old, the copra trade is dying, the phosphates will be finished in five years. Tahiti is like a beautiful and expensive mistress—she costs France four hundred million francs a year—and now she must help support herself."

Hard fact of life for the misty mistress who has to go to work: fewer than three thousand tourists get to Tahiti annually, by ship or island-hopping flying boat. "When the strip is finished," said the Frenchman, "we should get fifty thousand tourists a year."

Where they will be housed is a mystery at the moment. Of the handful of tiny hotels, only Les Tropiques can be classified, by a slight stretch of the imagination, as "luxury," and even Les Tropiques doesn't have hot water.

"We will have big hotels," the Frenchman went on confidently. "It is all but set for a French-American group to build a four-hundred-room hotel. And there will be others, many others."

There was a moment's silence, and then he shook his head sadly. "I'm sorry, too," he said, looking out of the window over the red roofs of Papeete. "I love Tahiti the way it is, the way it was."

And the way it will never be again, when the trucks stop rumbling, and the planes start landing, "for the economy."

But meanwhile the island drips greenly under the rain, or steams under the sun, much as it always has. There are only a few telephones, and they work about as well as their counterparts in France. The radio station broadcasts only half an hour or so a day. The only newspaper is a small mimeographed sheet. If you want the latest news you go to Vaihiria, the sidewalk café on the Quai Bir Hakeim, where you sip a *citronnade*, gossip with the golden-brown girls, find out who slept with whom last night, and gaze at the white yachts moored across the way.

It is a busy scene, one that becomes as familiar as home in twenty-four hours. San Francisco's Barnaby Conrad, the best-liked American on the island, walks past with his beautiful blond wife, and the Tahitian men stare at her. Sterling Hayden and his first mate, Spike Africa, climb down from their *Wanderer*—the port of hail, "San Francisco," is painted boldly on her stern—and thread their way through the endless torrent of bikes and motor scooters. Nita Wanamaker, the Tahitian-Chilean-Chinese beauty who is the most photographed girl in Tahiti, arrives with her fetching friends—Nicole, the girl friend of the young French doctor, and the doe-eyed eighteen-year-old who lives with the French baron.

Slumped in a chair nearby, bare to the waist, is Paul Gauguin's son, Emil, celebrated as "the only beggar in Tahiti." You may take a picture of his fat and flabby countenance for twenty francs, but it's hardly a bargain, with so much free beauty around. From the balcony of the old Cercle Polynésian, Ripley Gooding waves down—Tahitian Ripley, who once ran the original and unforgettable Tahiti Club at the foot of Broadway in San Francisco, and then the Blue Lagoon in Maiden Lane. Now, he boasts, he has three young girls living with him, one dedicated exclusively to the task of lighting his cigars. Ripley in his floppy white planter's hat, straight out of Somerset Maugham.

Papeete, Tahiti, where the livin' and the lovin' is easy, and the cloud-crowned island of Moorea lies offshore "like your conscience," as somebody once said. But Moorea, like your conscience, is always twelve miles away.

Emil Gauguin may be a bum, but, as you look around, you see how truly his father captured it: red earth, a profusion of waving banana leaves, hibiscus, bougainvillaea, poinsettia, and tiare making explosions as far as the eye can see, and a white horse grazing among the coconut trees. And the countryside: silvery waterfalls splashing down from the peaks, enchanted rivers snaking to the sea, and burnished girls splashing, bathing, and washing in the clear waters. Podesta Baldocchi, the florists, couldn't have arranged it more artfully—and by comparison Hawaii is a desert.

Deep night, the scent of gardenias, a girl's soft voice—and still the trucks raised their hateful dust, carrying the fill to the inching airstrip that will bring prosperity to the island that is already rich. And can only get poorer.

Now then, I can anticipate your next questions (or were they your first?). What about the women? What about the legendary golden girls who swam out to the incoming ships and disappeared, with whoops and shrieks, into the crews' quarters. What about love on the Island of Love—and is it really free?

At first flush the Tahitian girls are a disappointment. A lot of them are heavy-featured, some have bad teeth, quite a few flash dazzling smiles that reflect the gold in their mouths more brightly than the gold in their hearts. But in a surprisingly short time, your standards of beauty change. Suddenly you begin noticing the straightness of their backs, the magnificence of their carriage, and the satiny-silky smoothness of their skin. There is an ancient world of understanding in the way they look at you, a coolness in their touch, an aura of gardenias and cleanliness about them. Against the green and floral background of Tahiti, they fit perfectly. They are, in short, beautiful. (At the Vaihiria one day I met an American girl, a blonde, who, by San Francisco standards, is attractive, intelligent, and worldly. But, surrounded by chattering, laughing, eye-darting brown girls, she seemed all wrong—sadly out of place.)

Most of the girls are, to use a ridiculous euphemism, available. Many of them live with *popaas* (white men)—this is a mark of prestige—and are fairly faithful, by Tahitian standards, anyway. There are very few prostitutes, but the girls are pleased to accept gifts: island jewelry, a bolt of cloth (like women everywhere they love clothes). And even the prostitutes are socially acceptable; one, known inelegantly as "Black Back," is welcome at parties given by the very best *popaas*. In Tahiti every *tane* (man) is expected to have his *vahine* (woman)—and a man who sleeps alone is looked upon as a very strange article, indeed. If worst comes to worst, you can always go to Quinn's in Papeete—the most famous bar in the South Pacific—and pick up one of the "Quinn's Girls." These are not prostitutes, exactly. But they are always there, and waiting.

(Remarkably enough, Tahitian girls are not hard or harsh, strident or grasping. They are intensely feminine, even shy. When they go to bed, they keep their skirts on.)

A San Francisco psychiatrist, chatting over the morning coffee at Punaauia, the stylish Hillsborough-ish suburb of Papeete: "Love, by Western standards, doesn't exist here. If you fall in love, you'll only end up with a broken heart. The girls go from man to man—perfectly simply, honestly, without guilt, non-neurotically. They are never dependent on one man. As children they are handed around from group to group, from cousin to uncle to grandmother. They grow up outside of the family picture as we know it—and as a result, no mother complex, no father image, no complications. They need no one man to cling to."

Scene: The terrace of an attractive modern house rented by a wealthy popaa from Los Angeles. In the background, the crags and battlements of Moorea outlined against an extravagant sunset, all purples and pinks, oranges and mauves. A handsome, sad-eyed Frenchman named Mark Daunois sits on a low wall, playing his guitar, singing Sablon's "Maladie d'Amour." The popaas and their vahines listen quietly—and everywhere there is the international symbol of the cocktail party: cigarette in hand, hand around highball glass. A Swiss expatriate named Paul, who has just endeared himself to the crowd with a creditable imitation of Louis Armstrong, is talking about his Tahitian girl:

"When I met her, I felt sorry for her. So poor. She had only two dresses—faded, carefully patched, very clean. So, in a burst of generosity, I bought her ten dresses all at once. Ten! I thought her eyes would never stop bulging. A couple of weeks later, I told her we were invited to a party, and she screamed like an eagle. 'I can't go,' she said, 'I haven't got a thing to wear!' Funny, huh? And to think—that was one of the reasons I left the girls of Europe."

Scene: A neat thatched hut with pandanus roof near Point Venus, a few yards from the beach where the *Bounty*'s crew landed. No windows—just canvas blinds. A tiny bedroom. A tinier kitchen. This is the home of Baron Robert P., a French nobleman in his sixties—lean, ascetic, a man of great intelligence and sophistication. Books line the wall of his open, bare-floored sitting room: Proust, Balzac, his own biography of a relative who fought with Napoleon. In a glass case, a scale model of the *Bounty* that he made himself. And on the wall, a picture of his family's big château in Burgundy. Wearing only shorts, he sits in a canvas chair and smiles. "I came to Tahiti eight years ago, to write, to think, to just sit if I wish. Here I have found peace." His eighteen-year-old vahine, her neck as long and graceful as the stem of a flower, perches on the edge of his chair, listens silently, and runs her long fingers over his bald head. Baron Robert looks exactly like what he says he is: a happy man.

An American veteran of three campaigns in Tahiti: "When I came here the first time, I tried to treat them like American girls. Y'know, the old line, the build-up. They all walked away from me—thought I already had my vahine and was just flirting. Here, you use direct approach. You say right off, 'Will you be my vahine' or, 'I want you to stay with me.'"

And if that doesn't work, there are always the girls at Quinn's.

Fa'aa Airport, in a coral, coconut-fringed lagoon a few miles from the port town of Papeete, must be the most spectacular airport in the world. There is no airstrip—only a sparkling expanse of blue-green water. In the background the fantastic volcanic peaks of Tahiti reach to the rising sun—and across the way Moorea hides its jagged head in a nest of pink clouds. But for me, early on a Sunday morning, there was poignancy in all this beauty: Moored in the lagoon was a Teal flying boat, waiting to take me away from the barefoot days and the gardenia nights, away from the hibiscus and the frangipani and the golden-brown laughter. Away, away . . .

The strains of "Maururu a Vau," the Tahitian version of "Aloha," floated out over the lagoon. Arne Hogsted, the bearded Scandinavian who runs Les Tropiques, draped a tiare lei around my neck. In the open airport building I stood at the bar with Dale and Barnaby Conrad, Sterling Hayden, John and Purea Reasin, Nita Wanamaker, Betsy Pickering, and Mary Leeman and dolefully drank coffee and munched on croissants. After we'd toasted each other with straight shots of vodka, I fell into the arms of twenty people I'd never seen before and wept bitter tears. Then, kicking and screaming every inch of the way, I was dragged to the launch that ferries passengers to the plane.

Teal (this stands for Tasman Empire Airways, Ltd.) operates British Solent Mark IV flying boats from Tahiti to Western Samoa to Fiji—where I was scheduled to catch a Qantas 707 jet for San Francisco. The Solent is the kind of aircraft even Lucius Beebe, that confirmed plane hater, would have to approve of: double-decked, high-ceilinged, lots of leg room, comfortable chairs with headrests that really work—sort of a Pullman car among planes. But all these blandishments were lost on me, for this flying boat was headed in the wrong direction. I pressed a stricken face against the porthole, strained against the seat belt like a spoiled brat, and hollered, "No! No!"—but Captain Maury McGreal, the Teal skipper, showed no mercy. He poured on the coal and the Solent raced across the lagoon, shook the water from its tail, cleared the stone fingers of Moorea, and headed out across the South Pacific.

Some seven hundred miles out of Tahiti, Captain McGreal confided proudly, "Teal is the only airline in the world that lands at an uninhabited isle." So saying, he brought the Solent in to a silky-smooth, spray-filled landing in a lagoon of unbelievable aquamarine hue alongside a sliver of coral and sand. A crew from the nearby island of Aitutaki, in the Cook group, ferried us to the sliver while the aircraft was being refueled, and we drank orange juice and took a dip in the spectacular water. That coral strip has no name, no population, no *raison d'être* except the occasional servicing of a Teal flying boat. Needless to say, it's heavenly.

The Solent thummed on through the long afternoon, its four engines beating soporifically under the tropical sun. We lunched surpassingly on turkey, cheese, and tropical fruit, and 890 miles later began our descent to Western Samoa, where we would spend the night at Aggie Grey's renowned boardinghouse in the town of Apia.

Apia is forty-five minutes from Teal's landing place, and even in a jolting little Volkswagen bus, the ride is worth every second. The road twists through village after village, each one with its miniature church, its outhouses on stilts over the water, its dwellings open and propped up on stone blocks. It was now late on a Sunday afternoon, the sun was filtering through the trees and across the green grass, and the people, in their Sunday best, were strolling toward their churches— tall, handsome people in purples and yellows and oranges, some of them carrying big black umbrellas, all of them smiling and waving.

It looked disconcertingly like a scene from *South Pacific*.

I checked into Aggie Grey's, took a cold shower, and walked outside where a ten-year-old Samoan girl named Lucy was selling beads. "Did you make these yourself?" I asked. "No, sir," she answered in her careful grammar-school English. "They are made by the lady on Happy Island."

I went to bed. I don't mind Nature imitating Art, but when it starts imitating Rodgers & Hammerstein, I begin feeling a little unstrung.

Tahiti is hard to get to and harder to leave. Matson's *Monterey* sails straight out from the California coast, but it still takes her nine days to cover the 3600 miles—and coming back is even more of a project. First you go 2300 miles in the wrong direction: to Fiji. And in Fiji you wait till a Qantas jet comes along from Sydney to pluck you out of the jungle and fly you to San Francisco via Honolulu—another 5300 miles. Total miles in the air from Tahiti: 7600.

Now, then, where were we. Oh yes—Western Samoa. After a sleepless night of flailing at wasps in Mrs. Grey's boarding-house—Samoan wasps are bigger than 707s and much noisier —we forged our way back to the airport, where Teal's flying boat was waiting to take us on the final leg of the trip to Fiji. Samoa's biggest chief was there on the dock to bid us farewell —a large, handsome man, bald, broad of back and beam, with a short black lava-lava revealing his legs, sturdy as oak trees. He wore a heavy necklace and he posed graciously for photos, all the while clutching a pack of Camels. "Good-by, good-by," he called out as we piled into the launch. We waved our hands. He waved his Camels. Farewell, Samoa.

Suva, on the island of Viti Levu—the metropolis of the Fiji group: a bustling port town of forty-five thousand people, the majority East Indians, the old men wearing turbans, the women slim and graceful in saris. Suva is three times the size of Papeete, and three times as dull. Anglophile that I am, I hate to blame this on the British (Fiji is a crown colony), but there's no escaping the fact that everything shuts down in Suva at 10 P.M., and there's blessed little to shut down in the first place. The rain fell in cloudbursts and I spent a quiet evening in the new and antiseptic Club Hotel, shivering in the air-conditioned bar and wondering what the gang was up to back at Les Tropiques in Papeete.

Next morning Suva was steaming. I took a shower to dry off, emerged dripping, crawled in my wrinkled drip-dries, and struggled aboard the smallest four-engined plane I've ever seen—a De Havilland Heron—for Nadi Airport, on the other side of the island, there to await rescue by Qantas and its magic Boeing 707. The Qantas man who met me, all smiles and starched whites, was very polite—and very sorry. "Hurricane Dot is running around the Pacific," he said. "Our plane is staying in Sydney another twenty-four hours at least."

Well, if there's nothing to do in Suva, there's even less in Nadi. I moped around the Mocambo Hotel, a rambling, one-story wooden structure executed in a style that might be described as Early Fort Ord, and studied the countryside: mile after mile of sugar cane, coconut palms, and sturdy natives only two generations removed from cannibalism. I was happy to observe, in a loud voice and at frequent intervals, that they've certainly come a long way, they certainly have.

At 11 P.M. on the following night, deliverance arrived out of the dank, star-studded night. Its great landing lights agleam, its four jets whining, the Qantas 707 groped its way down to the ten-thousand-foot runway. A more thrilling sight would be hard to imagine: in the background a huge cane-sugar fire lighting the horizon, the vast ocean rolling nearby, the jungle brooding on the very edge of the strip, the natives presumably restless —and then suddenly, this shiny creature of civilization roaring in, a symbol of man's unconquerable urge to go wherever he damn well pleases, and in high style. Inside, the plane was all cool greens and blues, and the loudspeakers were softly playing a medley from *My Fair Lady*. As the 707 shot skyward again, with the soaring lift that only a jet can produce, an Australian stewardess tossed a blanket over me and I fell asleep, dreaming of a Cannibal Air Line on which the main course was guess who.

We dozed, we read, we ate and drank, we fought for the right to shave, and then, a mere six and a half hours later, Honolulu Airport, rain-swept and hanging on for dear life in the teeth of Hurricane Dot. Drenched, we struggled through the bottleneck called U. S. Customs, and then raced back to the plane. We were leaving early, before Dot could get nastier. In the teeth of a gale, we sailed aloft with only seconds to spare (bravo, Qantas!). Ten minutes later, our pilot announced with pardonable pride, the Honolulu Airport was closed.

The rest of the trip was all sunshine and soft feathers, the 707 cruising at 35,000 feet and 525 miles an hour with barely a waggle of its flexible wings. Less than five hours out of Honolulu we saw the wispy pennants of fog that mark the outskirts of Baghdad-by-the-Bay, and then the big bird was wheeling over the brown hills of San Mateo and straightening out over the Bay for its final descent. Traffic hurtled along Bayshore, the towers of the magic city blazed in the sunset's afterglow—and suddenly, in my wrinkled seersucker jacket and dirty white ducks, I felt the old familiar tug.

Rummaging through my brief case, I hauled out my black knit tie and hurriedly put it on. If there's one thing I learned on my trek through the far Pacific, it's that you gotta dress like the natives. Hello again, you dear old buttoned-down, black-tied, mink-stoled queen of a city!

20. PHYSICIANS, HEAL THYSELVES

(On the occasion of an American Medical Association Convention)

Welcome to San Francisco—a city that should fascinate any doctor, even those who are blue and cross and in a delegate condition for the American Medical Association. A city with a pulse; you can feel it throbbing in the cable-car slots. A city with a heart; it beats tirelessly across the hills and through the valleys, even though eminent practitioners have pronounced it dead a dozen times. A city with a voice, albeit slightly hoarse; its foghorns say, "Ahhh" and "Ooooo," disturbing everything except the fog, which comes in anyway. A city with an interesting set of psychosomatic illnesses, induced by keeping one foot planted firmly in the past and the other in its mouth—a particularly neat trick since its head is buried in the sand and lost in the clouds all at the same time.

Dear Doctor—up stethoscope and look around. At the Bay Bridge, the most spectacular bit of which goes only as far as Goat Island, where there is very little of interest; another part was tacked on to get you to Oakland, which is of interest only to Oaklanders. The Golden Gate Bridge takes most people to

Marin—except those few who decide t'heck with it halfway across and jump off; a Bridge of Size that became a Bridge of Sighs. From either bridge you get a fine view of Alcatraz, where the toughest cons in the country sit at sewing machines, making Ivy League pants for the Army; they also play the strangest kind of baseball there: the man who hits a ball over the fence— and into the Bay—is automatically out.

Browse around, merry medic, in this city of the world that contains the world in a city. History plucks at your sleeve: from Piltdown Man to Miltown Man, from Cro-Magnon Man to I. Magnin woman, through the eons to the neons. The Hamilton Field jets flying overhead at six hundred miles an hour, the cable cars crawling at nine miles an hour, exactly as they did in 1872. The fishy-tailed cars that will do a hundred, halted by bird-cage traffic signals installed in the 1920s. The most beautiful city hall in the country, its classic Renaissance dome buzzing with the kind of thinking that was popular in the Middle Ages. The Queen City of the Pacific, with more queens arriving every day, drawn, perhaps, by the ceaseless swish of the waves.

Physician, heal thyself in our therabeautiful city. Climb the hills, where a breath-taking view awaits you right around the next coronary. Telegraph Hill, where you can't send a telegram —but where you can get the message of San Francisco merely by looking. Nob Hill, whose crown jewel is the Pacific Union Club, housed in the brownstone mansion of "Bonanza Jim" Flood, who was much too busy making money to belong to clubs like this. Capitalistic Russian Hill, which slides down to a famed saloon featuring Irish coffee. And Twin Peaks, whose original Spanish name was much more colorful: The Breasts of the Indian Maiden; by all means go up there to be tempesttoss'd by the wind and the fog—the twin piques of Twin Peaks.

Doc, look at our docks, peer at our piers, funnel through our tunnel, get your lumps at Gump's, and claim your rightful share in Union Square—on a bench, where the old men who aren't going anywhere sit all day and contemplate the airline signs. Play the shell game at Fisherman's Wharf, land of the cracked crabitalists, and get your back-scratcher from a leg-puller in Chinatown. Eat sukiyaki with your shoes off and cioppino with a bib on. And on Grant Avenue in North Beach, don't raise your eyebrows, voice, or hackles when you're heckled as a tourist; this is the land of displeased persons—refugees from reality —and they're only trying to be like everybody else: nonconformist.

Prolific practitioner, may the city fill all your prescriptions. View the city under glass—like a slide—from behind a glass at Top o' the Mark. Don't complain of dizziness in the Fairmont's merry-go-round bar; the bar is going around, not you. Spare not the spareribs at Trader Vic's, and ask not the Trader about his wooden leg; "Don't get one of these things unless you really need it," he'll reply. Hurry for curry at India House, let yourself be charmed by Cherie at the Fleur de Lys and fawned upon by the Tangier's Alexis, the gorgeous Georgian whose Southern accent is Russian. May there be no gurneys at Ernie's, and nothing too messy at Vanessi. Even Ivy Leaguers fancy the cold salmon at David's—Yale Lox?—and there is no grease on at Grison's, even though that's the way you pronounce it. And may the food that melts in your mouth not turn to ashes when the check arrives.

San Francisco: It's good for what ails you, Doctor. Here we don't say the air is like wine; here, the wine, if it's fine, is like our air. Breathe deeply as you breeze through Golden Gate Park, where you can park on the grass any old time—but not in your car. Inhale the tang of the Pacific at Ocean Beach, exhale the garlic of Italy at Broadway and Columbus. Probe the mysteries of the ticker tapeworms on Montgomery Street, research the bar flies and lovebirds in the Iron Horse and Paoli's and ponder the people who live their lives on the side of hills without developing one leg longer than the other. And if you're serious about cirrhosis, there are always the Skid Rowgues of Howard between Third and Fourth—the end of the world in the middle of the city, full of faith, hope, and sherry.

Welcome, surgeons, specialists, pill rollers, clampers, and scalpel hunters—it's nice to have you doctors in the house. Start operating!

21. THE DAY BEFORE

(Old San Francisco—"the gayest, lightest-hearted, most pleasure-loving city of the Western continent"—died in the dawn of April 18, 1906. The day before, in the memory of those who survive, had been unforgettably brilliant. Spring was in the air and all San Francisco, poised unknowingly on the brink of chaos, was dizzy with pleasure. A modern column-about-town, written on that day, might have read something like this:)

IN ONE EAR: Young John Barrymore, appearing here in Richard Harding Davis's new play *The Dictator* (fair), is asking for trouble; or is his big romance with the fiancée of that Venetian-glass collector just another of his Tall Tales? . . . Bullock & Jones, the fancy tailors, are slapping a $465 suit on Wilson Mizner for a long-unpaid clothing bill; now that he's married to the rich Mrs. Charles Yerkes, you'd think the overdressed slob would pay up . . . Wondering muse: Does Mayor Eugene Schmitz know about the big crap games going on nightly in the basement of the new City Hall? Does he care?

. . . One of Nob Hill's snootiest matrons (Mrs. E.M.) claims that if Arnold Genthe tries to take Just One More picture of her on the street, she'll crack him over the head with her umbrella—and this I believe.

ADD INSIDEMS: Harry Coleman, the *Examiner*'s ace photographer, lost his shirt, his paycheck and his camera—betting on Bob Fitzsimmons to beat "Philadelphia Jack" O'Brien in their miserable battle at Mechanics Pavilion the other night (O'Brien won in the thirteenth). "Now will Fitzsimmons retire?" asks Coleman, "or will he go on making one farewell appearance after another like Schumann-Heink—who, incidentally, could beat him too?"

CAENFIDENTIALLY: Mrs. James Flood, Mrs. Herman Oelrichs, and Mrs. Frederick Kohl seem to be staging a private contest—to see who can wear the most jewels to the opera. At last night's performance of *Queen of Sheba,* Mrs. Flood won by three carats, but Mrs. Oelrichs, has a twenty-carat brooch she's holding in reserve for tonight's *Carmen,* starring Caruso as Don José . . . Incidentally, the party Caruso hosted at Zinkand's last night didn't break up until 4 A.M., and if Enrico's in good voice tonight, I'll be surprised. But critic Ashton Stevens, who has heard him before, predicts: "By the time Caruso gets through, they'll be calling it *Don José* instead of *Carmen.* He's magnificent."

MEDICAL NOTE: Dr. Arthur McGinty at Emergency Hospital will be happy when "Sunny Jim" Coffroth's Masked Roller Skating Carnival (currently at Mechanics Pavilion, with a $1000 first prize) is finally over. He's spending most of his time extracting splinters from contestants who slip and skid along the Pavilion's deplorable floor. "Frankly," sighs the doc,

"I'm pretty tired of getting to the bottom of Coffroth's problems."

SIGHTEMS: A mob at Market and New Montgomery, admiring Will Tevis' knobby new Winton touring car . . . Col. Kirkpatrick, the Palace boss, refusing to divulge the recipe for his latest concoction—a drink he simply calls "Number Six"; guaranteed to knock off your new Lundstrom hat . . . The elevator operator at the Poodle Dog, who wears three diamond rings and has reputedly made a fortune in real estate (on tips from the big Montgomery Streeters he hauls upstairs to Those Naughty Rooms—in return for which he keeps mum when their wives come sniffing around) . . . Craziest advertisement of the week (in an afternoon sheet): "Mr. and Mrs. Abraham Fournier—83 and 76—take pleasure in giving full credit for having prolonged their lives to Duffy's Pure Malt Whiskey." This I gotta try!

LA TRIVIATA: The Seattle-S.F. baseball series is drawing such poor crowds that a lot of crepe hangers are saying this might be the Coast League's last season . . . Attilio Fabri, the Italian consul here, is trying to raise money for the survivors of the Mt. Vesuvius eruption, hopes to get Caruso to sing at a benefit concert . . . Battling Nelson is threatening to knock Joaquin Miller's block off. Miller, who covered the Nelson-Willie Britt fight for the *Examiner*, described Nelson as "an abysmal brute"—and some wizeguy hadda go and explain to old Bat' what that meant! . . . How-swank-can-you-get dept.: The silk-robed Chinese porters who follow the horse-drawn cabs through the Palace's courtyard are now using manure scoops with plush handles! . . . Will Irwin nominates the Hotel de France (on California, near Old St. Mary's) for the best dinner deal in town—and maybe he's right: all the soup you want, fish with a French sauce, meat, two vegetables, salad, fresh fruit, and a pint of claret, all for fifteen cents.

(Such, in part, was the atmosphere of Old San Francisco on April 17, 1906. Late on a starry night, the city went to bed— to be awakened at 5:12 A.M. with the jolt that shook it almost to death.)

22. CONFESSIONS OF A CABBY

(Being a few anecdotes culled from the notes of Jack Kramer, a San Francisco cabdriver who is, of course, writing a book) :

Sentiment Department: One cabby pal of Kramer's had two shivery experiences in the same week. One spring night he drove an elderly man out to the rhododendron gardens in Golden Gate Park—so the oldster could sprinkle his wife's ashes over the flowers she loved so well. "Her dying wish," explained the widower. A few days later, he drove a woman to a cemetery and watched in amazed silence while she poured a quart of bourbon over her late husband's grave. "His dying wish," explained the widow.

Character Cabbies: The driver named Eddie. His favorite gag is to get down on his knees in front of the Southern Pacific Station or the bus depot and shout, "Ride in Shorty's cab, ride in Shorty's cab!" . . . The eccentric cab jockey known simply as "The Russian." On cold rainy nights, he parks near a big hotel, rolls up his windows, lights a big cigar, and calmly reads a paper—all this while potential customers are huddled under the marquee, dying for a cab. If the doorman asks what goes, he grunts, "Look, when I want customers, nobody rides with me. Now they all wanna go—and I don't. T'hell with 'em."

Bagatelle: One night a Pacific Heights matron called a cab and said to the driver, "I know this is unusual, but you've got to help me. My husband is out drinking somewhere, and I'm going to find him if I have to go to every bar in town. I know his favorite places. I'll give you five dollars every time you go in and see if he's there." Well, they cruised from joint to joint—and the cabby was doing fine. He was twenty dollars to the good when he walked into a Fillmore Street bar—and there was a man answering the husband's description. But the husband, who'd gone through this before, spoke first. "Here's twenty dollars," he said to the cabby. "Tell her I'm not here, either!" The cabby made a bundle that night, but he hated himself in the morning. About this much.

Meet the People: Author Kramer's favorite customer was a young sailor—a wide-eyed, pink-cheeked kid from a small town in the South. The kid kept leaning over the front seat, watching the meter with great concentration. And every time it registered an additional ten cents, he'd reach out and drop a dime on it.

Animal Fare: A big downtown department store hired a taxi one day to drive a baby elephant out to the S. F. Zoo (the elephant sat in the back seat, cramped but majestic, and stopped traffic for smiles around). The driver later tried to collect an extra fifty cents on the fare. "We're allowed that," he argued manfully, "for carrying a trunk!"

The Gabby Cabbies: They call a new driver "a green pea."
A passenger who doesn't pay is a "stiff," and a short haul is a
"jerk" (the haul, not the passenger). Most drivers call themselves "the boy" ("This is for the boy," they say when they're
dividing their money from the company's). "The stub shift"
is the period from 11 P.M. to 8 A.M., and a driver who keeps
his meter off while carrying a passenger, thereby gypping the
company, is "high-flagging." When you call a cab and then
don't show up, you're a "No go." Smart cabbies cruise around
looking for people wearing what they call "the taxi look." (Explains one: "They look like they're about to yell or whistle, but
probably won't because they're too polite.")

Add Laughs: Old-time cabbies like to play this trick on a
"green pea" who's dozing at his wheel. They sneak up, open
the back door, shout, "Ferry Building!" and slam the door.
Then they stand there and roar while the "green pea" awakens
with a start and lurches away—empty.

Efficiency: One night a driver picked up a mink-clad,
slightly tipsy doll in front of a Postreet bar and drove her to
her home in Sea Cliff. As she got out to pay him, he noticed
that, although she was still wearing her mink, she had all her
other clothes, down to bra and panties, over her arm. "Don't
worry about it," she giggled, noting his stare. "I always undress
on the way home. That way I can get to bed SO much faster!"

They're Only Human: A cabby named Joe was so afraid that
he'd be shot from the back seat (there was an epidemic of these
crimes a few years ago) that he had his cap lined with steel.
It weighed five pounds, and he threw it away after a week. The
headaches were worse than the fear . . . One day, a woman
called one of the big cab outfits and said she'd given a driver

a used streetcar transfer instead of a dollar bill—and she'd like to make good. Her message was put on the company bulletin board, but the cabby never identified himself. His buddies understood. "The ribbing he'd take wouldn't be worth it!" . . . A lonely, wealthy San Franciscan calls a certain cabdriver every time it rains and has him come over to his home to play casino all day (meanwhile paying full meter rates on his idle cab). He always explains, "I love the rain—because I grow asparagus. When it rains, I make nothing but money. Now then, whose deal?"

Ah Yes, the Drunks: The town's cabdrivers meet more souses (sice?) than the cops on Skid Row. Most of them are problems, but a few are funny. For example . . . One night a drunk got into Kramer's cab, gave an address, lurched against the other door, and fell out on the street. As he pulled himself to his feet, he said, "Thash purty fasht work, driver. How much I owe ya?" . . . And another customer, equally fractured, burbled to a cabby on Powell, "Howdja like a trip up Nob Hill?" "Fine," shrugged the driver, starting to open the back door. Whereupon the drunk handed him a dollar, murmured, "Enjoy the trip," and staggered away.

23. THE GOOD OLD SUMMERTIME

Summer never really comes to San Francisco. In July, there are warm days, certainly, and the bench warmers luxuriate in Union Square, the girls stretch their legs on the Marina Green, and the fortunate few with sun decks put them to good use;

and a few hardy beach athletes, with rippling muscles and hair to match, even take dips in the ocean, braving the icy breakers and bobbing around with the sea lions.

But it isn't really summer, in the great American tradition. There aren't the long hot nights in the back yard, with the kids shooting watermelon seeds at each other, and the June bugs sounding like jet fighters as they whiz past your ear. Even on a quiet night, you can't hear crickets chirping in the near distance, or the mighty bullfrog in the pond getting off a throaty croak.

The kids don't stand around barefoot at the corner, chewing tar pried up from the warm, cracking streets, and the stillness of a deep summer night is hardly ever broken by the sound of a mother calling, "Henry, Hennnnnery, time to come in now."

In the summertime, a halo of fog, rather than a cluster of beetles, is quite likely to gather around the corner street lamps of San Francisco. I don't mean this is bad. As a matter of fact, it's good. But it's not summer.

For a kid, there's nothing quite like the hot, endless summers of a small town, with the temperature hitting close to a hundred by mid-June, and staying there, as though painted on the glass tube, till mid-September. You had your hair cut off, you wore sneakers all day (even though they burned your feet and smelled awful), and for kicks you chased the ice wagon down the street and stole a chunk to chew on. There was always a quarry to swim in, a river to pull stripers out of, a vacant lot to play One Ol' Cat on, and a can to kick. Life was simple. Most of the time, you just sprawled around on the lawn under a big tree, chewing on a blade of grass, studying a small white cloud on the horizon, and wondering whether it meant that it might rain tomorrow. But it never rained tomorrow. For a kid in the summertime of a small American town, the sun shone endlessly.

Maybe there isn't enough room these days for summer. There are highways and super-highways and freeways so the people can speed to nowhere and back again. Tract houses are fanning out all over the meadows where a kid might lie and study a cloud in the sky. You don't have to clamber down a hot ravine in search of adventure when TV brings it into your living room. You can't even enjoy the tiny triumph of swatting a mosquito and shouting, "Got it!" These days, you take a can of something with a long name, aim, and fire. Psst. It's all over.

Only beyond the fringes of the great, summerless city does the good old summertime live on in something of its former glory.

On the slopes of Tamalpais, the kids still manage to get themselves an old-fashioned dose of poison oak, despite the shots, the pills, and the plant killers. Along the leafy, winding byways of Skyline Boulevard, you now and again see a bunch of barefoot, towheaded boys wandering along, and one of them might even be wearing a bandage on his big toe. Blessings on thee, anonymous barefoot boy with cheeks of tan. You are the living spirit of a summertime that has almost vanished.

Once in a while, near Woodside, you might see a boy in jeans, struggling through the underbrush with a .22 rifle over his shoulder and a dog at his side. And in the Santa Cruz mountains, a couple of freckle-faced kids—Hiya, Red! Hiya, Pinky!—with homemade fishing rods and lines of string and hooks of bent pins. And in the Los Gatos hills, a pig-tailed girl riding an old horse—bareback.

But you've got to look a long, long time to find a boy who can go through the ritualistic mumbo-jumbo of mumblety-peg (don't forget the toe-knee-chest-nut). Or a girl who can do the

casaba over the bibbety-spout. And has anybody heard the
shout of "Oley, Oley, Olsen free!" lately?

For most of the kids I know, summer is a pretty stylish,
sophisticated season.

The little ladies loll around kidney-shaped swimming pools,
anointing themselves with bronzing oil and changing their
suits every hour on the hour. The little boys, having had les-
sons from the time they were two, do one-and-a-halves, jack-
knives, and half-gainers off the diving board and finish up with
a crawl that wouldn't have looked bad on Johnny Weissmuller
in his prime.

The slightly older kids play expert tennis on a court worthy
of Pancho Gonzales, relax with a Coke served in a silvery glass,
and talk about the time when they can hit the old man for a
Thunderbird or a Corvette.

As evening falls over the idyllic scene, the charcoal fires
spring to life in 1001 barbecue pits from San Rafael to Carmel
Valley, and the New York cuts and the filets begin to sputter
and sizzle. It's the best beef in the world and it cuts like butter.
And you've got to be a sentimental fool, with an unreliable
memory to boot, to think that the barbaric wiener roasts and
potato bakes of your own youth were a little more fun.

This is the good old summertime, circa 1960. You can find
it, done up brown in aluminum foil, on any week or weekend—
down the Peninsula, behind a rambling ranch-style house,
alongside a hygienically pure swimming pool, underneath an
old wired, cemented oak that has been kept alive through the
skill of a dozen tree surgeons. It's nice, it's modern, it's clean,
and you can get an even tan all over.

But as you drive home toward the drifting fog, bumper-to-
bumper on the cold stone freeway, you keep thinking about the

kid with the big bandage on his toe. And the long hot days of yesteryear. And the crickets chirping away in the black velvet of a summer night.

24. THESE THINGS I LIKE

At dusk, whitecapped longshoremen hurrying along the darkening Embarcadero to the nearest bar—whitecaps in search of nightcaps . . . A Chinese jam session (up a long flight of stairs, behind a locked door) making red and yellow flashes of sound in the 3 A.M. blackness of Waverly Place . . . The old, well-dressed men who stand silently all day in the rear of Montgomery Street's stocktail lounges, using opera glasses to watch the magic numbers come and go . . . A couple necking crookedly on the moonlit slant of the Green Street hill, a lone girl homeward bound in a cab at dawn, a tourist's delighted childlike smile as he waits to board a cable for the first time at the Powell-Market merry-go-round for grownups.

These things I never tire of: The outdoor lunch counters along Market Street where a lonely man can swallow an oyster and watch the world (which isn't his oyster) run, walk, hobble, and limp past . . . The Sunday roar of the pro football mob at Kezar, spilling over the concrete sides and flooding through the trees—loud enough, almost, to make the leaves tremble . . . The patrician majesty of 945 Green, first of the palatial Russian Hill apartment houses, looking as remote and inaccessible as a castle in an autumn night's half-light, half-fog . . . A hi-fi playing Wagner in a tiny, wooden house (down a flight of wooden stairs) on Telegraph Thrill, a poodle walking a chauffeur on

Pacific Avenue (while the dowager queen watches sternly from her black limousine), midnight laughter (his, hers, theirs) from somewhere inside a boat bobbing gently in Yacht Harbor.

These things give me a lift: The metropolitan clanging of the fire bells along Market, and the cops striding out (like commanders in the field) to battle traffic to a halt . . . 450 Sutter's army of doctors straggling into the jammed elevators at day's end, looking more worn and haggard than their patients —and somehow noble, dedicated, extradimensional . . . The Broadwayesque excitement on Geary, Mason, and O'Farrell when three hits are running in the city's now-buckling theater belt . . . The passers-by standing to stare at the sippers sitting to stare at the passers-by in front of Enrico's Coffee House, sea gulls playing like children in the spray of a sprinkler in Civic Center, old men (looking wise as patriarchs) sitting along the wall of the Public Library in olden silence.

These things make me stop, look, listen: A woman slumped like a sack in the rear of a police paddy wagon, half-dead except for eyes dancing with hate for the world following behind in shiny cars . . . A loner leaning against a brick wall at Mission and the Embarcadero, hands in empty pockets, defeat in empty eyes, with no place to go but home for the night—the nearby doorway, where he'll eventually curl up to sleep like a street animal . . . Ladies of the night, heads swathed in black kerchiefs, emerging from Tenderloin hotels into the thin, midafternoon sun and disappearing into the velvet-curtained darkness of the nearest bar for a shot of breakfast . . . The fading glories of Franklin Street (only two mansions of note now, where once there were dozens), beacon lights flashing atop tall apartment houses (the red-light district of the skies), a general driving out of the Presidio, taking salutes, nodding slightly, lordly as a conqueror in a chariot.

These things I note in passing and pass as notes: The Cauca-

sian bars with Chinese cocktail waitresses—and the Chinatown
bar (the Ricksha) with Caucasian waitresses . . . Thin people
prowling around health-food stores, looking as though they got
there Just Too Late . . . The pewter tankards behind the bar
at India House, engraved with their owners' names (except for
Chauncey McKeever's, which reads "ANY McKeever"), the
old-time outhouse behind the Red Garter on Broadway (complete with crescent moon on the door), the amazing blind men
behind the cigar stands in public buildings, who feel their way
to the brand of cigarette you order, reach unerringly for the
magazine they can't see, swiftly make change—all without hesi-
tation, all with a friendly smile, all with a warm "Thank you."

These things paint little pictures: Ella Fitzgerald settling herself down on a stool to sing torch songs in the Venetian Room
—all the while dabbing daintily at her damp forehead with a
chiffon hanky . . . At the annual, riotous rummage sale in
Larkin Hall, Clarence Slade, most elegant of decorators, pricing
a Russian broadtail throw—for use as a lap rug in his Rolls-
Royce . . . Novelist Erskine Caldwell squirming uncomfortably in the First and Last Chance Saloon in Oakland as his wife
and a friend enter the powder room—where their conversation
is amplified and broadcast to the other howling customers . . .
King, the cutest waiter in Chinatown (at Tao Tao), singing
American rock 'n' roll folk songs—"There's a ling alound your
finger"—in the most outrageously delightful pidgin English,
and dissolving in giggles like a schoolboy.

The falling sun of rising fall casting reflected glory on the
East Bay hills, Christmas's red and green harbingers creeping
on sneaktoes into the downtown shopwindows, the first hint of
winter's chill fogging the cold breath of night—these are the
patterns of the city, these are the things I like.

25. THE MAN IN ROOM 359

They put ice packs on his feverish forehead and they tucked a faded blue blanket around his wasted body to ward off the chills —and they smiled at him and said, "You're doing fine." They put thermometers in his mouth and they felt his pulse and they took a blood sample in case he needed a transfusion and, in a corner, they dangled a bottle of saline solution from the branch of a metal tree, for intravenous feeding. And the crew-cut intern with the good smile listened with his stethoscope and said reassuringly, "Okay." But there was no doubt of it—

The man in Room 359 at Mt. Zion Hospital was dying. . . .

A tiny breeze rustled the curtain of the window overlooking Scott Street. The day—and it had been a beautiful day—was dying too. The homeward-bound traffic hummed steadily westward on Post and now and then the blast of a horn would reverberate with obscene pointlessness through the room, drowning, for a moment, the labored breathing. In the street below, two small boys wearing Giants caps were playing catch—and one shouted, "Hurry up, you think I got all day?" The man who was facing eternity stirred slightly under his blanket, under the great blind eye of the television set, and his own eyes stared up at the ceiling he had been looking at for months. He managed a tiny smile—

The man in Room 359 who was dying.

The sounds in the hospital corridor grew preternaturally loud. Visitors, fleeing in relief toward the elevators, babbled of the friend they had just seen, "She never looked better, I told her. That's all she needed, I told her, a good, long rest, that's what I told her." The metal dinner carts, noisy as garbage trucks at dawn, rattled and clattered over the hard floors, and the smell of food clashed with the odor of disinfectant. A nurse poked her head into Room 359 and asked, "Is Mr. W. having dinner tonight?" No, Mr. W. wasn't having dinner tonight, for—

Mr. W., the man in Room 359, was dying.

Under the harsh overhead light, the hollow cheeks were dark caverns. The cheekbones glistened under their coating of perspiration. Once he had weighed 170; now he weighed less than 100. Through the thin, lank, whitening hair—once it had been thick—you could see the scars where they had operated in an attempt to relieve the pain. Scars on his neck, where they had operated again. An attendant came in to change the dressing on his side. More scars—the landmarks of a losing battle against cancer. The attendant smoothed back the blankets over the body that now made scarcely a bulge. And the wilting flowers on top of the television set shook their heads as though mourning—

The man in Room 359 who was dying.

The doctors walked along the hallway, looking grave and thoughtful. In the phone booth you could hear one doctor saying in desperation to another, "I've tried everything. I don't know what's going on with her." A trim doctor in a trim suit studied his trim shoes and said, in something like embarrassment, to a widow-to-be, "We don't know how long it will last. The body—it's a pretty remarkable mechanism." An ambulatory patient, wearing a bathrobe and a purposeful smile on his red face, shuffled from room to room with a word of cheer. He peeked into Room 359, started to grin something, changed his mind, shuffled awkwardly on. On the radio across the hall, you could hear Russ Hodges and Lon Simmons broadcasting the Giants-Pirates game, and the roar of the crowd was a threnody for—

The man in Room 359 who lay dying.

His name: Mason Weymouth. His age: forty-four. He was my brother-in-law. It's traditional, and a traditionally bum joke, to hate your brother-in-law—or, at the very least, to make fun of him. But there was nothing traditional (except courage) about Mason, and we liked each other. He started from scratch with one camera and became one of the best-known free-lance photographers on the Coast; his pictures appeared in *The Saturday Evening Post*, the old *Collier's*, *Better Homes & Gardens*, and any number of national magazines. Loving husband, fond father, good guy. Through the pains that began raking him three years ago he could still make the joke, make the martini, make the effort. I never saw a man fight harder, and always with the tiny grin that you could still see on the whitening face of—

The man who was dying in Room 359.

He made a little sound and his wife bent over him tenderly and whispered, "Yes, darling." His right arm came up from beneath the covers, in a caressing gesture, and fell back; she folded it under the faded blue blanket. His tired eyes opened, closed, and he seemed to be sleeping. The chimes—all ashore that's going ashore—announced the end of visiting hours, but one visitor remained for one passenger who was not going ashore. He died as uncomplainingly as he had fought, still with the tiny grin on his lips. "Good-by, darling," his widow whispered.

All quiet now in the darkened hallways of Third Floor South.

The dead flowers stood in a row on the floor, and they wheeled the metal tree, with the saline solution, out of Room 359. The night nurse clasped the widow to her bosom and said softly, "We all loved him so very much."

Epitaph for the man who had just died in Room 359.

26. GREAT LIFE IF YOU DON'T WEEKEND

Aptos, in case you've never heard of it, is an ingrown little community on the shores of the Pacific near Santa Cruz, of which, possibly you've never heard either—in which case we're wasting each other's time, aren't we? But let us assume you HAVE heard of Aptos, and that you know it for what it is: a loosely strung together collection of middling-to-elegant beach houses, rather like those on the Channel coast of France—or are we losing you again?

At any rate, some of the more dashing San Franciscans maintain what we might call *pieds à plage* at Aptos—and weekends of the type that might have appealed to the late Scott Fitzgerald are staged there with astonishing regularity, considering the high rate of attrition among the participants.

Such a rout generally starts something like this:

"Come, come to our house in Aptos for a long, long weekend," sang out Virginia and Harry—and, knowing them to be the host and hostess to the toast and toastess of two continents, what could we do but accept?

So, gaily throwing shorts, raincoats, dinner jackets, and waders into our Good Will bag—you NEVER know about the weather in Aptos—we hopped into our merry Nosemobile and were away. Our route was a perilous one, down Skid Row and out the James Lick Memorial Freeway past International Airport, where you never know when you'll be hit by a low-flying press agent, but in due time we made it—and happy to be there, too.

The scene that greeted our gimlet eyes was straight out of a low-budget British movie for the export trade.

Virginia's and Harry's home is a two-story rambling structure on the beach front, and already it was teeming with two-story, rambling characters. There was Neddy-boy, wearing a red jacket with Thunderbird to match. And Peter and Jean, who arrived in a baby-blue Cadillac that matched her eyes. And Rex and Peggy, who steamed up in a dusty black Cadillac that matched his shoes. And Dodie, Neddy-boy's wife, who arrived a little later in a gleaming black Coupe de Ville with solid gold fittings. And Jack, who slunk up on a set of four white side-walls topped by a relatively unknown American car called a Ford, I believe. As Harry observed, surveying the parked cars, it looked like a meeting of a cold-rod club.

Oh, about those gimlet eyes that we looked around with. They're two parts watery gin, topped with a slice of jaundice.

But don't get me wrong—if you're getting me at all. A house party is real fun time, as they say in The Set, especially in the capable hands of a hostess like Virginia.

What I mean is, she has something planned for every minute. If you're not out chopping driftwood, you're making the beds. If you're not washing the dishes, you're running half a mile down the road to borrow a bottle of Vermouth from the Kuechlers (I always thought that a bottle of Vermouth lasted forever, too, especially among martini drinkers). If you're not stacking records on the phonograph, you're standing on your head with your shoes off as part of a charade nobody can decipher.

But that's not all. She's a project-type hostess, too.

"Now, my new project," she announced gaily, "is a piano for the house, so the guests can sit around all day with something to do besides stare at each other's wives. Not a new piano, mind you. Just any old piano. And the way we're going to raise the money is that anybody who says 'I' has to contribute a quarter to the kitty. Got that, now? All right, everybody *en garde!* (I forgot to say that Virginia is multilingual, especially in English.) *Mooshy-mooshy!* (This is a quaint Japanese phrase.) *Onee-ney!* (Ditto.) Game's on!"

A heavy silence descended over the handsomely appointed room, with its uncluttered view of the wide Pacific. Nothing was heard except the stertorous breathing of Neddy-boy, sprawled out on the sofa with his head dangling (every house party has one guest who can sleep anywhere any time). After half an hour, the game was abandoned. Nobody had said a word.

"I'll have to think of another way to get a piano," said Virginia blackly, mixing herself a whitely martini on the rocks.

A long weekend is divided into short afternoons, about fifteen nights, and no mornings at all.

The first night, about 10 P.M.—after each of the guests had tiptoed tipsily into the kitchen at various intervals and discovered, to their mutual horror, that nothing was cooking—it was decided that we should have dinner in a colorful restaurant stashed in the middle of an artichoke plantation near Watsonville. "Oh, goody, we LOVE artichokes!" said everybody, clapping each other's hands, backs, wives.

The place turned out to have everything BUT artichokes, and for a very good reason. Artichokes the chef couldn't have ruined. The evening was topped off rippingly with a spot of dancing in a smart Watsonville boîte called the Corral, which features a four-piece band from San Francisco. Everybody fell into bed at 4 A.M., set their alarms for 10 A.M., and slept till 2.

Saturday, what was left of it, was everything the Aptos Chamber of Commerce could have hoped for, plus hangovers. The sun beat down brilliantly, lighting up a scene of abject misery on the terrace. Groaning and whimpering, the guests, curled up like anchovies behind their dark glasses, lay strewn about on the terrace, trying to drown themselves in jugs of strong black coffee. Healthier than the rest, Harry the Host, otherwise known as Harry the Horse, split driftwood on the beach, every blow of his sledge hammer driving the wedge deep into our throbbing skulls. Then he walked briskly to the barbecue pit and built a roaring fire on which to cook a sirloin strip big enough to kill a cow. Come to think of it, it MUST have killed a cow.

Virginia, meanwhile, sat around in her zebra-striped sunglasses, thinking up new ways for getting a piano. "I think we'll play a secret-word game, like they do on the Groucho Marx program," she announced at length. "I'll write a word on a piece of paper—a common word, something you always have with you—and whoever says it pays a dollar and writes another secret word and whoever says THAT pays a dollar and so on."

Everybody said, "Yes, Virginia" and "Oh, Virginia" and forgot about it.

On Sunday, everybody was overjoyed to discover, about noon, that it was raining violently, and slept until 4 P.M. After a mad last-minute scramble of eggs, changing the beds, coffee, washing the dishes, coffee, packing each other's belongings, and more coffee, we were away, away to the blessed city of the north.

I don't know about the other guests, but I had a wonderful time, and a splitting headache to prove it. And if I ever find an old piano lying around the house, Virginia is welcome to it.

27. A QUIET DAY

"Not a thing doin'—man, I've never seen the town so dull." The reporter stares at his silent telephone, stares at the blank paper in his typewriter, stares out his window at the gray city, rain-pelted, impassive, faceless. But even as he looks, he knows the stories are breaking somewhere and everywhere, stories that (like a noise in an empty room) will die even as they are born, unseen, unheard, unreported . . .

"Yes, it's very quiet," agrees the dapper lawyer as he stands on Montgomery Street, staring up at the skyscrapers. A racketeer with Eastern connections has been to see him for advice on how to open the town, a socially prominent woman has just phoned him about the divorce she wants him to file, a tycoon stopped him only a block away to ask if he knows anybody to "talk" to in Internal Revenue about a certain income-tax problem . . . But he merely stands there, jingling the change in his pocket, and shrugs. "Real quiet today. If I hear anything I'll call you . . ."

"What's happened to this town, Mac?" grouses the cabdriver, slumping down behind the wheel, tilting his cap over his eyes. "Guy can't make a buck on a day like this." He has just delivered a Sea Cliff matron to the St. Francis for her weekly rendezvous with a big-name Geary Streeter, an hour earlier he drove a tourist (in return for a whopping tip) to a certain house in the alley off upper Market Street, and he's waiting for that married doctor to come rushing out of his Post Street office and hop into his cab for a fast ride to the airport; the doc's girl friend is a pretty big name in Hollywood, and she hates to be kept waiting . . . Yet the cabby goes on feigning drowsiness under his cap and groans, "It ain't like the good old days, Mac."

The Geary Street bartender, a not-so-former bookie, looks up from his bottles and smiles his fishy smile. "Have I heard any good stories? Uncle, I haven't even heard any bad ones." The phone jangles at the far end of the bar and he cups it to his face, his eyes half closed. Whisperwhisper "No baby like I toldja he's at the Mark" bzzbzz "That's right, he's registered as" mumblemumble "so what you're in Oakland take a cab he'll pay" dronedronedrone "f'get it you can settle with me later" nodnodnod "Okay baby" click. He saunters back to his station and begins polishing a glass. "My wife," he says with his fishy smile . . .

Rain in North Beach, the neon mirrored in splash-dab colors on the sidewalk, the little corner place on Grant Avenue smelling hotly of stale clothes, dirty necks, beards. The noisome odor has the color of yellow, and it hangs in the air. "Tourists are ruining this joint," the young man says. "They come in here looking for the Beat Generation. What's a Beat Generation, Daddy?" The fat man with the incongruous crew cut is saying to the girl across the table, "Stay at my pad again tonight?" She deadpans, "Why not?" A kid with a big tear in his old Ivy

League jacket asks, "Buy me a beer?" He takes a sip of it and says in a friendly voice, "I used to be an IBM operator. Man, a drag. One day I just cut out and now I hang around here and write a little poetry and sleep anywhere I can—on the floor, mostly. I wrote a poem about a lizard that's pretty good. Wanna hear it?" He looks at his beer bottle. "What I'd really like to be is an English teacher—I think it would help my vocabulary." Scratching himself assiduously. "Man, I've worn this same shirt for ten days." The reporter steps out into Grant and takes a deep breath of wet air. Stories, stories everywhere, but not a line of news . . .

"Naw, nothin' doin', and it's all right with me," grunts the cop on the Skid Row beat, waving his arms back and forth to keep warm; the homeless bodies are sleeping peacefully in the doorways, the female faces are peering down from the windows in the rooming houses, the empty bottles stand bravely dead against the lampposts. He moves away, the light glinting off his raincoat. "Only five dolla's fo' a good time, Papa," the dark voice slithers down from the raised window. In Mother Nellie Richardson's bar, a derelict girl is sobbing and Nellie is saying, "Poor kid, poor kid, all alone, in trouble, no dough." A skinny cat slinks out of an alley, knocks over a wine bottle, and yowls up a telephone pole. A drunk stirs in his sleep. Quiet, quiet . . .

A cocktail party in a beautful old Willis Polk house overlooking the Presidio, the butler passing trays of drinks, the beautiful blonde holding her lawyer's hand and beaming, "He's getting my divorce for me next week," the beautiful redhead glaring at the brunette whose husband is her lover, the chic hostess remarking airily, "I had that cold so long it was SUCH a relief to get pneumonia, finally," the talk all smooth and endless and unrecordable. In Doro's, the chief of Homicide sits in his booth, reminiscing about the Baer-Campbell fight that ended in Campbell's death. At the bar, the district attorney, discreet in his dark suit, talking faraway politics. In the St. Francis Grill, the governor and a senator with their heads together, laughing. At the City Hall, the mayor staring moodily down at Mole Hall—proving he knows an asset from a hole in the ground. Everywhere, the people who make news, making no news.

"Nothing doing today." The reporter goes back to his type-writer, throws his empty note pad into the wastebasket, stares at the blank copy paper. He knows that out among the metro-politan million the stories are breaking everywhere, like the waves against the Cliff House rocks, but, also like the waves, breaking unseen, unheard, and washing away forever. He lights a cigarette, runs a nervous hand through his hair, and begins typing: "A Quiet Day" . . .

28. MRS. WINCHELL'S LITTLE BOY

For me, the high spot of the 1956 Republican National Convention was not the abortive boom for Harold Stassen, the Sixth Street saloon that advised in large letters "Republicans— Stay Out!" or the way President Eisenhower's spectacles kept falling down his nose while he was delivering his acceptance speech. My most memorable moments began at noon on the third day of the convention when the phone rang and I picked it up to hear that unmistakable, staccato voice rasping:

"Hey, you silly son of a bitch, get the hell out of there and come down to Jack's for lunch."

"I'm sorry," I answered. "I'm tied up for lunch."

There was a moment's silence while the party at the other end absorbed this example of lese majeste. "Whadda you, big man or something?" the voice crackled. "BE there!"

And with that, Winchell hung up. I sat back and smiled. The Old Gray Ghost of Gotham was obviously in high spirits. The better he feels the more abusive he gets with his friends— and I was flattered that he thought enough of me to call me a son of a bitch.

Winchell is, after all, the father of us all.

I rushed much too fast through an altogether pleasant lunch with ABC's John Daly at the Bohemian Club and grabbed a cab to Jack's.

The old Sacramento Street restaurant should have been re-named Walter's for the day, for his amazing high-voltage voice filled the place with static, and he himself bounded from table to table, shaking hands, slapping backs, and letting everybody know that Mrs. Winchell's little boy was on hand.

After this display of his pep and vinegar, the Bard of Broadway returned to his table—or rather, Louis Lurie's. On this occasion, however, the well-known San Francisco millionaire was strangely quiet and subservient—"Is everything all right, Walter?" "You getting everything you want, Walter?"—and there was little doubt that HE was sitting at Winchell's table.

I squeezed into a chair one place removed from Winchell's position of honor. Between us sat the young and attractive travel columnist of the Los Angeles *Times*, whose name, by unfortunate (it turned out) coincidence, happens to be Joan Winchell. Her face wreathed in happy smiles at her proximity to the great man, she was busy inscribing notes with a gold pencil in a dainty leather notebook, and you could see she was making plans for a column titled "Winchell Meets Winchell."

Turning to him winningly, she said, "Y'know, Mr. Winchell, a lot of people ask me if we're related—and I have to tell them no, darn it, because my name is REALLY Winchell and yours isn't."

I grabbed her arm in warning, but it was too late. Winchell shot straight to the ceiling, hovered in an angry cloud, and then whistled down to the attack.

Addressing the goggle-eyed Joan as though she were a microphone, he waggled a finger under her nose and snapped in the voice that has electrified millions:

"Young woman, I will pay yew one hundred thousand dollas—in Yewnited States Savings Bonds—if yew can prove that my name is NOT Winchell—spelled with one 'l'." Clickety-click-click.

Miss Winchell retreated in some confusion. "I'm sorry," she stuttered. "I'd just heard that——"

"Do you realize," continued Winchell, "that what you just said is very anti-Semitic? Whadda you think my real name is—Lipshitz, or something? By the way, what's YOUR real name?"

"Winchell," answered Joan, looking a little faint. "It's always been Winchell. My father's name is Ed Winchell, and——"

"Yeah, I know all about Ed Winchell," Walter said, leaning back. "Why we've got a dossier on him THIS thick." He snorted. "Ed Winchell!"

Joan rallied slightly. "He's a very respected man in Los Angeles," she said loyally, but already on the defensive. "Everybody knows him and likes him." Walter had probably never heard of Ed Winchell, but his use of the word "dossier" had already planted seeds of distrust in the minds of his listeners.

"Lissen, Winchell, or whatever your name is," snapped Walter, pressing the attack, "don'tcha think I know why they gave you that name? Because they want MY name in THEIR paper and they can't get ME, that's why. Say, why d'ya suppose your name is in that paper in such big type?"

"I don't know, really," murmured Joan, obviously flustered. "I don't have anything to do with the type. I——"

"Why, you're nothing but a punk," he concluded triumphantly. "If you hadn't picked the name Winchell, your by-line would be in type like this." He indicated the probable miniscule size with his thumb and forefinger. "Lissen, young lady," he said in a more friendly tone, "let me give you a little advice."

The wilting Joan revived slightly and she poised her pencil over her notebook.

"If you have to steal somebody's name," he said grandly, "steal a name with a little CLASS—something like Roosevelt!"

Winchell glanced around and laughed, his terrier eyes snapping. He could still go from hammering invective to his own unique brand of humor with the greatest of ease.

We walked out of Jack's into the early afternoon sunlight. The Gray Ghost, neat and trim in his usual blue suit, slapped a floppy white Panama hat on his pink and balding dome. He looked all of his sixty years—he had developed a long vertical crease down the right side of his cheek since I'd seen him last—but his energy was as unflagging as ever.

He did a little jig to underscore his boundless vitality, then turned suddenly and pressed Miss Winchell against the wall to make another point about his name. She pushed him away gently—at which point a cop happened to cruise slowly past on a three-wheeler.

In a typical Winchellian flash, Walter became the comedian again. "Hey, Officer!" he shouted, rushing into the street and grabbing the cop. "I want you to arrest this young woman— she's molesting me!"

The officer twisted around on his saddle, surveyed the generously endowed Miss Winchell, and then studied Winchell, whom he obviously didn't recognize.

"Pop," said the cop as he putt-puttered away, "you should live so long."

Winchell looked a little miffed. The rest of us—including Walter's daughter, Walda, and Lurie's daughter-in-law, Jane— were convulsed. We got into Lurie's waiting limousine (the millionaire himself had gone back to his skyscraper office) and started the long drive to the Cow Palace, scene of the convention.

As we inched through the heavy traffic, Winchell stared moodily out of the window. Walda leafed idly through a newspaper. The rest of us sat and waited—but not for long—for the next outburst of Winchellingo.

"Hey," he said to me suddenly, pulling a sheaf of notes out of his inside pocket. "I got an item for you. About the Runyon Cancer Fund. Look, here's the money we're giving to California schools—this much to Stanford, that much to Cal, that much to—" He looked up suddenly. "Take notes, take NOTES!" he shouted.

"Well," I ventured, not unmindful of Miss Winchell's recent fate, "I don't think I can use an item about that, Walter."

But he wasn't listening. "Whatsa matter," he crackled. "Alluva sudden you're too BIG to take notes?" He stuffed the papers back into his pocket and sighed. You could see by the pained look on his face what he thought of the new generation of columnists.

There was a moment's silence, broken when Jane Lurie began a conversation with a girl friend who had accompanied her. Winchell straightened up and grabbed Jane's arm. "Don't talk when Winchell is about to talk," he advised. "When Winchell doesn't hear himself talking, he gets awfully bored!" It was another of his little jokes, and everybody laughed dutifully.

Now that he had everybody's attention again, he announced in his best broadcaster's manner, "When I was in Los Angeles, I found out the name of the dirty, low-down, two-bit, second-rate gag-stealing comedian who's been spreading the lie that Richard Nixon is an anti-Semite. I can't wait to see the Vice-President and tell him his name."

"Why would you want to do that?" somebody wondered.

"Why?" sputtered Winchell in disbelief. "Why? Because I'm a patriot, THAT'S why!"

We ruminated on that for a few seconds and then Winchell shifting restlessly in his seat, sighed, and shook his head. "That Sullivan," he groaned. The name of Sullivan hadn't popped up in his previous monologues, but we knew he meant Ed Sullivan. "That Sullivan," Winchell went on lugubriously. "Why, he oughta get down on his knees by his bed every night and thank God there's a Walter Winchell!"

Then he added in another quick sample of his ingratiating humor. "Couldn't he at least give me back my three—little—dots?"

We arrived at last at the Cow Palace, and started up toward the entrance through a long line of newsboys. Winchell stopped and talked to every one. "What's your name, kid?" he asked the first. "Uh—Billy," came the answer. "My name's Walter, Billy," beamed Winchell, slipping him four bits and grabbing a handful of his papers.

He repeated this routine with every newsboy, and by the time we got to the last one, the columnist had a huge armload of newspapers. "What's your name, kid?" Winchell said kindly. "Charlie." "Well, Charlie," he continued, "I started out the way you did, but I got out of it—and y'know how?" Charlie, openmouthed, shook his head. "By learning to dance, that's how!" crowed Winchell. "Look, I'll show you."

Blissfully unmindful of the thousands of persons streaming into the Cow Palace, Winchell took a firmer grip on his bundle of newspapers and executed a very creditable time step. The newsboy grabbed his money and fled.

While we crowded around, Winchell selected a copy of the San Francisco *Call-Bulletin* and confided, "I'm supposed to be on a vacation, but I'm still a working newspaperman. Soon as I got in town I pounded out a special piece for the paper."

He surveyed the front page swiftly and said, "Hm." He studied the second and third pages a bit more anxiously. When he got to the end of the first section, he hurled it away in disgust.

He started on the second section and we held our breaths as he turned the pages faster and faster, his face growing ever whiter. At last he found his piece, below the fold of the television page. "Walda," he croaked in agony, "they BURIED me!" Hurriedly he read through the copy and yelled, "The dirty so-and-sos, they killed the item about Walda—look!"

Shifting his bundle of newspaper, he fished into his inner pocket, pulled out a carbon of his copy, and shoved it under my nose. "There!" he said, pointing to the last item, which was something to the effect that his Walda has been voted the most beautiful girl at the convention by the assembled correspondents. It had been killed, all right.

"Looks to me," I said guardedly, "as though they killed it for space."

Winchell glared at me. "You crazy?" he demanded. "They killed it because it was a nice item about Walda, that's why. Oh, the dirty——"

He flung his bundle of papers into the dust and headed toward the entrance gate. We all held our passes, but Winchell stuck his in the band of his hat, like a reporter in a movie.

As we moved through the turnstile, the ticket taker stopped Winchell.

"Where's your ticket?" he asked.

"Where d'ya suppose?" growled Winchell, jabbing at his hat. "Up here, up here."

The attendant stared in amazement at the ticket in the hatband. "What the hell is it doing THERE?" he asked in the incredulous tone of the man who has now seen everything.

Inside the Cow Palace, we headed for the press section, and I begged to be excused. "Before you go," said Winchell in a tone of confidence, "do me a favor. A lot of people are going around saying Winchell is a dead duck. Well, you tell 'em for me that Walter Winchell is the LIVEST dead duck you ever saw!"

And with that he disappeared into the crowd.

29. ELEANOR

HEADLINE: "Woman Beaten, Dies in Hospital; Assailant Sought."

It was a typical story off the police beat—a little seamy, a little sordid. Her name, the police said, was Eleanor Sheehy Warwick, she worked now and then as a switchboard operator, and she lived in one of the smaller Tenderloin hotels. Some guy had found her wandering along a street in a daze, or so the story went, and she died the next day in a hospital, her body black and blue with bruises.

That's about all—except that I remember Eleanor Sheehy. At Sacramento High—how many drinks, how many cigarettes,

how many centuries ago?—she was the queen of the campus.
A beautiful brunette with a dancing figure and the kind of clean-
cut Typical American Girl features that appealed to illustrators
like James Montgomery Flagg and Arthur William Brown. She
was The Date, the one you sent the Cape Jasmine gardenias to,
and the Evening in Paris perfume. We danced with Eleanor
and we necked with Eleanor (nervously, politely) and, after
midnight, when the boys talked about the girls along the hot
summer streets of Sacramento, we discussed Eleanor (politely,
nervously).

Eleanor would probably be a big movie star, we figured as
we puffed on our cigarettes behind the wheels of our Model
Ts. Or a singer with a famous dance band. Or maybe she'd run
off and marry somebody dashing, like F. Scott Fitzgerald. Anyway, we knew something wonderful would happen to Eleanor,
for she was touched with glamour, excitement, and beauty—and
Sacramento could never contain the likes of her.

I don't know how Eleanor came to wind up in San Francisco's
Tenderloin, wandering the dark and ugly streets, beaten, dying.
"The woman"—that's the way the newspaper and the police referred to her—but to us she will always be "the girl." The death
certificate listed her age as forty-six, but this isn't right. Eleanor
Sheehy and girls like her—girls who are part of your youth and
your long summer nights, with the crickets chirping and the
cigarettes glowing—are always eighteen.

30. HAPPY BIRTHDAY TO ME

(On the Twentieth Anniversary of My Column)

On July 5, 1938, this column first saw the dark of print in the cold light of day. It was the signal for a series of strange happenings. Shortly after its inception, Hitler decided everybody should have Anschluss without Weltschmerz, Churchill assumed control in Britain, a disastrous World War rocked the world, and the Atomic Age began. As thrones tumbled and crowned heads rolled, the column marched relentlessly on, like the brainless creature it is, and the conductor himself grew steadily in stature from postpubescence to preadolescence, where he remains to this day, head lolling as he attempts to sit upright in his high chair. Next stop, according to plan: the ol' rockin' chair.

Twenty years. A long time to stand in the corner of a newspaper, scrawling inanities, illiteracies, and even obscenities on a paper wall. Twenty years of unflagging devotion to items, tritems, sightems, slightems, and even frightems; to the highly forgettable fact, the reminiscence nobody remembers, the flash that didn't pan out, the fallen arch remark; to the flopsam and jetsam, the abjectrivial and the three-dotty ephemera of a city's day-by-daze. A long time to be coining words, turning a golden language into pure caenterfeit.

Twenty years. Almost six thousand columns and six million words. Put them all together and they smell, Mother. Who was dancing with whom and where, but why? Marriages recorded, births noted, divorces granted—sometimes all in the same

family, for this is a family town. Tycoons observed at work,
drunks observed at play—sometimes the same people, for this
is the city that never sleeps (and sometimes, as Frank Norris
observed bitterly, "the city that never thinks"). Two decades of
decadence and destiny, of beauty and beastliness in a fog-misted
dream world I like to think of as Baghdad-by-the-Bay—its pennants sometimes brave, sometimes drooping.

Twenty years—long enough to watch a city grow away from
you even as you stand in the middle of it. Long enough to have
memories that flash through your mind with the jerky speed
of an old newsreel: The Bay Bridge reaching out across the
water, its shadow lengthening gradually over the ferries it was
about to doom. The last ferry to Sausalito, the crowd singing
"Auld Lang Syne," whiskey bottles bobbing in the moonlit
wake, the skipper crying silently. Debutantes who are now
grandmothers dancing with the boys they didn't marry in the
Mark's Peacock Court. Little Joe Strauss, who built the "impossible" Golden Gate Bridge, shrugging—"The redwoods will
last longer." The rickety roller coaster at the Beach, the half
trolley, half cable on the Fillmore hill, the handsome mounted
cops on the downtown streets (especially Jack Allen, who broke
a thousand hearts), Jake Ehrlich and his toadies lunching daily
in old Fred Solari's in Maiden Lane, Joe Vanessi, Bill Saroyan
and Artie Shaw playing pool till 4 A.M. every night in Mike's on
Broadway, Harry Bridges winning the rumba contest at La
Fiesta on Bay, Sally Rand presiding daintily over her all-night
Blue Room in the back of the Music Box, the lavish gambling
casino at 111 O'Farrell, Sunday-night hobbyhorse races at
Roberts'-at-the-Beach, doorman Joe (Shreve) Foreman reign-
ing like a king at Post and Grant, Anita Zabala Howard slum-
ming at Izzy Gomez's (her boy friends, we said, were "running
the gamut from Anita to Zabala"), the last night of the fair on
Treasure Island, when the moon was full and the enchanting

lights went down one by one, and, as we headed home with one
last glance at the sudden darkness, we knew we would never be
so young again.

Twenty years at soft labor, chipping at a rock with a feather.
Answering the phone: "I'm jumping off the Bridge in twenty
minutes. Be there if you want the story" (no jump, no story,
ever); "If I don't get a plug for my client, I lose my job" (life
is rough); "Man, I've got the scoop of the year for you" (it
isn't); "Now, promise me you won't print this" (I won't, somebody else does); "How DARE you print that?" (I didn't, somebody else did); "I lost my dog (cat, parakeet, car, brief case,
bottle, wife) and you've gotta help me find it" (I'm lost myself,
friend); "I've got a gun and I'm on my way to your office to
kill you" (wait till the next edition, we just went to press).

And reading the mail: "I loved your column about——," "I
hated your column about——," "Why don't you write more
about——," "Why do you write so much about——," "What do
you have to do to get in your column——," "What do you have
to do to stay out——," "I've stopped reading your column, all
that scandal——," "I've stopped reading your column, not
enough dirt——," "I've stopped reading your column." I still
read the mail.

Twenty years of trying to keep in step with the passing parade. Of reporting that Hilton will build a hotel here, of saying
the city has grown too big for its bridges, of keeping a snore-
board at opera openings, of calling Bayshore Skyway the Bayshore Dieway, of making Berkeleyans mad by calling it Ber-
serkeley, Oaklanders mad by calling it Brookland, Sausalitans
mad by calling it Souselito. I apologize, twenty years' worth.

But best of all, twenty years of holding a mirror to the city
and never tiring of the sight, twenty years of being in love with
the view around the corner, streets that climb to the stars, hills
losing their heads in the fog, cables running from here to day

before yesterday, and history walking at your elbow down a dark alley at midnight. On any birthday—20th or 120th—the perfect gift.

31. THE SAN FRANCISCANS

If he's in his seventies, he's likely to be just a bit of a bore. "Remember the Fire?" with a hearty chuckle and a shake of his head. "Did I ever tell you how I ran into Caruso mornin' of the quake—boy, was HE scared—and I said, 'Don't worry about a thing, seenyor, it's just a real estate movement!'?" Sure, he told you about it—a hundred times—and he'll tell it some more: the tumbling chimneys, the fire chief killed in the first shock, the looters running wild—"Caught one myself, with his hand in the City of Paris window." And every time, you'll listen with respect, for there is something gallantly San Franciscan about the old boy: the daily carnation from the corner flower stand, the weekly dinner at Jack's, the way he removes his Homburg the moment a lady enters the elevator, the look of sadness when he sees the old mansions come tumbling down—"I remember every family that lived in those houses"—calling the roll of the dead. "City isn't what it used to be," he murmurs, "but neither am I." Brightening: "Say, I ever tell you about the Midwinter Fair of '94? City promoted the thing to advertise our fine winter weather, and y'know what happened? Rainiest winter in history! I ever tell you?" Sure. But tell it again, dear old twinkle-eyed souvenir of The City That Was . . .

If he's in his sixties, he watches the lights coming on at dusk, and remembers the lamplighters trooping along the cobbled streets, and he and his cronies whooping along behind, singing their doggerel of the flea, past the street-corner vendors selling wild ducks and hot tamales, past the Chinese with their long queues, past the newsboys hollering, "Wuxtry, read all about the big accident, Market Street runs into the Ferry," and wasn't that a hot one. His was the new young city of potato bakes in the Sunset sand dunes and swimming in the Bay near the mighty Union Iron Works—diving into the oily waters off the *Orizaba*, the Pacific Mail's beached ocean-going paddle-wheeler. He marched off to his war in wrap leggings and flat helmet—and he came back, after it was Over Over There, to find that his city had grown older and harder. And so had he.

If he's in his fifties, he managed, miraculously, to survive the Prohibition era, and the long nights over the bad gin at The Philosophers Inn (his favorite speak, right across the alley from the Hall of Justice). He watched the Barbary Coast die, but not before he'd had a chance to goggle at the enormous nude of Andromeda in Firecracker Jim Griffin's saloon, and he sometimes believes he remembers the dancing classes at the old Thalia: "Why, one night I saw Stanley Ketchel trying to teach the 'rag' to Harry B. Smith, and there was Wilson Mizner on the sidelines, watching 'em and splitting his sides." He bought a suit at Klassy Klancy the Kustom Klothier, tea-danced at Marquard's, luncheon-danced at the Lido, danced till dawn at the Broadway Roof Garden—and lost his monogrammed shirt (and his Jordan Playboy) in the stock-market crash. To this day he sighs, "If I'd only sold when Herbie Fleischhacker told me to . . ."

If he's in his forties, he rode the roller coaster at the beach and heard his first swing band (Goodman's) at McFadden's Ballroom in Oakland. When band leader Bunny Burson invented the Joe's Special one 2 A.M. at New Joe's, he was sitting right next to him—and when Lucius Beebe rolled all the

way down Telegraph Hill, after too much champagne, who was
waiting at the bottom to pick him up? Who else, indeed. Angelo Rossi was his mayor, Tamalpais his Annapurna, Griff
Williams his band leader, and Susie Jane and Jackie Quealy
his favorite dancing partners in the Mark's Peacock Court. He
fought his war, too, and came home to find that the city had
grown even older and stranger than he—a city that still laughed,
yes, but not the way he and Bill Saroyan remembered it. Now
the laughter had a brittle edge, and the girls were hard, and it
took more drinks (and money) to get that happy high-on-a-hill
feeling.

If he's in his twenties, he grew up with the bridges—and he
wonders what all the shouting's about when his parents get
misty-eyed about the ferries. In his Jag or his TR-3, he'd rather
roar across the Golden Gater to Marin, and what's all this jazz
about the fun of waiting in line for a ferry that took forever to
get somewhere? For the birdies, Charlie. He's the New Breed,
born of Depression's end and the inflation and Korea and now
we make it from day to day because maybe somebody drops
The Big One and then where are you, Charlie? Like nowhere,
yes? His Peacock Court is a beer joint where you can get loaded
cheap and his Sally Stanford's is a downtown bar where you
can pick up a chick who has already bought herself enough
drinks to be reasonable and there's a built-in shrug under his
natural-shouldered suit. Freeways? So what's wrong with them,
and who cares how they look? They get him where he's going
in one helluva hurry. Nowhere, Charlie.

If he's a brand-new Mr. San Francisco, we say welcome—
welcome to the world where you may or may not be welcome,
welcome to the city of the world, welcome to the alleys you
must explore, the cables you must save, the foghorns that will
be a part of your earliest recollections. Listen to the sentimen-
talists and the cynics and know that you have to be a little (or a

lot) of both to be a San Franciscan. And remember that the hills you'll climb lead both to the past and the future. Look both ways, and you'll always be a San Franciscan.

32. CRAZY DECEMBER

A strange Christmas season—the bells tinkling thickly in the muggy air, the traffic signals glimmering in their holiday reds and greens through the smaze, and Tommy's Joynt loudly advertising the Tom & Jerries that hardly anybody drinks any more. Even the rain won't make much difference now in this Crazy December, when you could get a sunburn in Union Square while trying to work up enough strength to totter into El Prado for a gin and tonic.

But still and all, the bells are ringing and the carols are floating out across Geary and Powell—the voices piping "Come All Ye Faithful" and the newsboy humming along as he arranges a Christmas wreath on his metal stand (although the headlines are about a love murder in Berkeley). In front of Blum's, an old man opens a box, sets a row of tiny toy dogs on the sidewalk and soon has them leaping about—but no child stops to watch. Only other old men who stare down with unsmiling eyes, remembering the Christmases of their childhood and the toys that were so lively on the street corner. And so silent and lifeless when they got them home.

Downtown at night, the tinsel and glitter and lights burning bright—and a Christmas party crowd trooping down Post Street in bottle array, going on a store-to-store hiccup, brushing aside the blind man who stands there with his hat in his hand. In

the City of Paris, a small boy looking up-up-up at the huge
Christmas tree and turning to his mother to nod solemnly:
"You're right—it IS too big for our living room." A little girl
and boy in an I. Magnin elevator, studying the floor indicator
above the door—and the girl asking, "What does 'M' stand for?"
Boy, all-knowingly: "Macy's." And in the window of a cubby-
hole jewelry shop: "Watches $3.88—Limited Time Only." The
perfect watch for the Christmas season, with its peace on earth
and good will to men, all neatly gift-wrapped. For a limited time
only.

Babble of many voices, faces floating past in a collideoscope.
The Emporium's Christmas lights, draped across its façade,
shining like mecca (the meccanized age?) at the end of a dark
Tenderloin street. "Gift-wrap, charge and send? . . . Yes, it's
returnable . . . Whaddya mean it's too late to get it to Sacramento on time? . . . Can't you put 'em all in one package, fev-
vinsakes, you think I'm an octopus? . . . But she looks awful
in pink. So get it anyway, she looks awful in anything." In
a toy department, Mrs. James Coleman shooting a rocket
through the air, and where it lands—I care? Six Russian scien-
tists off the Soviet ship *Witjaz* trooping up Columbus Avenue
and turning into the first store they come to—No. 735—to buy
fifty dollars' worth of baby dresses, sweaters, and stockings for
their families back home. And realtor Robert Amore rooting
around frantically in a trash can at Grant and Geary. "I threw
all my Christmas cards into this dambthing," he explained now
and then to staring passers-by. "Thought it was a mailbox."

Salvation Army belles a-tinkle, cash registers a-jingle, and
sweet-faced, old Mr. Whitehouse standing as usual at Fifth and
Market, trying to hand out the free Bible tracts he prints himself (outta my way, outta my way). Photographer Fred Lyon
gorging himself on delectable *huîtres miniatures* (awright, little
oysters) at Le Trianon—"Tis the season to be jowly"—and at

the Old Poodle Dog, three men who represent 308 years of San Francisco business drinking a toast of 1912 Korbel Secchampagne: John Menzies of Parrott & Co. (1856), Adolph Heck, president of ninety-six-year-old Korbel, and Louis Lalanne, whose doggy restaurant dates back to the Gold Rush days.

Christmas, the season of light and lights—but where is the giant tree that used to stand high and glow atop Twin Peaks? Beautiful blue lights in the window of the Korean Consulate, a tiny boat afire with thrillowatts in Yacht Harbor, the elaborate outdoor decorations in the far-reaching, star-reaching neighborhoods. A Santa Claus swinging a baseball bat at 144 Merced, the home of Mission High baseball coach Bill Mustanich—and Deputy Police Chief Al (Snooky) Nelder heckling: "Why don't you put up your batting average?" Nick Geracimos, pointing to the house number: "He did."

The mail trucks jammed into the dark streets around Rincon Annex, and a yellow bus grinding up Mission, filled with laughing nuns—one of whom is playing a harmonica. Doc Fleissig, boss of the St. Francis Barber Shop, getting set for the shop's traditional Christmas Eve party, with an assist from Max Sobel and Joe Vanessi (subbing for the late great Herbert Fleischhacker, whose pet party this always was). Sign on a Columbus Avenue bar: "Avoid the Christmas Rush—Drink Now." And in the mail: "This is a personal invitation to attend a cocktail party given by we radio station and TV representatives at the Commercial Club." Sorry. Us busy.

And so the season moves, on wings of song and light and cheer, toward its grand climax. And as you drive slowly through the night streets, with the trees blinking in friendliness and the living rooms warm and inviting, the meaning of it all reaches out to you, cutting through the silliness and frilliness. And suddenly anything seems possible: even peace, even love.

33. STARS ON TELEGRAPH HILL

I scaled Telegraph Hill Thursday afternoon to see how they make movies, and I must say it was all pretty impressive. Frank Sinatra showed up a little late, the wind blew Rita Hayworth's hair every which way, and they had to put up a rope to hold back the gawkers, but even so, a few seconds of an epic called *Pal Joey* was shot and the movie makers considered it a day well spent. Along with about $15,000.

I arrived in typical Hollywood style. In a black studio limousine, flanked by press agents to the right of me (Ted Galanter) and press agents to the left (Bob Yeager). As we reached the top of the hill, the crowd swarmed around the car, pencils and cameras at the ready, and peered inside.

"We're nobody, folks," shouted Yeager, getting out and pushing his way through. "We're just people, honest." The mob studied us carefully and silently agreed. All except one bobby-soxer with a bandanna around her head.

"These are people?" she asked.

Around the circle in front of Coit Tower, all was magnificent confusion. When Hollywood takes over, man, how it takes over. There were wardrobe trucks. And sound trucks. And light trucks and heavy trucks. One truck containing two powder rooms ("Men" on the right, "Women" on the left). And a long dressing-room trailer, from which Miss Hayworth presently emerged, wearing a cashmere sweater, camel's-hair skirt, beige leather shoes and a piece of gauze around her wavy titian tresses. Her face was heavily made up and she looked younger than springtime.

Even Coit Tower was made up for the occasion. For one thing, a new entrance had to be built. "The real doors," explained Galanter, "didn't look real enough." On the lawn behind the tower, a vast terrace had been built, of wood painted gray to simulate stone. "This is Rita's mansion on Telegraph Hill, see?" said Galanter. "She's a very rich woman who's in love with Sinatra, but it isn't mutual. Today she invites him to stay for lunch on the terrace, and he turns her down. He says, 'I've already got a date for lunch—with a dog.'"

It sounded sad. As we discussed the lugubrious scene, a studio technician in a white uniform arrived with a can of mud and began brushing the goo over the gray wood.

"What's HE doing?" I asked. Silly question. "Aging it," answered Galanter.

It was now past 4 P.M. and they were ready to shoot. Miss Hayworth, with the make-up man still brushing her hair, sat at a glass-topped table, set for luncheon, on the terrace. A technician put Scotch tape on the place mat to keep it from fluttering. Everybody shouted, "Quiet!" Miss Hayworth eyed her salad, examined the silverware, and called out, "Hey, which fork shall I use?"

"Take your choice," yelled director George Sidney. The cameras rolled and a butler strode onto the terrace and mumbled something to Miss Hayworth as she lifted a glass of orange juice. She mumbled something back and smiled into the distance. "Cut!" The cameraman squinted through his finder and asked plaintively, "Couldn't we move the bridge a little?"

Miss Hayworth arose and shivered. "I'm cold," she chattered. Sidney removed his heavy overcoat and hat. "There," he grinned. "Now do you feel warmer?"

At 5:15 P.M., Sinatra strolled gracefully onto the set, wearing make-up and a sharp gray suit and sipping a Coke out of a paper cup. "Good morning!" he greeted. "I think I'm gonna make it." He walked out onto the terrace, shook his fist at the skyline, and intoned for laughs, "San Francisco, I'll lick you yet!"

The bells of SS. Peter and Paul, in the valley below, began ringing. "Stop that infernal clanging," roared Sinatra. "Bells and sirens—that's all you hear in this town. Sounds like one big jail break!" The wind whistled across Telegraph Hill, rippling his trousers. "Hey," he called to director Sidney, "what are we waiting for—more wind?"

"Don't worry," said Sidney. "We'll put rocks in your shoes to keep you from blowing away." Sinatra shivered, walked into Coit Tower, and studied the old WPA class conflict murals on the walls. "I know who painted those," he observed. "Schickl-gruber."

"All right, let's do it," suggested Sidney. "And don't worry if the wind blows you away," he said to Sinatra. "We've got an anti-aircraft crew alerted to shoot you down over the Golden Gate Bridge." Everybody yelled, "Quiet!" and the cameras rolled.

"Can you stay for lunch?" asked Miss Hayworth winningly. Sinatra turned a withering glance on her. "I've already got a date for lunch—with a dog," he snapped, turning on his heel and striding down the garden path. Her eyes followed him, sadly, with just a touch of heartbreak. "Cut!"

It was now 6 P.M. "Hey," said Sinatra, eying his watch, "I think I'm through. Let's have dinner."

And that's how movies are made. Somehow.

34. I WONDER WHAT'S BECOME OF—

Men who remove their hats when there are ladies in the elevator . . . Opium smokers in Chinatown . . . The proposal for a horse-drawn-carriage concession in Golden Gate Park . . . Saturday-afternoon tea dances in hotels (and the kids who used to "lobby dance" to avoid the cover charge) . . . After-hours joints with peepholes and passwords . . . Erma Leach, the blonde who rose to fame as a flagpole sitter for Horsetrader Ed . . . The Government's hate affair with Harry Bridges . . . Parking spaces.

Whatever happened to hair stylists who used to feature "marcels" . . . The rage for Boston bulldogs . . . The man who announced he had perfected a self-lighting cigarette . . . Yellow slickers with bright sayings inked all over 'em . . . The plans for a playground and park on Angel Island . . . All the coffee you can drink for a nickel . . . And what happened to "Wha' hoppen?"

Long-gone but far from forgotten: Wooden hobbyhorse races in night clubs . . . Those "ruptured-duck" emblems you wore in your lapel to show you'd served in the armed services . . . The Bay Area's tennis supremacy . . . Scales that return your penny if you guess your own weight correctly . . . Fortune tellers who actually use crystal balls . . . Good hot jazz in the Fillmore District . . . Five-cent jukeboxes . . . Matching "Sweetheart Suits" for guys and dolls.

Where oh where has my little dog gone, and also the brave

girls who wore Empress Eugenie hats . . . Those cardboard
figures that fitted atop the spindle on your phonograph and
danced as the record revolved . . . "Elimination dance contests" in night spots (with a bottle of cheap champagne for the
winners) . . . The "call board" for limousines at the Opera
House . . . Free samples in candy stores (and free hunks of
bologna in butcher shops) . . . Orange Julius stands—and hot
summer nights to enjoy 'em during.

I wonder what happened to the overalls that somebody threw
into Mrs. Murphy's chowder . . . "My name is Yon Yonson,
I come from Wisconsin, I worked in the lumber mill there—"
. . . The days when it was hip to say "hep," and the jivey set
was bigger than the Ivy set . . . Platform shoes with ankle
straps, and little fat furs called "chubbies" . . . Boys who wore
long curls till they were five and thought they had it made when
their mothers took 'em out of Lord Fauntleroy suits and put
'em into Buster Brown collars . . . "Walk Upstairs and Save
$10."

Among my souvenirs are songs like "Among My Souvenirs"
. . . Live broadcasts by name bands from hotel supper rooms
. . . Wide hand-painted ties (featuring nudes) that would
never tie . . . Model T Fords with Ruckstel axles, gas tanks in
the rear, and rare witticisms painted all over the sides, i.e.,
"Abandon hope, all ye who enter here" . . . Milkshakes so
thick you had to spoon 'em . . . Clever chaps who knew all
the table-top tricks, especially how to flip a spoon into a glass
by using a fork for a lever . . . The nights when a certain cab
company's "celebrity tour" of the city included a visit to a
madam in a Russian Hill mansion.

I wonder what's become of Sally, also Mabel, Irene, and
Mary . . . "Little Audrey" stories (When the cannibals put her
in the pot, Little Audrey just laughed and laughed; she knew
there wasn't enough to go around) . . . Couples who practiced

at home so they could dance the Lambeth Walk, the Big Apple and the Balboa Hop in public . . . The game known as "Handies" . . . Cords with bell-bottom trousers—and stores that gave free baseball bats with boys' suits . . . Collar-button dispensers . . . Old ladies gliding around in electric cars that had silk curtains and cut-glass vases for flowers.

Put me out on a limbo with the excellent lads who bought Ruf-Neks and Home Run Kisses because they contained pictures of baseball players that, properly waxed, could be used for "laggers" . . . People who ended every argument with "So's your old man" . . . Big white lapel buttons with "Damfino" on them (to plug the candy bar of the same name) . . . The kids who'd holler, "Whadda ya feed yer mudder for breakfast?" just before the "Rags, bottles, and sacks" man would call out his miserable message . . . "Knock-knock." "Who's there?" "Albie." "Albie who?" "Albie down to getcha in a taxi, honey."

I wonder what's become of merry-go-round restaurants, with the food slowly moving past on a conveyor belt . . . Golden Gate Park squirrels that would dive into your coat pocket after a peanut . . . Ice that tastes as good as the ice you used to steal off the back of an ice wagon . . . Kids who were merely "crazy mixed up" instead of juvenile delinquents . . . Candy dispensers on the backs of theater seats . . . Drummers whose bass drums lighted up with each kick to show a couple drifting across a moon-swept lake in a canoe.

I wonder what you'll do today that'll help fill a chapter like the above—twenty years from now. I wonder if there'll be a twenty years from now.

35. COMING HOME

(On Returning to the Chronicle After An Eight-Year Absence)

San Francisco. Once, in a not very inspired moment, I described it as "ever-changing, never-changing." Like a lot of observations, this is corny enough to be true, and true enough to be corny. The face of the city undergoes constant revision—new buildings rise, landmarks crumble into dust, busses lurch along in the steel paths left by long-dead streetcars—but the heart of the city remains the same, singing from the hilltops, dancing across the eternal Bay. The city: as the Frenchman said, the more it changes, the more it remains the same. And now that I'm back in this corner I occupied for all the years I care to remember, I feel at home again in Baghdad-by-the Bay—and all its many faces seem to smile in the crisp January sunlight.

San Francisco, the ageless. The cable cars die one by one, the ferries fade into the dim past, the freeways snake their alien way across the soft hills—but the city clings to its golden yesterdays for all the shrilling of the manic-progressives. On a dark, still night the ghosts of Ralston, Sharon, and Giannini stalk the streets of the financial district, where the buildings look as ancient as Roman temples. The name of the Hop Sing Tong is still whispered fearfully in the back alleys of Chinatown—and on the Embarcadero the toy railroad's cheery clang and the moan of a departing freighter play a duet as timeless as the tides. Nothing ever changes: on Friday afternoons the fine ladies in their limousines still roll up to the Opera House for the symphony, just as they did in the days of Papa Alfred Hertz and Pierre Monteux. Monteux, who hated the Little Old Ladies. "They keep their gloves on all through the concert," he used to sigh. "I can never hear the applause."

San Francisco, the City That Was—and Is, always. Mrs. A. B. Spreckels gazing out at the Bay from her sugary-white mansion on Washington Street, and likewise gazing out across Union Square from the top of the Dewey Monument (that's her young face on the statue, but only the pigeons can enjoy it). Mrs. James Flood, daughter-in-law of Bonanza Jim, gazing from her Fairmont penthouse toward the nearby Pacific Union Club, which was once her home—as was Sacred Heart Convent on Broadway (her most famous remark: "I'm the only woman in town who had a son born in a convent and a daughter born in a men's club."). San Francisco, where the past is always present: You see Dr. Frank Norris astride a stool in the Hippo, munching a hamburger—and your thoughts race back to his famous uncle, novelist Frank "McTeague" Norris, who died at thirty-three of a ruptured appendix while on a pack trip. His nephew, sitting alone and staring into space, might have saved him, had he been there.

San Francisco, city of characters. Harry Bridges—"The Nose"—gaunt and gray now, but still walking with that waterfront swagger. Jake Ehrlich—"The Master"—his hair now glinting with silver, but his manner as cocky as ever as he strides into the Palace on high-heeled cowboy boots. Louis Lurie—"The Lucre"—at his table in Jack's, tearing up the menus and ordering for everybody (always the same: sole meunière and cheesecake). The socialite lawyer whose uncle was prize fighter Jim Corbett, the tycoon's widow and her fancy young boy friend, the wealthy gadabout dining at Amelio's with his wife and her lover—these are the counterparts of yesterday's fables, these are the legends of tomorrow.

San Francisco: "Here," a visiting Britisher observed, "there are fewer people one either envies or pities." You can feel that by the dawn's early light when the scavengers' trucks begin their raggle-taggle parade down Columbus Avenue—one driver wearing a high silk hat, another a rose behind his ear, a third bellowing "O Sole Mio." You can feel that on a crowded Powell cable, when the conductor pushes his way through the crowd and hollers wickedly, "Awright, letcher conscience be your guide!" And Johnny, the legless pencil peddler on his neat little cart in front of the Palace—don't pity HIM. "San Francisco girls have the prettiest ankles," he grins up. "And I see 'em all!"

San Francisco, the viewtiful. The Ferry Building, the town's grandfather's clock, standing defiantly straight at the foot of Market; its toy boats are gone and its face is hidden by a freeway, but if you're an old-timer, you still set your watch by its 4:30 siren. The Bay Bridge—that car-tangled spanner, I'm afraid I once called it—and the Gate Bridge, vibrant in its suspended animation (Small boy: "Daddy, why did they make the bridge towers so high?" Father: "So they could put a red light on top to keep the planes away."). The streets that are stairs on Telegraph Hill, the streets that are walls, the streets that are hills: the streets that poet George Sterling used to scale, shouting exultantly, "At the end of my streets are stars!" And, white, cold, perfect, Coit Tower—which Sydney Walton, no poet, he, insists on describing as "The Russ Building, after taxes."

"San Francisco is a wonderful place," William Saroyan once said to me, "but tell me—do you really think it's worth a full column every day?" I do, and I can only hope that you think so too. For it's good to be home again.

36. WEEKEND IN VEGAS

Memo to Billy Graham: I advise you to get down to Las Vegas as soon as possible. I spent a weekend there—I use the verb literally—and would like to report that Mammon has such a head start I don't think he'll EVER be overtaken. The only church I saw was a chapel made entirely of formica and featuring a complete marriage for twenty dollars. It's next door to a casino where you can get 8–1 the marriage doesn't last.

Las Vegas: So close to San Francisco, so far from reality. A trip to the moon, even on gossamer wings, no longer interests me. Vegas is far enough out of this world for anybody. If your TWA Connie gets a tail wind, you can be plunged into this seven-eleven heaven in an hour and a half—provided, of course, the Air Force and its protective circle of jets decides to let you through. I flew down in my usual state of suspended animation, with both eyes glued to the porthole, staring jets away. When we landed at Vegas, our doughty pilot, Captain Gilmore, headed straight for the quarter slot machines in the terminal—and I don't blame him. I felt pretty lucky myself.

Vegas: A gaudy splash in the Nevada desert. It still amazes me: Here, within a few square miles, on these balmy evenings, you have your choice of shows headed by Frank Sinatra, Martha Raye, Joe E. Lewis, Tony Martin, Frankie Laine, Ernie Kovacs and Edie Adams, Gordon MacRae, the Mary Kaye Trio. Ten years ago they were saying, "It'll never last." At this point I wouldn't even bet that it won't outlast that nearby man-made miracle, Boulder Dam, named in honor of ex-President Herbert Boulder.

Vegas: Where you sleep all day and play all night and never
hear a discouraging word, especially "Reno." It's unknown at
the Sands, my favorite spot in the heart of the Strip; the Sands,
which is big-league Vegas at its best, is having its biggest season
—as usual. The casino is as busy at 6 A.M. as it is at 6 P.M.
You might even wander in at 8 A.M. and find Sinatra and his
buddy, Joe Everglades Lewis, shooting dice at the end of an
all-night session. "I lose," Sinatra says pleasantly, "Joe wins
four thousand."

Vegas: Somehow the picture never changes. The same faceless men running the tables, as impersonal as funeral directors.
The same young blondes and their fat old men. The same old
dolls in (and with) their plastic heels, sitting at the roulette
tables, playing every number but the right one; they can't bet
their ages—the numbers stop at 36. The constant whirr of slot
machines, noisy as crickets on a summer night. Sex, like peni-
cillin, is a drug on the market here; beautiful girls sit alone and
unguarded at the bar while their men are at the crap tables,
striving mightily for the hard eight. There isn't much laughter
around the tables; gambling is night-blooming serious.

Vegas: In the Sands's well-appointed rooms, you wake up to
wired music—featuring the records of its great stars, Sinatra,
Lena Horne, Sammy Davis, Nat Cole. By midafternoon the
bodies drag themselves down to the pool, where everybody
hides behind dark glasses. Vegas, like Los Angeles, looks like
a city of the blind. The synthetic Vegas jokes float around in
the warm air. Tourist: "How old are you, little boy?" Boy:
"Four, the hard way." "I just met the mayor of Las Vegas and
he shook hands like this"—business of pumping a slot-machine
handle. "How much?" I said as I got out of my cab. The driver
squinted at the meter: "Three lemons—that'll be six bits."

Loss Vegas. Oy Vegas. Lost Wages. And so on.

The "Tournament of Champions" was on at Vegas. Golf,

you know. When the ball drops in the cup, the caddy lights
up, I suppose. But I didn't waste my time following Ken
Venturi or Porky Oliver. I listened in the Copa Room of the
Sands to the champion of them all. Sinatra—gaunt, intense, his
blue eyes flicking around the room, his suit black, shirt black,
tie pink. He sings with a restless, nervous drive: his shoulders
hunch, his fingers snap, he prowls the stage like a cat, he stamps
his foot suddenly to the beat, he stops the twenty-five-piece orchestra with a quick dart of a finger—and all the while he is
pouring sex out over the audience. If you're a man, you might as
well not be there. Every woman, from six to sixty, is along with
Sinatra, her eyes devouring him; the effect is unbelievable,
magical—and the men are not jealous, only impressed. "What's
he got?" they keep wondering, wishing they had it.

Downtown Las Vegas, a little like Reno. Here, the natives
wander around, the women in their house dresses, the men in
their wide-brimmed hats, leather jackets, and jeans. The casinos
are vast, neon-lighted caverns—like supermarkets featuring
specials on money; Hardway, not Safeway, Stores. Men playing
two slot machines at the same time—and a Little Old Lady
perched, appropriately on a high chair, playing a penny machine
and wearing an old glove on her right hand to protect it from
the handle. In the Horseshoe, a million dollars in cash is on
display under the glass, with a uniformed guard always on duty.
"Just to keep the kids away," he said, a little apologetically.
Naturally. In Vegas, only a kid would be interested in a mere
million dollars.

End of the weekend—and the San Franciscans piling back
into the white Constellation. The pilot swung around over the
glittering Strip and dipped his wings in a last gallant salute to
our money. In the dusk of Daylight Saving—we'd lost an hour,
along with everything else—we droned northward across Death
Valley, Mt. Whitney, and the grapes of Fresno and settled

down at last in San Francisco. Where the only slot machine in sight was the parking meter alongside my car—and I'd lost my bet on that, too.

37. THE BLIND MAN

He shuffled slowly along Geary Street near Stockton, being jostled now and then by the hurrying shoppers. With what I'm sure was unconscious irony, he was playing "When Irish Eyes Are Smiling," on his battered accordion. He walked a straight, unwavering line—and in front of I. Magnin, a well-dressed woman bumped into him. "Can't you watch where you're going?" she snapped, and then she noticed that he was blind. "I'm sorry," she said impatiently, and he stopped playing long enough to raise his greasy old cap to her . . .

I'm sorry, too, blind man. Sorry that the woman was short with you. Sorry that your tin cup contained only a quarter, two dimes, a nickel, and a smattering of pennies (I couldn't resist a peek). Sorry that you play the accordion so badly—and that you realize it, otherwise why would you play it so softly and hesitantly? But most of all, sorry that it was such a beautiful day and you are blind.

While you are waiting helplessly, blind man, to be led across the intersection, let me tell you about it . . .

Across the street in Union Square, a woman in a linen dress is sitting in the grass, methodically taking off her stockings, rolling them into neat little balls, and placing them in her shoes. Nearby, a man in shirt sleeves is asleep, his face turned to the sun. High in the blue, the jets are leaving their chalk marks—

and just a few hundred feet up, a single-engine plane putt-putts by, its propeller sounding oddly old-fashioned.

The mysterious banner of some minor foreign power flaps from the front of the St. Francis—and the people strolling past try to identify the country, and fail. You can hear the cars honking along Stockton Street—the traffic is miserable, blind man—and the cops are having their whistles full trying to keep Union Square Garage from causing more of a jam than it was supposed to solve in the first place.

The blind man has crossed Stockton, now, and you walk slowly beside him as he plays "Home on the Range." The people hurry past, their heads down, for it makes them uncomfortable to see a blind man on a beautiful spring day. A nickel drops into his cup, and he murmurs, "Thank you," but the donor doesn't hear him. He is too busy to slow down. He only hopes his nickel helps to even things up, a little . . .

There is so much to see, blind man with the sad accordion. The girls in the summer dresses, flashing past in convertibles. The windows raised in the skyscrapers, and the doors propped open—for on a warm day, the city is like a small town, and strangers speak to each other in the elevators about the heat.

As you walk slowly along, you feel that you can see the whole city, in a flash. The Bay quiet and blue, like a lake, and a freighter inching past the Marina. Children from Chinatown playing loudly in Portsmouth Square while their elders, dozing on the nearby benches, awaken just long enough to glare at them. Heat rising in waves from the white cubicles of the Sunset, and beyond, the various contraptions of Playland-at-the-Beach, writhing in a kaleidoscope of motion.

But meanwhile, the blind man shuffles straight ahead, his cap well down over his unseeing eyes, his fingers now playing something unrecognizable on his old accordion.

At the corner of Grant Avenue, the blind man stops and leans against a building. He takes off his hat and mops his forehead with a handkerchief. Then he reaches into his tin cup and feels the small change—but it is hard to tell whether he is pleased or disappointed by what he finds. His expression is unchanging. And he looks around, seeing nothing.

The windows of H. Liebes' and Livingston's, across the street, are full of the clothes known as "vacation togs," and the students, fresh out of school, look at them with hungry eyes. The wives of convention delegates study the wonders in the windows of Saks, and around the corner, at Brooks Brothers and Abercrombie & Fitch. For there's a holiday spirit in the air, blind man. Maybe you can feel it too.

In a hundred leafy corners of Golden Gate Park, the picnic cloths are spread. In a thousand secret gardens behind the houses that march across the city, barbecue fires are smoking. On the terraces of Telegraph Hill, on the balconies of Russian Hill, on the sun decks of Pacific Heights, on the green of Aquatic Park and the sands of Ocean Beach, the bodies are slowly turning and baking, with an occasional basting of suntan lotion.

The signs of the mellow vacation season are everywhere. The crowds standing in line for elevators to the Top o' the Mark, where you look out on a golden city under glass. The mobs wandering through the labyrinthine lobbies of the Fairmont and wondering "Where will it end?" (even Ben Swig wonders sometimes). The wide-eyed strangers straggling from bistro to bistro on Broadway in North Beach, gasping, "Gad, what characters" at natives who return the doubtful compliment.

At the end of the long day, the sun drifting down into the Pacific, as though reluctant to leave the scene it has made beautiful—and leaving a few glowing souvenirs in the high windows of the Berkeley hills.

Refreshed, the blind man adjusts his greasy cap over his eyes, shoulders his accordion, and shuffles on, playing with sublime inappropriateness "Jingle Bells." But it makes no difference. The people brushing past him are lost in their busy oblivion, as blind as the blind man to the sights of the city around them.

38. OUT OF MY MIND (CONT'D.)

I know they're corny, but gold anklets, on the proper trim ankle, still look sort of sexy to me.

This city would seem to be the perfect setting and atmosphere for coffeehouses, yet there aren't more than half a dozen —whereas Los Angeles has around fifty and New York over a hundred.

When the barber holds up a mirror so you can see the back of your head after a haircut, do you ever say, "Terrible! I don't like it!"? Neither do I, fellow mouse.

How can the Scots make such wonderful whiskey and such awful music?

Whoever had the idea of making the longshoremen wear white caps added a lot of color to our waterfront.

Add Sanfransimiles: As rare as a North Beach restaurant without at least one Mario on the staff.

With all that money, wouldn't you think Texans would live somewhere else?

Although I've been a resounding feminist all my life—look it up, wizeguy, it doesn't mean THAT at all—I must admit that women don't drive as well as men. They have fewer accidents, but heaven only knows how many accidents they cause. Besides, wise male drivers give a woman driver plenty of room, thereby making the girls look better than they are. None of the foregoing applies to your wife, of course.

I'm all in favor of the Cliff House, but I must say that the current edition leaves something to be desired. The Cliff House, to play its proper role in the mystique of San Francisco, should be all red plush and crystal chandeliers.

Let's face it, old-timers—the International Settlement looks much better since the fancy ladies moved out and the fancy lads moved in with all their interior decorative jazz. Pacific Street may no longer be Terrific Street, but at least it's got chic instead of cheek.

Victory in the newly gadgeted men's rooms: When your hands get dry at the same instant that the hot air blower turns itself off.

Men who were once married but now live alone are continually amazed at how long a tube of toothpaste can last.

I could qualify for those American Express ads featuring a celebrity who's saying, "I never carry more than $50 in cash." I never do, either. That's all I've got.

My idea of the grandest of Grandes Dames is eighty-year-old novelist Kathleen Norris, who, after a mellow lifetime of mansions and estates, now lives happily in one room at the old El Drisco Hotel on Pacific Avenue, where she flails away at her typewriter with arthritic fingers, plays solitaire between ideas, and is easily the most amusing conversationalist in town.

The loudspeakers at International Airport are tuned perfectly: just high enough to catch your ear, just low enough so you can't quite catch the announcement.

Real San Franciscan: One who looks at the fog on Monday (after a sunny Sunday) and moans, "Now why couldn't it have been a lovely day like this yesterday?"

I always wonder what chauffeurs are talking about when they

gather in knots around their limousines, waiting for Their Masters to emerge from a party.

A cable-car gripman throwing his lever at Powell and California looks as heroic, somehow, as the figures on the Mechanics Monument at Market and Battery.

I'm always surprised at the number of people I find shopping in the all-night groceries at 4 A.M.; I always figure everybody else in the world went to bed hours earlier.

Is there any stadium in the whole world as uncomfortable as Kezar?

I'm always afflicted with anthropomorphism when I see an old black limousine living out its last days as a jitney on Mission; I would like to hear the story of its elegant early days and its decline and fall.

Sodden thought: When Babe Pinelli retired as a baseball arbiter, was that "The Decline and Fall of the Roman Umpire"?

Being a San Franciscan is like belonging to a club that isn't as exclusive as it used to be, and whose original ideals are getting harder and harder to live up to.

Ballet lovers don't have much to look forward to any more; little did we know we were witnessing the end of the Golden Age when we saw Massine, Yousekevitch, Danilova, Toumanova, (and others of equal rank) dancing *Gaitié Parisienne* at the Opera House, with Monteux and the entire San Francisco Symphony in the pit.

A San Franciscan thinks of his city as being on the same level as New York, not as being in the same state as Los Angeles.

Add other worlds that few San Franciscans ever explore: the narrow, winding roads of Corinthian Isle, where a white-haired widow always seems to be out for a stroll, and you expect to see a peasant in a donkey cart (Positano? Taormina?) right around the next bend.

Chinatown on Saturday night always looks like a stage set for a Rodgers & Hammerstein musical—and I'd like to meet the director who never fails to add the final, obvious touch: two drunken sailors weaving happily through the throngs.

There are few things more depressing than a small Tenderloin bar on a week night, with its bartender staring down at the floor, one dyed blonde drinking beer (and constantly eying the door), and the jukebox playing something maudlin. Despair written in neon letters that bubble.

Call me misanthrope: I figure at least half the firms that cancel Christmas parties "in order to give the money to charity" really do nothing of the sort.

Wondering muse: Is mulled wine for people who think?

Even Skid Rowgues don't seem as tragic as very old people who work downtown as messengers.

I'll bet you didn't know there are left-handed men's suits. If the match pocket in your jacket is on the left side, that's what you got, friend.

I'm so chicken-hearted I find it difficult to hang up in the middle of a transcribed telephone announcement. You too?

If you look twice at a girl smoking a cigarette on the street, you're not as emancipated as you think you are.

Interested in automation? Well, the P.G. & E.'s $21,000,000 power unit at Hunters Point, taller than a ten-story building, is operated by only two men!

Sodden thought after struggling unsuccessfully to open a Christmas package: What kept this country together before Scotch tape?

My idea of poignancy: A crying child on the merry-go-round at the beach.

Whenever I see a man shopping for lingerie I wonder if the psychiatrists are right. I mean the ones who say you buy the kind of Christmas presents you'd like to receive.

A sailor and a girl walking down the street always look gayer than a soldier and a girl. Is this Hollywood's influence?

Was "sober as a judge" always a tongue-in-cheek cliché, or has it become a joke only in our generation?

My first day as a reporter for the Sacramento *Union* (in 1932), I whistled in the city room, whereupon an old-time copy-reader hurled a lead paperweight at my head, narrowly missing; I haven't whistled in a newspaper office since.

Every time I see a lunch counter advertising "Two eggs (any style) 40¢" I wonder what they'd do if I ordered eggs Benedict.

Hard to believe, these austere days, that San Francisco once had a rollicking race track in the Ingleside, a roaring gambling palace on Market, and a plush bagnio on Russian Hill.

Add names guaranteed to make you flip, the more you think about it: the grocery that calls itself the Little Giant Superette.

Why do people insist on calling the San Francisco Museum "The Museum of Modern Art"; it is, of course, but it isn't.

The Big Game seems more like the Big Game at Cal than it does at Stanford.

There's something authentically San Franciscoish about the match-book slogan for Valley Joe's saloon on Sutter: "Refreshments served during earthquakes."

People who like pigeons act as though people who don't like pigeons are un-American.

Something MUST be wrong with our traffic system when one Little Old Lady, meandering across an intersection, can tie up a whole string of cars waiting to make a right turn.

What did unemployed playgirls call themselves (for publication) before the word "model" was invented?

The most dangerous animals at the Zoo (far as the keepers are concerned) are the giraffes; a giraffe can kick in any direction—front, back, sideways, and especially your way.

I don't care what the psychiatrists say, a "syndrome" still sounds to me like a house of prostitution near the airport.

After listening (on the radio) to "April in Paris" followed by "I Love Paris in the Springtime" followed by "Paris in the Spring," I wonder what they do with the city in the winter. Close it?

I can't shake the feeling that people who say they "adore" caviar are kidding.

Add sounds you never hear in the streets of a big city: the whirr of a power saw cutting kindling, the tinkly bell of the street-corner scissors grinder, the loose slam of a screen door.

People riding alone in taxis always look sad.

I can understand almost anything except why people go into the embalming business.

Thanks to the sacred pigeons, walking through Union Square these days has all the charm of a stroll through a henhouse.

Names that sound rich: Paige Monteagle, Covington Janin, Starr Bruce.

"Public defender" is a title with a marvelous sound to it, but it's a misnomer. He defends people accused of crimes against the public. The district attorney is the actual public defender.

Time marches on, fashions change, landmarks vanish—but the downtown newsboys still shout, "Getcher papuhs, read awllll about it," and thereby have achieved the status of Charming Anachronisms, bless'm.

Seven out of ten San Franciscans have never visited Mission Dolores, but six out of ten have been to Top o' the Mark.

People rave about certain restaurants because "you can get a wonderful steak there"—as though that were a neat trick, which it isn't.

My theory that all the brown gravy served in the town's restaurants comes from a reservoir in Coit Tower prompts Howard

Gossage to wonder where the white sauce comes from. Easy. The swimming pool in the Pacific Union Club.

Ad-about-town: "You sleep better with a savings account at Bank of America." Sounds uncomfortable. And cold.

If you've listened to his confreres here and elsewhere, you have to agree: Don Sherwood, who calls himself "the world's greatest disc jockey," really is.

Motoring thrill that comes once in a lifetime: Arriving at an intersection (with a left turn in mind) just as the cop starts rolling away the "No Left Turn" sign.

How come you tip waiters, but not airline hostesses, who work as hard? And why is it you tip cabdrivers, but not gas-station attendants, who work even harder? And does it make any more sense to tip a hat-check girl than, say, a salesgirl?

Is this an epigram? "The dollar won't do as much for people as it once did because people won't do as much for a dollar." Or would you call that a half-aphorism?

A smart saloonkeeper is one who asks EVERY woman, no matter how old she looks, to show her ID card; nothing is more flattering. And a wise restaurateur is one who asks every customer, no matter how fat: "Losing weight?"

Dr. Hugh Medford's thought for today: If snow should fall heavily on San Francisco, only one vehicle would be able to go about its business as usual. Right again. The cable car.

Add archaic labels that refuse to die in the electronic age: icebox; even people who'd never SEEN an icebox call their refrigerators that.

At least twenty bistros cater to homosexuals, and an equal number won't allow unescorted women to sit at the bars. Is this fair?

Sea lions must be the most romantic animals in the world. Whenever you look at bare Seal Rocks—and they seem to be bare most of the time—somebody is sure to inform you, "It's mating season." Very fishy. But then, one sea lion's mate is another's *poisson*.

Why do pedestrians who stand off the curb look mad at cars that almost hit them?

There's still something grisly about the sight of a car being hoisted up and hauled off from a towaway zone; like it's being hung by the neck until dead.

Add great fiction: The theory that waiters, bellboys, cabbies, etc., don't "respect" people who overtip. Respect is hardly the word. They adore them.

A real San Franciscan, in a real San Francisco restaurant, doesn't grab the French bread and yank off a hunk. He picks up the loaf, hands it around the table (hanging on grimly) while the others tear off a slice, and then gives what's left to someone else to hold while HE gets his. This is breaking bread in the grand manner.

Among the secrets stolen from us by Russian spies seems to be Yankee know-how.

Some smart saloonkeeper oughta invent a drink called a "rain check." Then when one customer says to another, "I'll take a rain check"—why, it'd be worth it for the confusion alone.

Johnny Mathis is one of the nicest kids I ever met, but if anybody'd told me three years ago that he'd be one of the nation's top singers I'd have said awgwan. In fact, somebody told me that, and that's what I said. "Awgwan."

I'm tired of the phrase "outside of New York." San Francisco, it seems, always has the most something or the biggest whatnot or the best whatever "outside of New York." And I can't think of a better place to be.

39. EUROPEAN INTERLUDE

As I'm sure you've heard until you could retch at the sound of the words, everybody, but EVERYBODY, is going to Europe these days. Even I—and if that doesn't make it official, nothing will. I figure if I can make it across the big pond, anybody can.

The way it all came about was rather sudden.

"Caen," snapped the boss, chomping down on his cigar as though he hoped it was my finger, "it's time you took a trip. Column's getting stale. Nothing but crumbs about crumb-bums lately. Pack your bag and your wife—you should excuse the juxtaposition—and hit the road to Europe."

"Europe?" I whined. "You mean that place way over there that's full of foreigners? So what'll I do when I get there?"

"Anything, everything," said the boss grandiosely, waving his cigar without taking it out of his mouth. "Get to know the people. The big people, the little people. Have a glass of milk with Mendès-France. Have a heart-to-heart talk with Gina Lollaber-wotzername. Get the lowdown on lasagne and fettuccine and some of those other Italian politicians. Now get going."

"But haven't you forgotten one little thing?" I ventured. When he looked questioningly, I squeaked, "Money," in a wee voice.

He reached into his desk and tossed me a small envelope. I opened it, and out fluttered several stamps commemorating the invention of the sewing machine, some Confederate dollars, and a canceled membership card in TWA's Ambassadors Club.

"Boss," I said feelingly, "you're too good to me."

He nodded. "I know," he said. "Now go. Have the time of

your middle-aged life. Oh, and one more thing. Write every day. Columns, I mean."

I reached out to shake his hand, but he was gone in a puff of cigar smoke.

Europe. The very mention of the word brings back a flood of memories better off forgotten.

My first trip abroad, at the age of six, with mater, pater, and Sister Estelle. I called them mater and pater because I heard some other kid say it, and my mother and father wondered what was the mater with my pater. Anyway, they traveled first class. I went by steerage, because that's what I asked for. I thought they steered the ship from there and I didn't want to miss a thing.

My second trip, courtesy of Uncle Sam during World War II. Everybody else came back with harrowing tales of shot and shell and narrow escapes, but all I can remember is an incident in Luxembourg during the Battle of the Bulge. I was riding in a jeep along an icy road with Collie Small, the war correspondent, when suddenly the jeep spun around and Collie, who was sitting in the back seat, sailed out and landed head first in a pile of snow.

"Gee, Mr. Small," said the GI who dug him out, "that was some swan dive you just took."

"Y-yeah?" sputtered Collie, spitting snow in all directions. "T-tell me, did I keep my f-feet together?"

A trip in '49, on the fifth anniversary of D-Day, during which, I must report in all modesty, I was decorated by the French Government. For what and with what, I'm not sure. I think it was the Order of Christian Dior, made of spun sugar with the *pâté de foie gras* cluster.

The French official who pinned it on me kissed me on both

cheeks and then bent down and ate the decoration, so you'll just have to take my word for it.

I distinguished myself further on that particular trip. During a reception at the residence of then President Vincent Auriol, I found myself standing next to him with nothing, as usual, to say. "Any good entertainers in Paris at the moment?" I blurted. "Why, yes," he answered. "Yves Montand, for example. Very good indeed." At this point most of the other guests crowded round to hear what the President and I were talking about. "Yves Montand!" I said enthusiastically. "Why, I've always LOVED her records!"

The coronation in London in '53—and walking down Picca-dilly the day before the great event to marvel at the Londoners who had sat on the curbs for two solid nights, in a drizzle, to be sure of vantage points.

In front of the Ritz, I noticed a fresh-faced British girl sitting primly on a camp stool, reading Somerset Maugham. I intro-duced myself, and gushed, "I think it's so wonderful, the way you people have been sitting out here all this time, waiting to see the Queen. What I mean is, it's fantastic. That is—well, we'd NEVER think of doing such a thing back in the States."

Carefully placing a finger on the sentence she'd been reading, she looked up at me for the first time.

"Pity," she said, and went back to her reading.

With this background, you can see that I was ready for Eu-rope, but was Europe ready for me? First stop:

Florence, known to us Italians as Firenze. Queen city of the Tuscan Hills. Cradle of the Renaissance. Home of the Medicis and Michelangelo, Da Vinci and Raphael. And also of a small sidestreet bar called Bing Crosby's. If anybody in the place had spoken English, I might have been able to find out why.

Firenze. The San Francisco of Italy. Steeped in culture and

up to its fourteenth-century towers in tourists who arrive via bus, train, and car. There is no airport in Florence large enough to handle big planes. Even Italian airliners don't land here. There are all kinds of noises in Florence, but hardly ever the far-off drone of a multiengined plane passing overhead.

Florence, a serene rolling city of about 400,000 people, its skyline punctuated with campaniles, church towers, and Romanesque ruins. The streets are narrow and crooked, and lead you casually around a corner to one surprise after another, like the streets of San Francisco. You emerge from dark alleyways into wide squares, you step into winding lanes where George Eliot once strolled, or Elizabeth Barrett Browning. There is an ageless, romantic flavor about Florence—a pleasant change of pace from the hustle-bustle of, say, Rome.

The Arno River flows through Florence, and is an integral part of the city. The best hotels and some of the finest shops border it, and the traffic is heavy along the riverside street. The most famous old bridges across the Arno were destroyed by the Germans in their 1944 retreat, but the Ponte Vecchio, the oldest and most famous, was spared. It is lined on both sides with tiny shops, each one overflowing with gold and silver trinkets and tooled leather, and jammed with tourists, pawing through the items and groaning in dismay at the prices. Venice has the Bridge of Sighs. Florence's Ponte Vecchio, at least at this season, is the Bridge of Wails.

The most pleasant square in Florence—a chance for a bum joke here, but I'm avoiding it manfully—is the Piazza della Signoria, dominated by the Palazzo Vecchio, a fourteenth-century building. When the Medicis ran the whole Tuscany show, they did their business here. Now it's the city hall, but majestic nonetheless.

The square is dotted with enough great statuary to fill a couple of ordinary museums at home. There's a big marble fountain featuring Neptune in all his manly glory, an equestrian statue of Cosimo de' Medici, a few lions here and there—and, under an open arcade, a dozen or so heroic classical statues, any one of which would have a whole park built around it in the States.

Across the street from this marble factory is an open-air bazaar, selling everything from bags to straw skirts, and vice versa. And when your feet get tired, there are a couple of sidewalk cafés where you can force down the strong, bitter Italian coffee and whisper as you look around "Golly, look at all the tourists, willya?" The tourists at the next table are looking at you and saying exactly the same thing.

From the Piazza della Signoria it's only a short walk to the Church of Santa Croce, and it's worth every winding step of the way. For within the soaring walls of Santa Croce are the great marble tombs of Michelangelo, Dante Alighieri and Leonardo da Vinci, Galileo and Rossini. Oddly enough, Michelangelo's tomb, surrounded by three grieving figures, is the smallest of the group. But someone had remembered to leave a small bunch of blue cornflowers at its base, a gesture that made Michelangelo the most important man in this burial place of immortals. There were no flowers on the other tombs.

Florence is no different from other European cities that attract visitors in driven droves. There's a hotel shortage here, too. The well-known hotels are booked solid—and I'm lucky enough to be installed in a smallish place called the Lucchesi, rather far from the center of town but overlooking the Arno. Directly across from me is a medieval tower, apparently all that remains of what must have been a fortified wall. And on the green bank on the opposite side of the river, small, barefoot boys stand in the sun, fishing with throw lines, and families gather in the early evening to sit, laugh, and eat, while the many bells of Florence chime softly in the distance.

It's fun to sit on the tiny tiled balcony and watch the changing scenes across the river, and the busy traffic in the street below. Motor scooters, with the inevitable girl on the back saddle. All manner of people on bicycles—old women with laundry bundles on the handle bars, well-dressed businessmen with brief cases, artisans with gold mirror frames over their shoulders. Trolley busses rumble past, a few feet away from the balcony, shaking the whole building. And now and then, the long, narrow Florentine streetcars with one row of seats on each side. They have to be narrow. The streets are the same.

Florence. A city of music and masterpieces, of shops crammed with fine antiques and palpable junk, of ancient towers at intersections and statues in corners, of square, gray stone buildings that look like prisons from the outside and palaces on the inside, of frescoes, murals, Della Robbias, and carved doors in such profusion that soon you take them for granted. That's Florence, otherwise known as Firenze.

I went to a cocktail party in a countess's fifteenth-century palace on the south bank of the Arno River.

It was more or less like a cocktail party in San Francisco, except that when you dropped an ash on the floor, it landed on a carpet that Joseph Bonaparte had once trod on, and the table top your glass left a ring on dated back at least six hundred years and was probably designed by Michelangelo. Everything else in Florence was.

The guests were typical cocktail-party types too, in a chic, Florentine way. Every other man was a count, at the very least, and if all the women weren't countesses, they at least looked like countesses. Through the first round of martinis, anyway.

The party proper, or improper, was staged in several small rooms about the size of the Rome railroad station, comprising the state apartment in the palace of the Countess Serristori.

Why it is called a state apartment, I have no idea—unless it's because that's what the guests were soon in.

The countess, a really marvelous-looking octogenarian, had turned over her place for the evening to her good friends, designers Richard Mayo and Marshall Williams, who were the hosts. I was the guest of honor, but nobody knew it except Mayo, Williams, and me. And I didn't say a word. All the other people thought the party was for THEM.

I'm beginning to hope it was.

Quite a few people from San Francisco were crawling around the woodwork, but after the second martini, I was in no shape to take notes. Or rather, I thought I was until the next morning, when I looked at the notes and read that Scrtlf Krtny was there with Plority Trghsv. I don't remember seeing THEM at all.

However, I do have some slight recall of a large group of decorators, who were traveling through Europe with an even larger group of decorators under the auspices of A.I.D. (American Institute of Decorators). I think I saw George Brown and Beauchamp Alexander and ever so many people from Knoedler-Fauchere and somebody from Frances Mihailoff's studio and a nice girl from Berkeley named something like Elizabeth Elston. Good luck to the A.I.D., which is exactly what its members needed after this evening.

Frank Chapman and his wife, singer Gladys Swarthout, arrived and snared a drink and a canapé with grace, dexterity, and an Italian friend named Gino. And the belle of the ball was the beautiful Countess Figlinesi, known in San Francisco as Simonetta Schubert, who is here with her two small children—and the nicest thing that has happened to Florence since the Germans retreated to the north.

But back to the palace, which has gone through a lot in its five-hundred-odd years, but very few routs like this, I trust.

The state apartment is a glittering layout with tremendous

crystal chandeliers, mirrors as high as the guests got on two drinks, red brocade walls, a bedroom with a canopied bed large enough for a football game, and about ten jillion dollars' worth of art treasures strewn about as though they didn't mean a thing, which indeed they do.

While they were still able to walk, the guests paraded around from room to room, goggling at the masterpieces, and saying in awed tones to Mr. Mayo and Mr. Williams: "Gee, some place you have here!"

At this, while Richard and Marshall were bowing gravely, a Duchess Diana Something-Hyphen-Something would laugh raucously. This Diana was a caution. "I just LOVE people from San Francisco. Where are all the people from San Francisco?"

As soon as the drinks got low, she left for Harry's Bar, where she has unlimited credit to match Harry's unlimited patience.

The party staggered on, far into the night, without the gracious presence of the countess, who had long since gone to bed.

The hors d'oeuvres disappeared, and people moistened their index fingers and picked up the crumbs. Rows of empty scotch and bourbon bottles were lined up beneath a priceless sixteenth-century table that had probably had a peace treaty written on it. Nothing was left except half a pitcher of warm martinis, and the survivors fought over it like hungry cannibals over a fat missionary.

A nice expatriate named Mrs. Glugg (that's what my notes say) banged her empty glass on the parquet floor and called out imperiously, "Dick! Marshall! If I don't get another drink, I shall leave immediately." Since she'd been saying this for quite some time without leaving, nobody rushed to her assistance, least of all Dick and Marshall.

Two decorators walked through the room, carrying a third decorator who had decorated his interior too lavishly. "Poor fellow," somebody observed. "Hasn't been the same since his nervous breakdown. Now, twenty drinks and—pouf!"

Somebody named George was lounging against a fireplace and observing loftily, "My dear, I'm so TIRED of ruins I could SCREAM. Why don't these people keep UP their buildings? Look at the White House in Washington. It's EVER so old but they take care of it, and it's still BEAUTiful."

Fortunately, nobody seemed to be listening to him.

The last drop was drained from the martini pitcher, the last crumb was picked up (from under the table by a guest who happened to be there), and the bottle-scarred veterans slithered out. We can imagine the look on the countess's face when she inspected her palace next morning. It was an antique to start with, but it's EVER so much older now. HONestly.

Avignon, France—Well, you can't stay in Florence forever— especially if you're allergic to Italian gin—so I got myself a car in Monte Carlo and began driving toward Paris.

This might turn out to be the smartest thing I ever did. The highway from Monte Carlo to Nice and Cannes and along the Riviera coast is a many-splendored thing, and my hat is off to the engineers. I don't know how they managed to carve this winding ribbon out of sheer rock overhanging the Mediterranean, but they did, and anybody who has the privilege of driving along it should be grateful forevermore.

I'm also grateful to the crews who installed the guard rails and banked the turns. There are so many things to see—the blue waters pounding on the rocks below, the ancient ruins on the rocks above, the crazy motorcyclists directly in front of your bumper—that it's hard to keep your hands on the wheel and your eyes on the road.

Heard any good old saws lately? My old saw for today is "You can't get a bad meal in France." Francophiles have been

saying this for years to all and sundry—also on mondry and tues-
dry—and on this trip, I had a chance to test it.

A few miles out of Cannes, as the Ford flies, there's a tiny
village called Anthéor—population maybe three hundred,
maybe. It's barely listed on the map, and if you have weak eyes,
you'd never notice it at all. The famed Michelin guide, the bible
for all travelers in France, lists one hotel there as passable, but
says absolutely nothing about the food. Which is a sure sign
that there's nothing edible, by Michelin standards.

However, I was hungry as hell, by anybody's standard, so I
stopped at a little roadside place that, so far as I could see,
doesn't even have a name. It's a "Bar-Restaurant," of which
there are thousands in France.

A dark-haired, dark-eyed waitress who could have played the
second lead in any B picture served me the complete luncheon.
First, pink slices of cold ham, with olives, pickles, and radishes
that were artfully carved and arranged. Plus the usual superla-
tive French butter and coarse-textured bread. After that, a large
and flaky patty shell, filled with ham and olives in a white sauce.
Then breaded veal chops in a butter and parsley sauce. Gruyère
and Camembert cheese, a good wine of the region, and coffee.

The check came to about $2.25. And the quality? Well, off-
hand, I can think of only half a dozen San Francisco restaurants
that do better. And at least a dozen so-called "famous" restaurants that do only half as well for twice as much.

I cut away from the Mediterranean and rolled through the
Provence countryside, passing up Citroëns, Renaults, and Dela-
hayes as though they were standing still. As a matter of fact,
several of them were, but no matter.

Feeling the pangs of hunger again, I stopped for tea and fruit-
cake at Les Deux Garçons in Aix-en-Provence, a notable old
French city near Aix-en-your-Beer, or any other horrible pun
you feel inclined to inflict upon yourself. Here, I took the op-

portunity of inspecting what is commonly known as the W.C., and discovered a large white implement manufactured in England and labeled in large blue letters, "The Adamant."

Ah, the British.

At Avignon, I checked into the Hôtel d'Europe, a fine old auberge of pre-Hilton vintage, and then walked along the cobbled streets, crossed the town square past Dead End-type kids who speak French (this always comes as a great surprise), and walked up a long flight of stairs to a restaurant called the Lucullus.

The mighty Michelin guidebook gives this a favorable rating, but in San Francisco, the Lucullus would give Trader Vic a pretty fair run for his money. And Avignon is, after all, a very small town.

While the thunder roared in the Provence hills and the rain pelted down on Avignon's cobblestones, I sat alongside an open window—despite all this weather, it was still warm—and dined elegantly on asparagus with an unbelievably smooth cream, egg, and lemon sauce; *l'agneau des Alpilles grillé sur feu de bois* (okay, a sort of lamb chop grilled over a wood fire) with artichoke hearts filled with a butter sauce; a *meringue glâcée* with almonds; a bottle of Châteauneuf-du-Pape; and coffee.

This cost me slightly more than lunch—about five dollars—but believe me, Dad, you've got to go a long way to find food like this. All the way to Avignon, in a merry Fordmobile.

Avignon is, of course, most famous for a bridge, and I wasn't going to leave without at least a stroll across it. However, it's a good thing I stopped about halfway across the Rhône, because that's where the bridge stops. The rest of it has simply fallen off.

This is no scoop, though. It happened several centuries ago, and I'm sure somebody has mentioned it by now.

Saulieu, France—Driving north toward Paris from the Riviera is like rolling endlessly through a great park.

The fields are green and idyllic, as in a bad oil painting. Coal barges move slowly along the Rhône, just as they're supposed to. Glamorous-looking cows graze peacefully on meadows as flat and smooth as billiard tables, right at the edge of the winding Saône River. Poplars, elms, and chestnut trees wave gently along the highway.

You round a bend, and there, on a hilltop to your right, stands a great château, its spires gleaming in the sun. All that is missing, to make the scene complete, is the sight of long pennants fluttering from the towers, and a knight in shining armor charging across the moat on a white stallion.

After the drawbridge has been lowered, of course. Dredging a waterlogged knight out of the moat is one helluva job, involving a tow truck, the AAA, and all that. Sometimes it's hardly worth the trouble. Leave the blighter there to rust, I say.

The villages flash past as you purr along Highway N7. Endearing villages, each with its tiny square and its gray monument to the fallen heroes of World War I, and its old, bright-eyed men sitting on the benches, silently watching the traffic and the world pass them by. The grandmothers teeter past on bicycles—the grandmammas who aren't out working in the vineyards, that is—and the small children play in blue smocks that button up the back.

And here and there, a tremendous cathedral, with the village's tiny houses clustered close around it, as though for protection.

There are no billboards along N7 to clutter the view of vineyards, meadows, winding rivers, and far-off mountains. There is however, an endless series of roadside signs, to tell you such things as that Mobiloil is Bi-Actif, and that Shell has ICA (the French version of TCP, I guess) and that Vittel is "L'eau qui *danse et qui chante*," in case you've been looking for water that dances and sings. Shades of Crazy Water Crystals!

A word, incidentally, about the highway direction signs in France. They're so clear and graphic that only a fool could get lost, and what if I did? With my masterful grasp of the French language, it was no problem finding my way back to the wrong highway.

As a matter of fact, I didn't know I was lost till I stopped a man and said, "*Pardonnez-moi, m'sieu, mais connaissez-vous la route à Paris?*" and he answered, "*Jawohl, mein Herr*," took off his Alpine cap and waved it in the opposite direction.

So far as the gourmet is concerned, the most important stop along N7 is at Vienne, a small town with a world-famed restaurant called the Pyramide—not because its founder was an Egyptologist, but because a pyramid-like tower stands half a block away.

The owner and guiding genius of the Pyramide, Fernande Point, died a few years ago, but the restaurant is as celebrated as ever, and the Michelin guide does right well by it, awarding it four crossed forks and spoons (meaning de luxe) and three stars (meaning worth a special trip, even from San Francisco, I presume).

I had the light luncheon. Three hors d'oeuvres—a duck *pâté* in a pastry shell, a *pâté de foie gras* encased in brioche and a trout mousse with a fine truffle sauce. Then came turbot in champagne sauce, followed by a very tender, very juicy *entre-côte* with a wine sauce, and asparagus. For dessert, there was an array of fresh strawberries, sliced oranges, a chocolate cake, ice cream, four cheeses, and half a dozen varieties of tiny French pastries, all delectable.

For 2500 francs a person (about $8), plus wine, plus coffee, plus tips, you can have any or all of these things. I skipped the ice cream, the fruit, and a couple of the pastries, much to the rather disapproving surprise of the waiter. The French people all around me were eating everything in sight and coming back for seconds.

Filling the Ford (with Mobiloil Bi-Actif, quoi else?) to match my stomach, I took off through the Burgundy country-side, where the weather turned out to be as rich as the lunch. First brilliant sunshine, then fast-moving clouds, then thunder-claps and driving rain. At one exciting point, the sun was shin-ing brightly while the rain was practically jamming the wind-shield wipers, and in the distance, a rainbow arched across a mountaintop.

I stopped for the night at the Côte d'Or, a charming auberge in Saulieu with a first-rate restaurant run by chef Alexandre Dumaine, who has received so many diplomas for his culinary achievements that they line the dining-room walls. I settled for a vegetable soup, cold boiled chicken (with slices of truffles un-der the skin), a green salad, a bottle of Pouilly-Fuissé, and so to bed. All first-rate, including the beds.

Next morning I drove on through the sun, the rain, the hail, and the still-magnificent countryside—and then the traffic be-gan to get heavier, the buildings larger, the gendarmes more frequent, and there, in the distance, rose the Eiffel Tower. At last—Paris. Where the French are loaded on American money, and the Americans are loaded on French champagne. Or so the story goes. We shall see.

Paris—Somebody once said, "Everybody has two home towns—his own, and Paris." At least, I think somebody said it. If not, it's been said now, and not very well.

My own home town was Sacramento, which is a long way from Paris in about every way I can think of. Nobody writes any songs about Sacramento and nobody ever called it "La Ville Lumière," but I do recall that its slogan is "The Heart of California" and that during the Depression, the one with the capital D, it was the nation's white spot.

However, Sacramento is a nice, healthy, growing city and a great place for trees. I'll bet there are more trees per capita in Sacramento than people per capita. It is also the per capita of California.

Well, so much for Sacramento. I don't know how it got in here in the first place, except that somebody once said, "Everybody has two home towns—his own and Sacramento."

What I started to talk about was Paris. In my own small way, I'm sort of an old Paris hand. When I say, "Donnay mwah l'addeesseeown, seel voo play," the French waiters know they're not dealing with a greenhorn. After they examine the tip, they realize they're dealing with a tinhorn.

I came to Paris the first time when I was six. With my parents. It's a waste of time to come to Paris when you're six, and you shouldn't come with your parents at any age. If you do, you never get to Place Pigalle to see the bareback riders who are bare in front, too.

As I remember it, my father, who was a native-born Frenchman, spent all my time walking me around the Arc de Triomphe, up the Eiffel Tower, through the palace at Versailles, and down to Napoleon's tomb. I couldn't have cared less.

I just wanted to be back playing in the vacant lot in Sacramento with Jack and Clarence Lavelle, who always beat the hell out of me, but only because they liked me so much.

The second time I came to Paris I was old enough to appreciate it, but there happened to be a war going on at the time. I arrived in the city on the heels of Ernest Hemingway and a few other war correspondents, who, with occasional help from the Allied armies, had liberated Paris.

It was all very exciting. There was still intermittent firing in

the streets, heard only by the newspapermen, and every time
a champagne bottle popped, somebody would fall off a bar stool
and put in for a Purple Heart. The girls started out kissing
everybody for free, but pretty soon they went back to charging
for it, and the GIs began complaining just like the tourists do
today.

In fact, there were so many soldiers around the place that
before long it was a pleasure to be out of Paris. The Americans
were spoiling it for each other, as usual. The city was soon full
of restrictions and generals in limousines, and in no time at
all, the better-looking French girls were living as well as they
did under the Germans.

I got back into Paris on V-E Day, which I think was May
7, 1945, and on that occasion the city was at its best. The sun
was shining, the streets were jammed with cheering people,
and some of the girls were kissing everybody for free again.

And this time, not even the sharpest-eared journalists could
hear any intermittent firing on the outskirts.

The third time I came to Paris was in 1949, on the fifth
anniversary of D-Day, and it rained every day. La Ville
Lumière was gray and dismal, and the people seemed likewise.
Prices were high, nobody had any money, and every time you
stepped out of your hotel, you'd be surrounded by an army of
black marketeers.

I was with a group of American newspapermen, and one
drizzly afternoon, we lined up in the courtyard of some big old
building and received medals from the French Government for
the part we played in the Liberation. In my case, the medal
was bigger than the part.

The French, however, give nothing away without extracting
something in return. In this instance, the French minister of
war jabbed the medal straight at me, so that the prongs went
through my suit and shirt and into my skin, making two small,

neat holes. In the language of war correspondents, I bled profusely.

That's how I became the first American to be wounded in France five years after the war had ended.

Now on my fourth trip to Paris, I found the city the way I had always imagined it (except, of course, for the now-muted symphony of the auto horns). The *flics*, in their capes, standing at the intersections, waving traffic along with their white batons. In front of the government buildings, the guards, magnificent in plumed hats and red sashes. The weasel-faced types in long, thick overcoats skulking along the streets of Pigalle, inviting you to see "curiosites" unheard of outside of Paris. The limousines double-parked in front of Christian Dior, and the hotels and chic restaurants crowded with the bejeweled elite of five continents and certain parts of New Jersey. In Place de la Concorde and along the Champs Élysées, the fountains playing in a sea of light, and the great public buildings bathed in a silvery glow.

Here is Paris, at last, at its magnificent best. And here was I, at last, not quite too old to enjoy it. But almost, Son, almost.

I love Paris in the morning . . .

In the narrow streets, the shadows are still long—and it is cool under the trees along the great boulevards. The bareheaded *midinettes* sing on their way to work, the hotel chambermaids holler at each other across the courtyards, and at the sidewalk cafés, white-jacketed waiters begin wheeling out the tiny tables and setting up the chairs that have been stacked against the front windows all night. The flics stand in pairs at the street corners, chatting of this, that, and the other passing girl, and every now and then, one idly waves his white baton to keep the traffic moving along.

I love Paris in the morning, when the city still belongs to the

French. The tourists don't see much of Paris in the morning.

I love Paris in the afternoon . . .

Now the traffic is approaching its normal state of madness, and the sidewalks are jammed with people hurrying to lunch. The shopkeepers are locking up and closing the grilled shutters over the windows. There is excitement in the air, for the *déjeuner* is an affair of great importance, and there are only two or three hours to devote to it.

The sun is shining, so you pick a sidewalk café on the Avenue Matignon. Already most of the tables are taken, and the people are studying the menu and discussing the items as seriously as they read their newspapers and trade opinions on the news. The waiters stand by respectfully, trying not to hurry them, because they know that vital decisions are being made.

And after that, there must be a searching study of the wine list, interspersed with little arguments about the '53s as opposed to the '50s, and the Loires versus the Rhônes.

You decide to eat lightly. Just a *salade niçoise*, frog legs *Provençale, Pouilly-Fumé*, a strawberry tart, and coffee. The waiter looks inquiringly. Perhaps you are on a diet? Meanwhile, the French around you are eating slowly and tremendously, with concentration. A *pâté*, a fish with sauce, a steak with *béarnaise*, two kinds of wine, cheese, strawberries and ice cream, a liqueur, and finally, *eh bien*, a *petit café noir*.

And yet you see very few fat Frenchmen. But so many fat Americans, including yourself.

Paris in the afternoon . . .

You take a deep breath, cross your fingers, close your eyes, and drive headlong into the mass of traffic swinging slowly around the Arc de Triomphe. As the auto-go-round reaches the other side, you drop out, head down the Avenue of the Grande Armée, and turn into the Bois de Boulogne.

You pay a thousand-franc deposit, get a rowboat, and drift

idly along, under old trees that spread far out over the water. The banks are as neat and green and as artfully planted with flowers as though John McLaren had tended them himself. Ducks paddle alongside your boat. And in the distance, through a gap in the trees, the Eiffel Tower rears its tall, gaunt frame.

You drive back toward the heart of the city along the Avenue George V. The Duchess of Windsor, thin as a mannequin, is walking into Balenciaga. The crowds are already thick at the cafés on the Champs Élysées, sipping an apéritif, or examining the pastries displayed on trays by girls in white jackets.

The sun is getting lower, and the white spires of Sacré-Coeur on Montmartre are turning golden.

I love Paris in the evening . . .

The lights are on, and there is already a hint of perfume and champagne in the air. In the George Cinq lobby, the tourists are babbling, and in a corner of the Ritz bar, a bewildered young Frenchman looks this way and that, studying every face, and finally explains, "I was trying to see if there's another Frenchman in the room. There isn't."

In the Tour d'Argent, a marvelous view of Notre Dame and the gaily lighted excursion boats floating down the Seine. At the Café de Paris, the lights are dimmed and the orchestra plays its specialty—a long, dreamy, heavily arranged Viennese waltz. As the leader, a violinist, walks around the floor, his eyes closed, pouring his heart into his solo, a woman at ringside says loudly to her husband at the far end of the table, "Heyyy, don't he look just like Sam Slotkin?"

You move on to the Monseigneur on Rue d'Amsterdam, with its oil paintings and its chandeliers and its small army of fiddlers who rove around the room, playing one song after another, expertly, without pause. The cellist props his instrument on your table and whirls it around as he plays, never missing a note. There are other kinds of notes at the Monseigneur, too.

Thousand-franc notes, tucked into the violins and displayed meaningfully and often to the customers. So you shouldn't miss the point.

In the Left Bank's Latin Quarter, you drop in at the Hôtel Aux États-Unis, where most of the customers are Negro and a young man plays "How High the Moon" and "The Lady Is a Tramp" on a French horn. And finally a small, dark bar called the Club St. Germain, where there are photos of tousle-haired girls on the walls, and the bartender is a woman, and the girls dance with each other to hillbillyish American records.

I love Paris every minute. Even at 2 A.M. in a smelly Left Bank club, to the accompaniment of music you wouldn't listen to back home. Because soon the sun will rise, and the magic will begin all over again.

Paris—I have had several angry letters from ex-subscribers, all asking approximately the same question, to wit: "How come you never tell us anything about the lives of the average French couple? That's the kind of thing we're interested in—and not the things you've been writing about, such as Who Threw the Haricots in Mrs. Dumont's Champignons."

Well, if there's one thing I'm sensitive to, and I doubt it, it's the hoarse voice of public opinion, so I've been looking around for an average French couple. Without much success. If there's one thing the French aren't, it's average, and a French couple is twice as unaverage.

So I'll tell you, instead, about Mr. et Mme. S., who are neither average nor typical. But on the other hand, in France one never knows. Does one?

I met Mr. et Mme. S. through a mutual friend who lives in San Francisco.

Mr. S. is, I would judge, in his late forties. Tall, husky, with graying hair, a mustache, red cheeks, and a hearty manner. He is in the textile business, and important. When he calls up Maxim's for a table at the last minute, they either have one— or they build one. If every hotel in Paris is full and you want a room, you mention his name. *Violà.* You get the suite the manager has hastily vacated.

Mme. S. is a tall, striking redhead, with her hair cut short in the chic French style. Her diamonds and rubies look as though they were paid for because they were. She is always greeted warmly at Balmain and Christian Dior because she not only looks, she buys.

Mr. et Mme. S. are often seen at Longchamps and Auteuil race tracks. They go to Deauville when it is fashionable to go there, and they spend a few holidays on the Riviera, although they complain it is usually overcrowded with people who aren't altogether acceptable.

Mr. et Mme. S. are very nice, very warm, and very rich.

Their home is the kind of place you can't believe exists, even while you're in it.

It's in St. Germain-en-Laye, a picturesque village overlooking the Seine, about forty-five minutes from the heart of Paris. To get there, you drive in one of Mr. S.'s cars, an American convertible, through the Bois de Boulogne, across the Ponte de Neuilly, past Puteaux, and, from Bougival on, along the Seine to St. Germain.

You drive up to a high gate, and a servant in a white uniform swings it open for you. You roll through to enchantment.

The home of the S.'s is a comparatively small, delicate, stone structure that was once part of a tremendous, rambling castle built by Henry IV in the sixteenth century. It is surrounded by acres of formal gardens with beautiful clipped hedges and statuary, flower gardens, ancient walls, and an extensive vegetable garden.

The house is officially a French national monument (on a

hill just above is the Pavillon Henri-Quatre, where Louis XIV
was born). Mr. S. bought the place from the Government, and,
in return, must keep it in perfect repair. Also, he must maintain the vast grounds. If he asks for financial help from the
Government, he would have to open the place to the public
once a week, and who wants the public tromping through your
gardens?

"We know you are tired of all that rich food in the Paris
restaurants," said the S.'s as they welcomed me, "so all we will
have is a light lunch. Not much wine. A little nothing."

We sat at a table under a huge crystal chandelier. There was
a centerpiece of calla lilies and blue cornflowers from the garden. A butler and a maid, both wearing white gloves, began
serving the light lunch, the little nothing. The snacque, as it
were.

First, the small French cantaloupes, filled with port wine.
Then great slices of smoked salmon, with toast and that incomparable French butter. The wine became a Mersault, and the
course changed to chicken, done to a golden turn, and tiny
potatoes, crisp and buttery. And a marvelous green salad, fresh
from the garden. The white wine disappeared, a red burgundy
took its place, and a wide tray of cheeses appeared—Camembert, Brie, Gruyère, and an unbelievably delicate goat cheese.

The servants took away the silver plates on which we'd been
served, and replaced them with gold plates, with gold knives,
forks, and spoons. It was the time for dessert—a strawberry tart
as big as the sun, on a thin crust to end all crusts. With whipped
cream, thick and so rich it was almost yellow. And to fill the
huge goblets in front of us, a rare Louis Roederer champagne,
very *brut*, in clear bottles.

"As we said," the host and hostess kept murmuring, "a very
light lunch. We hope you are getting enough to eat. We apologize."

I was getting enough to eat.

After the potluck lunch, we looked around the house at the treasures, the paintings, the antiques, the old prints showing the palace as it was in the days of Henry IV. We saw the carriage house, which has been converted by the S.'s into an elegant bar and hunt room. A twin carriage house is the servants' quarters. There is a stable where Mme. S. keeps her riding horse. And a great Dane and a boxer.

"It is exactly what we want," said Mr. S. "A small place. Just enough room for the two of us."

In the late afternoon sun, the tall gate swung open again, and I drove away from the enchanted world of Mr. et Mme. S., who are very nice, very warm, and very rich. Not the average French couple, perhaps, but on the other hand, in France one never knows. Does one?

Besides, as I learned later, they weren't really married.

A fine day in Paris—and the last one. If you're the sentimental type (and who isn't, in this beautiful city?), you can work up quite a lump for your throat at the prospect of leaving. Especially when the sun is shining through the trees all golden and dancing—and a bareheaded street singer is walking along the Faubourg St. Honoré, giving a new lift to the tired strains of "La Vie en Rose." The air is a wonderful mixture of wine and coffee and fresh bread in the corner *boulangerie*, and the cops are all handsome and gallant, and the girls are chic and looking at you with mischief in their eyes.

Or so it seems on a fine day in Paris—and the last one.

You drive slowly around the Arc de Triomphe, with its eternal flame to the unknown soldier, and even the names on the nearby street signs seem touched with a special glory. Foch, Victor Hugo, Kléber, Haussmann, Wagram, Clemenceau. All the greatness of France, synthesized in a city that has lived so long and seen so much and still seems so young.

You move down the Champs Élysées to the gardens of the Louvre, where the first guillotine was set up during the Revolution. And you gaze out toward Place de la Concorde, where other guillotines continued their bloody work. In the background, a palace of Louis XIV, and on a nearby wall, a large concrete L—for Louis—almost buried under the huge N that Napoleon arrogantly placed on top of it. In the near distance, the golden statue of Jeanne d'Arc on horseback glints in the sun, and at Place Vendôme, a pigeon roosts atop the statue of Napoleon done up as a Roman emperor.

Everywhere you look, there is a page from history. And you see and feel it all—on your last day in Paris.

You stroll along the narrow street known as Rue Danou, past the original Harry's Bar at No. 5 (on the window, it still says "Sank Roo Danoo," for the phonetic benefit of Americans who can't pronounce French addresses), and you remember the Paris of the Twenties and Scott Fitzgerald and his lost people trying to find themselves up and down the long, dark streets, somewhere between midnight and dawn.

You turn into the wide and elegant Rue de la Paix, and look into Cartier's windows, where the only shabby thing is your reflection in the glass. And then the Ritz Hotel, around the corner.

On a day like this, you must have lunch at the Ritz. In the open-air restaurant, under the trees, near those two very French statues—women's heads on the bodies of lions couchant. You toy with a *pâté en croûte* and look at the people—the men bowing from the waist to kiss a woman's hand, the hand of a woman created by Dior, perfumed by Balenciaga, and adorned by Van Cleef.

Was there ever such chic as this—or is it only because it's your last day in Paris?

You leave the Ritz, through revolving doors spun by page boys, and head for the very top of Montmartre. Slowly through the busy streets, weaving in and out among the tiny cars and the bicyclists and the women selling ice cream from gleaming chrome pushcarts.

There are flower vendors on the corners of Place Clichy, and on the Butte Montmartre, the church of the Sacré-Coeur gleams new and white in the sunshine.

You walk along the narrow streets at the crest of Montmartre, and the scene seems ageless and as alive as tomorrow. A blonde runs into an apartment house to keep a tryst with an artist. Young lovers walk arm in arm. A poodle runs down an alley to bark at a goat that lives in a bar. A tall man wearing home-made sandals—a political refugee from the United States—pushes a baby carriage.

In Butte Montmartre's main square, dating back almost ten centuries, you sit under an umbrella at A La Mère Cathérine (founded 1793) and sip a cup of tea. A young artist wearing house slippers and long hair sits on the curbstone and sketches the street scene, as countless thousands of artists have done before him and thousands will in the future. At his side, a girl with shoulder-length orange hair sits in her black slacks and watches his work and murmurs encouragement, in the manner of girls in 955, 1955, and, God willing, 2955.

Montmartre, one of the few places in the world where you can still be young and alive and free. Or so it seems, on a fine day in Paris.

It's hard to get to Paris, even today, when the jets fly high, wide, and handsome. And it's hard to get to know Paris, in a few days, or even a few weeks.

But you can get the feel of the city, just by walking and

riding around its streets, and crossing the bridges from the
Right Bank to the Left. Paris seems to be pulsatingly alive all
around you, wherever you happen to be. The *Parisiens* do things
with great gusto, and it's fun just to sit and watch them—speaking their language lovingly, with their teeth sunk deeply into
every word; waving their arms in rapid outbursts of emotion;
eating their way through dish after dish, and discussing each
spice and each herb; and drinking their way through one wine
after another, and reciting the background and the fable of
every grape.

The Parisiens enjoy life, even in these times when life is
hard. They can sip an apéritif, and make it look like the greatest pleasure in the world. They can watch a pretty girl walk past,
and savor every little movement. They can sing and laugh and
talk endlessly—and they are forever aware that they are living
in the most beautiful city in the world.

Or so it seems on a fine day in Paris—and the last one.

London—This isn't the most beautiful city in the world. Nor
is it the most charming, delightful, or winning. But it's undoubtedly the most impressive. Eight million people, living in
streets, squares, circles, hills, gates, and mews that cover almost
seven hundred square miles of flats, houses, monuments, parks,
undergrounds, terminals, pubs (beer and wine only), pubs
(fully licensed), clubs, palaces, tenements, and stores, stores,
stores selling everything from comestibles to wet goods to boots
and spurs.

London is great and gray, even in the occasional sunshine.
Along the muddy Thames, the Houses of Parliament stand as
square and straight as the British conscience. The Gothic pile
of Westminster Abbey rears up in a mass too solid to take in
with a single pair of eyes. Big Ben frowns, fat and stolid. The
Tower of London and Tower Bridge seem far away and of an-

other world, even when they're close at hand. In Trafalgar Square, Nelson stands at the top of his tall column, gazing endlessly out to sea, and the huge black lions of Landseer crouch forevermore around the base—looking even more forbidding, if possible, on a sunny Sunday when London's children clamber over their backs and reach into their mouths.

London is big and old, with the musty smell of age. History marches along on its street signs—Grosvenor and Berkeley, Wellington, George, Oxford, and Chesterfield. In Grosvenor Square, Franklin Delano Roosevelt stands in bronze on a marble pedestal whose base still shows traces of the red paint that was hurled at it after the Yalta papers were published. In Berkeley Square, the trees are in full leaf and people sit quietly on benches—listening perhaps for the nightingale that never sings. Here and there, as you wander through the endless city, you find gaps in the solid rows of buildings—the holes left by German bombs that whistled down almost two decades ago. And now and again, rising on a site that had been cleared by Hermann Goering in 1941, a modern white office building or hotel, looking as out of place as a neon sign on Buckingham Palace.

London is orderly, and so are Londoners. They queue up for busses and theater tickets in a long, straight line, and the Londoner who would try to shove in ahead of somebody else doesn't exist. The bobbies walk along under their black helmets with slow, measured steps—and they never, never run, even to the scene of an accident. Running is against regulations, on the theory that it excites people and police to the detriment of efficiency. Cabs waiting for fares line up in a rank in the middle of the streets, and, unlike Paris, there is no regulation against the blowing of automobile horns. There doesn't have to be. No matter what the hour, you hardly ever hear the toot of a horn. Bad manners.

London is not a gay city. It is a soldier in a resplendent red uniform and black bearskin shako, marching slowly along with fixed bayonet in front of a stone barracks. It is a bobby standing at grim-faced attention outside No. 10 Downing Street. It is a gray lady riding solemnly past in a black, hearse-like limousine driven by a cadaverous chauffeur, and an old man with a long beard and broken shoes carrying a sandwich board—advertising "Old Clothes for Sale"—along Oxford Street. It is little, dingy restaurants filled with strange odors and limp water cress, and it is dirty barges on the Thames. It is an old, proud, unvanquished city—and a city that seldom smiles.

London is a tradition. Men in bowler hats, stepping into their clubs for lunch. Old waiters in Simpson's in the Strand, slicing the roast beef razor-thin with shaking hands. Beef and kidney pie at the Connaught, and tea that has been carefully steeped. Fine old pubs, like the King Lud and the Coach and Horses and the Pig in the Pond, where the martinis taste strongly of vermouth and the whisky is poured straight and iceless into a goblet. The golden figure of the armored knight above the gleaming chrome marquees of the Savoy Hotel, the top-hatted doormen at Claridge's, and, of course, the clerks in cutaways and striped pants in the ground floor grocery section at Fortnum & Mason, selling fruit and flowers and canned cockles with all the punctiliousness of salesmen selling diamonds at Cartier's. And the omnipresent crowds at the gates to Buckingham Palace, waiting quietly and patiently for a glimpse of the royal family—and, if they fail to get it, walking away with the hope of better luck next time.

London is a miracle of transportation. The best cabs in the world, fulfilling every requirement of a good taxi: plenty of leg room, seats for five people, space next to the driver for luggage, and a short wheel base for turning around on a farthing. And, for the final triumph, low fares and helpful drivers. Almost as good as the cabs: the familiar red double-decker busses, rumbling along one after the other—and for some reason that perhaps the Municipal Railway can explain, requiring a stopping zone only half the size of San Francisco's. A ride through downtown London in the upper front seats is worth a hundred times the fare, which starts at tuppence (less than three cents). And if you can't get there by cab or bus—the marvelous underground railway system, with its escalators, its clear, simple maps, its follow-the-colored-lights system for passengers, and its red trains rocketing from station to station.

London is a teeming world of somber buildings and quiet people. It doesn't have the chic of Paris, particularly in its food and dress, but it has more stability. It doesn't have the crumbling glories of Rome, but it lives more strongly in the present. It doesn't have the flavor of Madrid, the pace and excitement of New York, or the sheer beauty of San Francisco. But it has the majesty and serenity that befits the biggest city in the world. And, in the slow judgment of history, perhaps the greatest.

There are several ways to come back to San Francisco after a couple of months in Europe.

You can come back as the worldly-wise place dropper, in the following manner:

"Ah, it's good to be home again" (pronounce it "agayn" for added effect). "I see at last what people mean when they call San Francisco an international city. The rolling countryside around the airport—how like Surrey! Or even Montecatini. And the city itself, almost Roman on its hills. I took a walk down Columbus Avenue, and felt that I was strolling once agayn on the Via Manzoni—Milano, you know. Post Street and New Bond Street, how much they have in common. Quite amazing."

Driving through Golden Gate Park, you glance around, shake your head as in disbelief, and murmur, "But it's the Bois, almost to a T! Except, of course, for those dear restaurants that put the Bois in a class by itself. Pre Catalan or the Pavillon d'Armenonville would look right at home here, don't you think? Oh, but I forgot. I suppose it's YEARS since you've been to Paris. If ever."

At Trader Vic's, you scan the menu critically, toss it aside and purr to the waiter, "Would you just ask the chef to whip up a little *ratatouille niçoise* in the manner of Jarrasse at Deauville. I'm sure he knows how it's done. That is, if he's a chef of any standing at all." And at the Blue Fox, Alexis' Tangier, or Amelio's, you tear up the wine list, sail it across the room and smile faintly, "A *demi-bouteille* of Pouilly-Fumé, and make sure it's one of the GREAT years."

When he brings a 1948, you blanch and snort, "Good heavens, man, you call '48 a great year? If you don't have a '47, bring *la cuenta*—that is, *il conto*—I mean, the check, and we'll be going."

So go. Nobody will mind.

Or you can come back as the big international funnyman.

"Hey, nice little town you have here," you say after an appraising look around. "Natives seem friendly and anxious to please. Tell me, do they hate Americans here? Don't like to stay long in places where they hate Americans."

If this fails to get a snicker, you rattle on:

"Not funny, eh? Guess it's the same old problem. Language barrier. All I can speak is English, and my humor loses something in the translation, hahaha. Whaddya call that patois you people speak here—Friscoese? Well, I'll pick it up in no time. Real ear for languages. Just tell me how to ask for the check in Friscoese, and I'll get by, never you fear."

A little later, you pull a wad of one-dollar bills out of your pocket and say:

"Man, the exchange rate here is terrible. This funny money —whaddya call 'em, Yanqui dolars, or somethin'?—doesn't go

very far. Oh well. I suppose they have one price here for the
tourists and another for the Americans. Anyway, this is the most
expensive place I've been in yet. I was gonna stay here the
rest of my life—but I'll be lucky if I can afford a week."

Upon leaving a restaurant, you press a British ten-shilling
note into the waiter's hand and snicker:

"Sorry, haven't had a chance to change my money. But this
scrap of paper is good as gold. Ten bob. Worth ten bob the
world over. Yes, sir, you can be a big man in the corner pub
tonight."

You'll finally get your laugh. Waiters are trained to laugh at
anything, even a ten-bob tip.

Or you can return to San Francisco as the 200-per-cent
American. With your eyes flashing red, white, and blue, you say
intensely:

"Well, sir, I can't tell you how it feels to be back in the good
old U.S.A. Back in God's country, I always say—and believe
you me, I told those foreigners over there that the good old
U.S.A. IS God's country, by golly. And don't think they don't
know it, either.

"Why d'ya think they hate us so much over there? Jealousy,
that's all. When I got through telling 'em about the things we
take for granted over here—telephones that really work, a
chicken in every pot, an old-fashioned family dinner straight
out of the deep freeze, with your loved ones gathered around
the TV—when I got through telling 'em how we live, I could
see they hated me.

"Ya think that bothered me? Not on your life. I just feel
sorry for 'em. Europe is washed up, done for, and why good
Americans even go over there and throw their money away
is beyond me."

Obviously.

Or you can just come back the way most travelers come back.

A little tired, a little overweight, with your clothes, your baggage, and your bank account in a slight state of disrepair. With a faintly dizzy appreciation of the speed of air travel that whisks you across oceans and continents, cultures and customs in less than twenty-four hours.

You come back with a few palpable things—gifts that cracked in your baggage somewhere between Florence and Paris, souvenir ash trays that stubbornly survived all sorts of banging around, dog-eared menus from memorable restaurants, terribly out-of-focus snapshots of palaces, monuments, and ruins, and a name-and-address list of new friends you hope to see again someday but probably never will.

And you come back with other, even more valuable mementos—kaleidescopic memories of far and beautiful places, recollections of warm people doing their best to make you feel at home, and a fresh awareness of other worlds that lie across the oceans. Only a few hours away, as the jets fly. And only a few minutes away, as the rockets fly.

Ideally, to travel is to learn—about other people, about yourself. And perhaps, if the lesson is learned well enough on both sides of the shrinking world, the rockets will never fly again. The tourist can yet be mightier than the hydrogen bomb.

40. THIS IS SAN FRANCISCO

Eight hundred thousand people, 400,000 phones, 300,000 cars fighting for 15,000 parking places, garages you can't tell from a hole in the ground, saloons on roof tops, mansions built on sand, hovels resting on rock, man-made islands, a real island full of man-made misfits, the Ferry Building clock telling time for the ghosts of yesterday—and the memory of the last lone ferryboat shrugging its way to Oakland and back on invisible tracks.

San Francisco. Geraniums growing in tomato cans on tenement windows, lush invisible gardens behind stone mansions, families of twelve living in basement rooms around the corner from community apartments with empty floors, oil paintings on grocery-store walls, artists growing beards to cover their confusion, $5000-a-year city employees riding in $5000 city limousines, and the traffic circling Union Square like a mongoose around a snake, looking for an opening.

San Francisco. Sailors on horseback in Golden Gate Park, off-duty cops riding the merry-go-round at Ocean Beach, ugly pelicans suddenly becoming graceful as they swoop for fish around Seal Rocks, the Legion of Honor looking ancient and ageless under a fog-shrouded moon, golfers in Lincoln Park turning their backs on a view that tourists travel thousands of miles to see—and trudging along with heads down, looking for lost balls.

San Francisco. The clatter of dice in an Embarcadero shed, the murmur of midnight voices behind drawn shades in a Telegraph Hill byway, the oily swish of the Bay around a Yacht Harbor piling, a child's delighted scream as the Powell cable lurches suddenly into Jackson, the Sacramento bus groaning up Nob Hill, the bells of Macy's playing "I'll Take You Home Again, Kathleen" as the husbands arrive to pick up their working wives, not all of whom are named Kathleen.

San Francisco. Women in mink sitting at the counter in David's, shopgirls having a lunch of five martinis at El Prado, $50,000-a-year execs having a sandwich at their desks in the Standard Oil Building, gaunt, birdlike women feeding bread to fat pigeons, bums pawing through garbage cans in the alleys off Mission, the matronly cats of North Beach waddling around—too overfed to look twice at the rats that scuttle past, toujours gray and unafraid.

San Francisco. The new and aloof elegance of the once-strident International Settlement, a smell of peanuts at the foot of Broadway, a cloud of black smoke hanging heavy over the bleakness of Treasure Island, steel bones of a burned-out mansion standing bare on Washington Street, uniformed chauffeurs walking dogs near the Presidio wall, stern nurses in white walking children through Lafayette Park, the kids of the far Mission playing tag in the middle of flat streets, looking almost abnormal in their normalcy.

San Francisco. The "new" 12 Adler Place (once an artists' hangout) without a picture on its white walls, Josephine Premice shouting, "*Olé!*" during the bullfight movies at the Matador, Lili St. Cyr bundled up in mink from ears to ankles (the rewards of a bare existence) as she leaves the 365, Inez Torres sitting on a guy's lap at 3 A.M. in the Papagayo Room, the George Christophers standing in a swirl of people on a Broadway street corner at midnight, the silence at 5 A.M. when nothing seems to be awake except the blinking eye of Alcatraz —looking around at nothing.

San Francisco. Convention delegates "seeing" San Francisco through a glass darkly in the long bars of the Palace, pedestrians marooned on desert islands of concrete in the carbon-monoxide sea of Market Street, women under umbrellas warmly appraising the spring styles in the Geary Street shopwindows, old men wearing hats sitting in the drab lobbies of small hotels and staring into infinity, old ladies eating lonely dinners in cafeterias and staring into mirrors that reflect their emptiness with pitiless accuracy.

San Francisco. An empty scotch bottle bobbing in the wake of a tipsy yacht, trucks double-parked alongside limousines on Montgomery Street, cars parked on sidewalks in Maiden Lane, lovers parked in cars on Twin Peaks, tourists parked in front of telescopes on Telegraph Hill (where the best sights keep their shades pulled down), motorcycle cops parked in dark service stations (their white helmets giving them away).

San Francisco. Yesterday's treasures turning to junk in the windows of the antique dealers along McAllister, somebody's valuables becoming valueless in the Third Street pawnshops, some mother's son turning into the old man on Howard Street, the flag at half-staff on the Pacific Union Club (a rich man has died), the nose-curling odors of Fisherman's Wharf (a thousand crabs have perished), the honking of horns, the blowing of whistles, the slap of cables, the scream of sea gulls —the babble, the confusion, the heartbreak, the joy of the world we call San Francisco.

41. ANYONE FOR DUCKS?

I don't know what YOU were doing at 4:15 A.M. on a certain Saturday—sleeping, probably—but I can tell you that your fearful correspondent wasn't snoozing peacefully between the percales.

He was being rousted out of the kip by Walter McGowan to go out and shoot down a few innocent ducks. This unlikely scene, staged at this ungodly hour, took place on Mr. McGowan's ranch near Princeton. If you've never heard of Princeton, it's near Butte City. If you've never heard of Butte City, we're in the same boat, friend, and a little crowded, isn't it?

Anyway, Mr. McGowan is a very strong and persuasive man, and, after allowing me fifteen minutes in which to whimper and protest, he threw me out of bed and got me into a reasonably upright position.

From that moment on, there wasn't a duck for miles around that wasn't in mortal danger. To say nothing of duck hunters.

If you've never been duck hunting in the predawn hours, let me tell you that it has its moments of strange and haunting beauty, none of which is reflected in the hunters. Sartorially speaking, our intrepid little band would've made Abercrombie & Fitch flinch.

There was Trader Vic Bergeron, the noted restaurateur, done up to the teeth in a blood-spattered jacket and waders that reached to his honest, stubbly chin. There were Mr. and Mrs. Paul Bancroft, looking like the Bobbsey Twins on safari. And Joe Knowles, wearing a khaki uniform of the type that was declared obsolete shortly before the Crimean War. Mrs. Bergeron's formidable beauty was artlessly concealed in what must have once been a Bundle for Britain until the British rejected it. The host, Mr. McGowan, looked every other inch the Great White Hunter. As for your sleep-drugged correspondent, whose participation in the rugged life had been limited heretofore to several sips of a Gun Club punch at Mr. Bergeron's restaurant, he looked just as you'd expect.

Miserable.

After a hearty breakfast of coffee, grunts, and groans, our party piled into station wagons and rattled twenty miles over Glenn County's finest back roads to some place or other, where we transferred to an outboard motor with boat attached.

Then we putt-putted along a beautiful tulle-lined canal to the duck blinds. A duck blind, according to the legend, is where duck hunters sit and get blind while waiting for a duck to fly within range. I wouldn't know about that. Our group was strictly non-alcoholic. Not even a can of Sterno.

We broke up into twos and threes and took our stations in the concealing underbrush on the shores of a big pond dotted with decoys.

As the sun started rising wanly—how else could it rise at 5:30 A.M.?—great flights of birds appeared overhead, majestic and impressive in the half-light. Fortunately, my shooting partner was Trader Vic, and here's a man who can spot birds.

"Sand-hill cranes," he said as a mighty flock drifted past, a good thousand feet in the cold air. "Snow geese," he pointed out a moment later. "No," he corrected. "Spotted geese." As though I were about to put up an argument. Two large white shapes floated eerily over the pond and two shots rang out. "No, no!" he shouted. "Swans! Five-hundred-dollar fine!" The swans were perfectly safe. I couldn't have hit the barnside of a broad if it had flown past my muzzle.

Then the ducks began appearing (the smart little quackers had grabbed an extra hour's sleep on us). Vic produced a duck call—a short black pipelike affair—and let out a few blasts, cupping his hands around it to create various effects. I listened entranced. Harry James in his finest moments never sounded any better.

As four mallards hove into view, fairly low, Vic whispered, "Watch. I'll call these babies right around over our head."

He played a short, soulful Concerto for Ducks, in E flat, and sure enough they hesitated in their flight and started swinging around. They floated past at the other end of the pond and Vic blew what must have been the mating call, for they wheeled suddenly and came straight for us, as though they were on wires. I grabbed my Daisy air rifle, prepared to sell my life dearly.

"Now!" snapped Vic, and as the four mallards passed over-head, four shots rang out and two of the birds dropped straight down into the water in front of us.

"Wow!" shouted the Trader triumphantly. "I got both of 'em!"

I reloaded silently. Who am I to argue?

After what seemed like several days had passed by, I glanced at my watch and saw it was 10 A.M. Teal, spoonbills, widgeon, sprig, and mallard had been flying past at a great rate, and our anti-duckcraft battalion had managed to bring about eighteen out of the sky.

I can't take credit for any of the kills, mainly because my partner, no doubt jealous of my incipient skill, wasn't giving me many chances to shoot. Mr. Bergeron is the kind of hunter who credits the ducks with better eyesight than a jet pilot. Every time a duck would come nearby and then scoot away, Vic would look at me balefully and complain, "He saw you turn your head." When I sneezed once, he acted as though I'd made a thousand ducks change course. "Here," he finally said. "You go sit on that box. I'll tell you when." You know, I'm still waiting?

But I'm not complaining. For four solid hours, he blew on that duck call, and it was remarkable. Even the ducks who didn't turn around seemed to enjoy it. They say that birds come from as far north as Ashland, Oregon, just to hear Vic play.

Looking back on it all, I'd say it was a worth-while experience. The only thing I object to is the early hours. I think the ducks would appreciate a later start, too. I know I would, and I'm

strictly on the side of the ducks, as they could tell by the way
I wasn't shooting at them.

42. WARM WONDERFUL WEEKEND

Early on Friday evening you could tell already it was going to
be one of those weekends—velvety warm, mellow as a memory
of childhood. Indian summer drowsed on the hills, and the
dying sun set fire to the East Bay before burning itself out in
the far waters. There was no breeze to stir the Columbus Day
banners along Columbus Avenue, no breeze to flutter the curtains at a million open windows, no breeze to ruffle the pond-
like waters of the Bay. The city sparkled, beaded with perspiration.

On a corner in North Beach, where it always looks like
summer, a beautiful girl ran her fingers through her hair and
said in wonderment, "It's just like Europe"—and so it
seemed. By the thousands the people were out and strolling,
hand in hand, arm in arm. They jammed the sidewalks and
spilled over into the streets, dodging like kids at play among
the slow-moving cars. Girls in shorts, showing their fine legs,
and shirtless men in Bermudas, and Chinese kids running in
barefoot bursts of a musical laughter. And there were songs
in the air—even though some were only the Tin Panalities of
a jukebox, floating out through the propped-open doors of panting saloons.

Velvet night, streaked with sweat. At "L'Amore dei Tre

Re," the culture vultures ran fingers around the boiling edges of their boiled shirts, and Giorgio Tozzi sang mightily as the heat condensed and danced off the tip of his nose.

In the Blackhawk the jazz cultists shed coats and then ties, while Oscar Peterson bent ponderously over his piano, grunting loudly to himself; the sheets of water pouring off his forehead made the keys slippery as an ice rink, but he skated magnificently, with never a slip.

At Fack's, rivulets ran down Annie Ross's heroic cleavage as the high priestess of bop-and-Basie blasted like a trumpet in full cry—and her devotees mopped and bopped their brows and loved her in the steamy stickiness of it all.

The city slept restlessly, kicking off its covers, and the Saturday dawn came up in warm wonder, the temperature rising with it. Heat waves and white-clad players danced on the courts at the Mill Valley Tennis Club, and the splashing of bodies into pools could be heard clearly from Los Altos to the shaded lanes of Ross. The football fans, dressed for baseball, trooped to the weekly slaying of the Bear in Memorial Stadium—and far out in the soupy Bay you could see the painted boats on the painted waters, their sails forlornly dead. And late in the day, a thousand people rimmed Coit Tower to watch the sun go to blazes, trailing angry bursts of glory.

Once again the streets came alive. Old people dragged pathetic dining-room chairs out to the sidewalk to watch the Coney Island parade. And a Ferris wheel, all green and red, spun slow as a boyhood dream alongside SS. Peter and Paul.

Sunday—and again no breeze save that made by the rustling of a million comic sections. No sound broke the Sabbath silence except the groans of the hung-over. The freeways and skyways dozed like concrete boa constrictors that had had their fill of automobiles. The October sun rose mercilessly, drawing the night people out of their holes with a great blinking of slitted eyes through slatted blinds.

High in the beautiful hills of Berkeley, the University professors began the rites of the Bloody Mary. Eggs Benedict jiggled forth under waves of yellow hollandaise, hands and heads trembling in unison. The warm air became a living thing, heavy with the perfume of coffee, the song of birds, the laughter of children—and Lunik seemed exactly as far away as it is.

In the thin, Italianate shadow of the Campanile the shirt-sleeved thousands began winding slowly up the campus hill-sides to the Greek Theater. On and on they came, like acolytes to mass, like pilgrims to Mecca, like aficionados to a sporting event. For, under the unbelieving summer sun, the San Francisco Opera Company was presenting *Aïda*.

Oddly enough, on this oddest of weekends the Italian's story of ancient Egypt never came more magnificently to life than it did against this backdrop of Greek columns on an American campus before an audience that sprawled on grassy knolls, squirmed on stone seats, put paper bags over its heads to ward off the sun, and perspired and wept to the heartfelt outpourings of Leontyne Price, Jon Vickers, Irene Dalis, Lawrence Winters, and Giorgio Tozzi.

It was an electric performance. Even the hard-bitten veterans of the orchestra were carried away, even the booming Dr. Robert Sproul seemed strangely subdued (for Robert Gordon Sproul), even a Cal touchdown in the Big Game couldn't have produced louder cheers than those that rang out at the finale, spreading slowly over the old campus to die at last among the autumn leaves.

The crowd filed quietly down the hillside, filled with beauty, glowing with contentment.

Warm and wonderful weekend, a long drink at sunset with old friends, the twilight sky fading through a stand of eucalyptus, and somewhere in the near distance the smell of burning leaves, the bark of a dog, the small, satisfying sounds of our little world settling down for the night. The East Bay lights began twinkling under the eternal stars—and suddenly peace seemed not too distant a dream in the Indian summer of our lives.

43. THE DANCING YEARS

San Francisco is a city of memories—and they can be stirred, sometimes, even by something as unimaginative as a press release beginning: "Freddy Martin and his orchestra open November 12 in the Venetian Room of the Fairmont Hotel" . . .

After all these years a "name" band playing in a hotel's supper room. That doesn't do anything to you? It does something to me, dear heart, for I misspent my youth in the era of Big Bands—and although it left me with kidneys that rattle and arches that have fallen flatter than a soufflé in an earthquake, I regret not a minute of it. Of all the fabulous foolishness we've known in our generation, this was one of the most foolish. All of us survived it. Not one of us wasn't marked by it.

These were the short, swift years before World War II—and this was our youth in Baghdad-by-the-Bay. The long-legged girls in their Empress Eugenie hats and tight-fitting suits. Platina fox and chubby lynx jackets—these were all the rage. The nights were heady with Evening in Paris and Christmas Night and Cape Jasmine gardenias, but every once in a while you went all the way with a big purple orchid. And everybody had a favorite band (there was no singer in the world then except Crosby) and the arguments raged as you set out to make the rounds.

It's hard to believe now that so much could have been going on in the space of a few blocks, a few years. Into the Palace's Rose Room Bowl, one upon the other came Artie Shaw, Vincent Lopez, Casa Loma, Paul Whiteman, Henry Busse, Ray Noble. At the St. Francis, Guy Lombardo, Jan Garber, Ted Weems, Lawrence Welk, Dick Jurgens, Richard Himber, Xavier Cugat, Freddy Martin. In the Drake Persian Room, Carl Ravazza, Joe Sudy, ice shows, girlie shows, all kinds of shows. Benny Goodman, Griff Williams, Hal Kemp, Skinnay Ennis, and Veloz and Yolanda in the Mark's Peacock Court. Across the street at the Fairmont, Henry King, Joe Reichman, the De Marcos. When you made the rounds then, there was really a round to make—and every opening night was an event. Or so we thought. We'd rather have been caught dead there than anywhere else.

Sweet nights of innocence: The lower bar of the Mark was our meeting place on Friday nights, and it was noisier than a YMCA pool at noon. Jake Ehrlich, Jr., and Reed Funsten and Frank McGinnis always seemed to be arguing while the rest of us were trying to get dances with Kathie Thompson or Theo Taft Brown or Susie Jane or Jackie. If we were on the shorts, we tried to "lobby dance"—sneaking into the room past Fritz, the stiffly Prussian maître d'hôtel, as soon as the music started. Half the time he'd throw us out, half the time he'd look the other way—it all depended on his Teutonic mood. Old Fritz. He terrified us all, like a German schoolteacher. We never tipped him, but he retired rich anyway.

And the tea dances on Saturday afternoon. Visualize, if you will, the Palace's Rose Room jammed with five hundred girls, all of them forking creamed chicken in patty shells and gazing adoringly at Artie Shaw, who stared back with unconcealed disdain. There was a big picture at the entrance, and always a smear of lipstick across his mouth where some girl had planted a frustrated kiss. "Little morons," he'd snap, laying down his clarinet at the end of the session. "Let's get the hell out of here" —and I'd walk out behind him stiffly self-conscious at being thus honored by so great a man. In those days there was nobody so celebrated as a band leader.

The dancing years—how fast they vanished, to the beat of a cymbal, the wail of a saxophone. We did the shag and the Dipsy-Doodle, we formed circles for the Big Apple, and we put our little foot right there for the Maxixe. Like lost children, we clung to each other through the great new tunes—"What's New" and "Blue Orchids" and "I Didn't Know What Time It Was," which summed us up perfectly. And at 1 A.M. in the darkened rooms all over town the bands swung into their "Moonlight Medleys," and the jeweled globes on the ceiling cast glittery reflections over the couples that pressed against each other in love's young agony. "Sweetheart of Sigma Chi" to "Sleepy Time Gal" to "Good Night Sweetheart"—and it was all so tender and beautiful that you could cry, almost. Then, in a cruel instant, the lights came on blindingly as we all stood and stared at each other, wiping off the lipstick while the girls fussed with their hair and talked in unnaturally loud voices.

Nobody seems to know how or why it happened, but suddenly it was over. The big bands vanished and the great rooms, the magical, romantic rooms, fell into disuse one by one. A generation that had danced learned to march and came back too old for all that—and an era was filed away forever, along with the bids and programs you used to stick in the frame of your dresser mirror. The gardenias turned brown, the cloying scent of Evening in Paris faded away, and Artie Shaw's clarinet was heard no more down the drafty halls of the Palace.

But on November 12, says the press release, Freddy Martin's band opens in the Fairmont's Venetian Room—and when it's "Moonlight Medley" time, perhaps my youth will come back "like the rains of spring, my loves like the wild geese flying." Stephen Vincent Benét said that. He was a poet who understood the dancing years.

44. ON A SEPTEMBER NIGHT

An Indian-summer haze hanging over the night-lighted hills, a full moon lavishing its reflection of the black Bay, the city that knows no seasons drowsing and dreaming in the lull that comes before the rise of fall . . .

Dreaming? Yes, a city can dream, fitful under a warm blanket —dreams of golden yesterdays, dreams of old glories on a day such as this, dreams of an exposition glowing on a man-made island in the Bay, dreams of clipper ships flying grandly through the bridgeless gate, Portsmouth Square alive with Chinese mandarins, Plunger Bill Ralston and Bonanza Jim Flood striding across California and Montgomery as though they owned it—which might very well have been the case.

A city asleep with a smile on its face—a smile for "China Mary," the queen of the Chinatown lotteries (but she gave more to charities than many a Nob Hill nabob). A smile for Gertrude Atherton and poet George Sterling taking a daily downtown stroll together, Gertrude striding along like a man and Sterling scrambling to keep up with her. A smile for the wizened newsboy who marched into the old Coffee Dan's on O'Farrell each midnight and, as the crowd paid respectful si-

lence, read off the Page One headlines in a stentorian voice
—after which, wild applause. A smile for Bill Saroyan arriving
at the Mark with a greasy bagful of shrimp (which he insisted
on passing out to the debs), a grin for little Yehudi Menuhin
stopping in the middle of a recital to blow his nose industri-
ously, a wistful half-smile for sad, thin Robert Louis Stevenson
crossing the Bay for a rendezvous with his Oakland sweetheart.

So much to look back on, from high on a late September
hill. Peacocks preening along the dawn pathways of Golden
Gate Park and Uncle John McLaren, the park's genius, looking hatefully at Kezar Stadium and spitting, "I'd rather have
a bed of petunias there any day." The St. Marys of Slip
Madigan and the Santa Claras of Clipper Smith playing their
Little Big Games under the Sunday sun (gladiators all, nine
feet tall) and a marvelous fullback named Ernie Nevers leading the Stanfords to the 20–20 tie on an autumn afternoon
when the world of Berkeley was filled with innocence and
simple courage.

Indian summer, thick and heavy, blurring the sharp edges
of the present, bringing the past into soft focus. We laughed
at the lovelorn swain who threw himself off the bow of a
ferryboat, floated beneath it, and was dredged up, choking and
gasping, as he bobbed to the surface at the stern; he laughed
at himself, too—eventually. We hustled through the Ferry
Building and were impressed afresh each time at the great
circle of car tracks and the ceaseless roar of the Noisiest Main
Street in the World and the endless adventures waiting at our
very fingertips. The streets led anywhere—and that's where we
were content to go, anywhere in the young city: to the States
Hof Brau, with its big concert orchestra (and booths named
after German cities), to the Capitol to hear "Two Boys and a
Piano" (one of the boys was Crosby), to Recreation Park to
watch Kid Mohler (who might have been forty, but looked

sixty) slam a ball like it has never been slammed since. It was
a city for the enthusiastic, and everybody was.

The old, slow yesterdays—how they come to life on a velvety
September midnight when even the cables seem to sleep in
their slots. After the fire-quake, John Tait running down Powell
to his beloved restaurant, looking at its undamaged façade and
exulting: "Thank God, I've been spared," then he unlocked
the front door and stepped into what lay behind: nothing but
rubble. Sunny Jim Rolph cracking his usual joke (and getting
his usual laugh) before a crowd in North Beach: "I am a son
of California, I am a son of San Francisco—and I am a son of
this beach!" Garbage horses breaking their legs on the slippery
streets, and mounted policemen shooting them then and there.
The great saloons along Kearny and Sutter filled with great men
patting their great bellies, and twirling their mustaches at the
beauties of 1910, who held a nosegay of violets to their faces
and peeked daringly through the swinging doors.

The sleepy mind of a city curled up like a child, dreaming
childlike of days that were warm and endless and nights that
were endlessly gay (the word hangover hadn't even been invented, so nobody had them). The tentative slam of a screen
door on a wide, wooden porch, the kids playing mumblety-peg
under a tree, the Winton (or the Durant or the Chalmers)
parked at the curb, and you didn't get mad when somebody
called it "Frisco," because it didn't seem important then. More
important was a Sunday silver fizz at the Cliff House, looking
out over the broad ocean that would keep the world away from
us forever—so we could live, laugh, and love in the best of all
possible cities.

Indian summer, and the old city asleep and dreaming—silent,
white, perfect as the moon overhead.

45. DEATH OF THE SEALS

In 1958, major-league baseball, in the form of the transplanted New York Giants, came to San Francisco. Their arrival, to the accompaniment of more overblown civic oratory than you would have thought possible in a reasonably sophisticated community, spelled the end for the city's beloved (when they won) minor-league team, the Seals—surely one of the most felicitous nicknames in baseball history. After a particularly dismal performance, it was, of course, pointed out that they also performed like seals.

On the team's final day of action, however, everybody loved the Seals, and my report went like this:

The city was small and warm Sunday. Like an American village on Sunday anywhere, any time, all roads led to the ball park. For the Seals were about to die, and everybody (well everybody to whom the Seals meant something) wanted to be in on the kill, for sentimental reasons.

It was not the Sunday crowd of the bullfight, intense, a little bloodthirsty, nervous. And not the Sunday crowd of football, tough, cocky, pushy, and even, in its own curious way, stylish. It was the most American crowd of them all—the baseball mob, and what a wondrous crew:

The kids carrying their gloves and their dreams, the old men who talk of Harry Wolverton and Willie Kamm and Ping Bodie, the fat old women grinning toothless grins at everybody, the furtive eccentrics with their secret bottles, their darting eyes, their sudden hoarse shouts.

These are the Americans, and Sunday they were out in force

at the village ball yard to say good-by to the Seals—a group of men who mean nothing in themselves, but who, merely by wearing the name, have become part of the mystique of San Francisco. It doesn't matter whether the town will be better or worse without them.

What matters is that it will be different without them.

Somewhere a foghorn was calling, but not at Seals Stadium. The sun was hot, and a Little Old Lady in front of me began fashioning a hat out of the Sunday classified-ads section. She had a sweet, lined face; she looked like somebody's mother. Her pale blue eyes roved over the playing field and then she glanced at the watch on her thin wrist.

"C'mon, ya crummy bums," she yelled in a voice that set the light towers to swaying. "Le's play ball!"

All the beautiful, ageless pageantry of baseball began. The Municipal Band took a healthy cut at "Take Me Out to the Ball Game." The three umpires marched out, and the crowd dutifully booed, as crowds have done for a hundred years. A man named Tommy Maloney advanced to a microphone near home plate and announced "Today is I Am an American Day. Turn to your neighbor on your right and say, 'I am glad to be an American.'"

I turned to the man on my right and said, "I am glad to be an American."

"Glad to know you, McCann," he said, pumping my hand. "McGuire's the name, McGuire."

The game proceeded pleasantly, in the meandering way base-ball has. A wonderful, nostalgic haze of peanuts, hot dogs, mustard, and beer settled over the stadium. The sky was blue, the grass was green, and there were the timeless sounds of base-balls thwacking into oiled leather, bats connecting solidly with horsehide, rumps sliding along in the dirt.

A few yards outside the stadium, cars were hurtling across the skyway, horns were honking, and nerves were knotting, but inside, it might have been 1927 or 1907—for the same old chatter was filling the air: "Give'm the high hard one, Jack boy," "Put on the squeeze, ya dummy," "All the way, Bill, all the way," "Back to the Three-Eye League, ya donkey."

Across the aisle from me, a small boy wearing glasses was slumped down in his seat, peering at the sky and identifying planes. "Douglas Skyraiders," he announced loudly as a group of jets swept past. An old twin-engine job lumbered into view. "C-47," he intoned, "otherwise known as the DC-3." On the far horizon above Alameda, a high-tailed job appeared. "PBY," he said.

His mother, a leather-lunged Seal rooter, suddenly wheeled around and looked at him in disgust. "Why don'tcha go home and practice the piano?" she suggested.

The Sacramentos won the first game by virtue of a ninth-inning home run, and everybody began milling around. The old-timers trooped across the street to the Double Play and Flukie's Third Base for a quick shot of bourbon, followed by a beer. A fat man wearing an undershirt flabbed his way across Sixteenth and Bryant. "Lose your shirt, mister?" asked the cop on the beat. "Yeah!" roared the fat man, his belly shaking with mirth. "I bet on the Seals." The cop shook his head and turned away.

Inside the stadium, a village clown, wearing a long coat and a silk top hat, appeared from out of nowhere, grimacing, leaping up and down the stairs like a jumping jack, making faces at the girls, grabbing a beer bottle out of somebody's hand and emptying it.

The crowd applauded his antics and laughed—the kind of laughter that goes back beyond TV and radio, back beyond movie and telephones, back to something early and real and almost lost: the laughter of people sitting together in the afternoon sun, under a blue sky, with the band playing and the flag rippling on the pole in center field.

And so it finally ended. The Seals died like champions, and the crowd filed out silently, leaving the stadium empty except for the peanut shells in the aisles and the smell of baseball slowly fading away. Next year there will be more baseball—major-league, minor-league, some kind—but it doesn't really matter. For the game is only made up, after all, of the dreams and memories of the people who watch it, and these will never die.

46. DOWN THE ROAD A PIECE

I'm as devoted to progress as the next liar, but there are several hallowed items I think should be left strictly alone—disregarding, for the moment, such obvious candidates for perpetuity as the cable car and Kathleen Norris. At the moment, the objects of my concern are Highway No. 1, Carmel and the Del Monte Forest, three vital links in the escape route for anyone who enjoys an occasional flight from reality. I have spent a weekend checking diligently into the status quo of these three indispensables, and it seems to me that status isn't quite as quo as it once was.

For more years than I care to think about, I have considered Highway 1 to be "my" highway. I feel possessive about it because for all those years you hardly ever saw another car on it. In the fishy eye of a highway engineer, I suppose it was pretty awful: narrow, bumpy, pitted, barely two-laned, covered with fallen rocks and fraught with blind hairpin turns.

But that was the charm of Highway 1. You tooled along at the pace of a snail with tired blood, with the Pacific gleaming at your right and an occasional cow grazing at your left. Grazing your car, I mean. With no traffic fore or aft, you were free to drink in some of the most remarkable scenery in the world; farms spreading greenly to the very edge of the ocean, white lighthouses shining atop sheer cliffs, secret beaches where the hand of man seemed never to have set foot, veritable Fingal's Caves of rocky grottoes with the surf roaring into them, wild and free.

And the wonderful array of little landmarks along the way. Rockaway Beach, quiet and sleepy, turning its back on the continent. Half Moon Bay, with its fine, forthright smell of fresh fish. Davenport, nestling in the shadow of the mighty Santa Cruz-Portland Cement plant, its houses and melodramatic church covered with a fine film of cement dust. Moss Landing: lighted towers of the P.G. & E. power plant reflected in the tiny bay where fishing boats ride at anchor. And Watsonville, with its farm hands lolling in the shade of the hot main street, or, ablaze with cheap wine, brawling in the gutters.

Once there was time to drink it all in. Now, endearingly archaic Highway 1 is being "improved." Horrendous curves that once forced you to take a firmer grip on the wheel and really drive are being straightened out. There are divided stretches of banked, four-lane highway that could be any highway anywhere—with distracting views moved safely out of sight. The result, inevitable, is more traffic, all of it moving at about ninety miles an hour.

Highway 1 is no longer "my" highway, or yours. Now it's everybody's. The most scenic drive this side of the Grande

Corniche between Monaco and Nice will soon be as exciting as the Embarcadero Freeway.

Carmel, the enchanted village, is doing its best to keep the clock turned to yesterday, but this looks like a losing fight too. The cracker-box houses are springing up in sterile and orderly rows across the road, a shopping center goes up at the end of Ocean Avenue, and the traffic is so heavy that cops on three-wheelers putter back and forth all day long, slapping pink tickets on windshields. Parking meters will be next.

Here and there, of course, the old line is being held with remarkable fortitude. Harrison Godwin's Pine Inn is as rich in Victorian charm as ever, and you can still gather around the blazing fireplace in his taproom and sip a highball made with the last full measure of devotion. Such true believers as Stuyvesant Fish, Edison Holt, and Walt Hecox still forgather in Sade's, which, as I recall, was once just about the only bar in Carmel; and Gallatin's, in Monterey, and John Gardiner's Tennis Ranch, in the valley, go on proving with reassuring results that you can observe the niceties and still make a buck.

But Carmel is changing. I knew it for certain when I saw a fine-looking old duffer strolling past the Pine Inn, his tweed jacket properly tacky, his cashmere sweater properly baggy, his jodhpur boots properly shined. There was only one jarring note in this walking picture of Old Carmel. He was wearing a Giants' rooter's cap.

As you drive past the entrance to Sam Morse's Del Monte Forest, you will see a sight to bring tears to the eyes of the hardest-hearted subdivision builder. Hundreds of great pines have been uprooted, great gouges have been carved into the primeval hillsides, and the ubiquitous bulldozers are hard at work. For the State Highway Department (Division of Havoc) has decreed that here, of all lovely places, a freeway should go through. I don't know where the freeway will end—somewhere down the road in a bottleneck, I'm sure—but meanwhile, the devastation is appalling, and a small atom bomb could hardly have created a scene of greater desolation.

Once you are deep inside the forest, however, the past returns with a rush in this last outpost of escape. Quail scuttle across the roads, golf balls sing through the air, tennis balls ping, and you can sit at night in the lodge and listen to the best little dance band in the land and look out over the cove and watch a great moon rise, silvery white, out of the ancient pines that are probably already marked for destruction.

And as you listen to the old songs in the old surroundings, you can only reflect that even the moon isn't beyond reach. Soon it, too, will be pock-marked, blighted, and crisscrossed with freeways—never to rise again.

47. WONDERFUL WORLD OF WALT

To launch his '59–'60 season, Mr. Walt Disney summoned the press to his Disneyland, and let me say that we all scrambled like puppies to accept his invitation. To reject Mr. Disney would be like rejecting motherhood, fatherhood, and Liberace, all at once, for he occupies a position roughly analogous to the American flag and Santa Claus, with Albert Schweitzer thrown in.

He may be Uncle Walt to the kiddies, but to us older earthlings he is the last of the father figures—the last magician, the last creator of razzle-dazzle and fantasy, of his world and yet slightly apart from it, like the Wizard of Oz.

I look at him with awe. And so, I noticed, did another invited guest, Richard Nixon, who gazed upon Mr. Disney with
shining eyes and treated him with great respect—as though he
were afraid that if he didn't behave Father would rub his
magic cash register and turn him into Dumbo.

Anyway, despite my well-known aversion to children, dogs,
and Southern California, there I was on the guest list, so, without further adieu, I took off early in the morning for the Walter-
works, dragging Daughter Deborah behind me in a cloud of
comic books and giggles. We boarded a Western Airliner—the
one featuring "Hunt Breakfasts"—and headed South, while I
sat there in a trance, hunting for the reason they call them
Hunt Breakfasts. I was still hunting when we passed over a
wall of smog as high as a space monkey's eye, and soddenly we
were at Los Angeles Airport.

Chewing the last of our pig sausages, we ran for the helicopter, and soon we were beating our way across the mysterious
countryside, gazing down on mile after mile of tiny one-story
houses, each with its tiny swimming pool pressed alongside
for cold comfort. Thousands of cars—all of them red or yellow,
for Southern Californians prefer bright colors—darted up and
down the new streets, which had lately been peaceful orange
groves. It was an overwhelming sight, and I was quite dumb-
struck. In fact, I was struck so dumb I was still wondering why
they call them Hunt Club Breakfasts when, a scant twenty
minutes later, the towers and pennants of Disneyland—
Graustark, Mecca, Xanadu—rose out of the haze to welcome
us.

Or rather, there to meet us was Disneyland's dauntless chief
of publicity, Mr. Edward Meck, who has worked so long for
Mr. Disney that he is beginning to look like Mickey Mouse.
And what a perfect name for the job. Mr. Meck—in charge of
meck-believe.

Disneyland is four years old, and, having been admirably built to start with, now looks both brand new and ageless. I suppose it is a commentary on the whole Southlandish scene that it seems more permanent and believable than the tract houses we had just flown over.

In a world going around in dizzy circles, Disneyland stands serene under the broiling sun, a crazy, well-ordered monument to childlike sophistication. Perhaps THIS is where the Summit meetings should be held, here where elephants fly and a mouse cracks a whip over the merry-go-round.

It has always been my contention that Disneyland is for grown-ups, not children.

Oh, children love it—naturally—as they would love any great amusement park, with its color and motion and gay music. But for the adults (who outnumber the children by three to one) it is something much more. It is the reaffirmation of their childhood dreams, the rebirth of their youth, all packed into a few magic hours, a few magic acres.

The Jungle Cruise (still the best ride of all, for my money —or Mr. Disney's), the spectacular paddle-wheel river boat and memories of Tom Sawyer and Huck Finn, the old-time show in the soda-pop saloon, the turn-of-the-century village, the Keystone Kops, the silent movies, the barbershop quartets on the street corners, and the brass bands marching—these are not for kids. These are for the kid in all of us, and here is Mr. Disney's triumph.

It was hot in Disneyland that day, but the show went on any way. Under the broiling noonday sun, Father Walt staged a parade to end all parades—and how long has it been since we've had a good parade in San Francisco? This one had it all: the prancing horses, the dozen bands, the dancers in the streets, the strutting drum majors, and, most important, the proper pace. The climax was unforgettable: seventy-six trombonists in top hats, white tie, and tails, playing, of course, "76 Trombones," while composer Meredith Willson, a kid like the rest of us, waved his arms happily and had the finest time of his life. And then ten thousand balloons floated out across the crowd, out across the snow-capped Matterhorn ride, out across the new Monorail and submarines, out across the castles and minarets—and the Vice-President and the other kids sat there silently in the sun and watched them till they disappeared, one by one, like the laughing years of parades down the hot summer streets.

Dusk now—Disneyland's most beautiful hour. With the gaslights coming on and a band, somewhere playing "Swanee River," and the couples strolling along the lagoons, we climbed back into our helicopter and rose slowly into the gathering night, leaving the dreams and the legends behind—but in good hands. The hands of the wizard known as Walt.

48. FUNNY OLD TOWN

Freeways that aren't safeways, Safeways that aren't freeways, pigeons overfed by people that are underfed, two mints minting nothing but dust, Ferry Building piers-with-tears reaching out empty arms for boats that will never return, expensively ornate lampposts lighting up a Market Street that has turned tacky, idiots blowing horns in the tiled latrine whiteness of the Stockton Tunnel, inscrutable Oriental ladies jaywalking across

Jackson on feet that were once bound, sentries at stiff attention in the Presidio saluting an army of colonels in a peaceful post of the past.

Mansions hidden behind mansions in the discreet sterility of Pacific Heights, passengers fighting for seats on busses and for the privilege of standing up on cable cars, the Market Street midget reading *Mad* at the biggest newsstand in town (his), cops strolling in pairs past the slobsided bars where you can arrange for everything from a "fix" to an abortion, Coit Tower dimly seen through the snarling mists of February, weak and pale, as though only half its light bill had been paid.

Revolting shreds of filthy curtain fluttering at broken windows in A. A. Tiscornia's monument to grime at California and Kearny, old watchtower rising with Rhineland romanticism out of the hilltop foliage on Yerba Buena Island, dusty golden steeds charging at each other over the Opera House proscenium while the symphony thunders below, teen-aged deadpanned girls with thick legs and thin smiles drinking stocking-black coffee on slack-jaw, lackluster Grant Avenue, a sudden Sunday rain squall driving the sea gulls, screaming, across the empty, dripping decks of Telegraph Hill; inside, the hi-fi and the low fireplace crackling away against the storm.

The earthquake-tested, fire-tested, time-tested Montgomery Block doomed to die because automobiles must park though their owners have no place to go, tethered boats bobbing like drunken sailors in Yacht Harbor, the Sunday Bay throwing itself in white fury against Alcatraz as though trying to get in, a spin-wheeled cab struggling like a fly in a spiderweb on the dripping flank of the Taylor Street hill, the well-fed burghers of Marina Boulevard, standing in snug smugness at their picture windows, staring out at the picture of passers-by staring back at them. The Saturday-night "No Vacancy" signs on the Lombard motels (for love will find a way one night a week),

Ricksha-bound bar belles and boys streaming through the
Chinatown alleys with heels clicking like mahjong tiles on the
ancient bricks, black-suited skin-divers frightening the sea lions
off Seal Rocks under the watchful windows of the Cliff House,
the many towers of Parkmerced and Stonestown looking faraway and concretely unreal in the dark Sunday gloom, a lost
city marching in circles on the edge of Suburbia.

A tug battling its way bravely across the Bay with only its
red stack showing above the spray, the 3 A.M. Sunday hubba-
hubbub in the Papagayo Room (the customers outscreeching
the parrots), "new" Geary Boulevard looking like a street im-
ported from some other city, with its streetcar tracks gone, its
lights too bright, its traffic islands snaking down the center
with raw efficiency—a street oddly at odds with the odd old
buildings of the Richmond District.

Lovers locked in arms and cars under the spreading trees of
Golden Gate Park, drunken drivers weaving home at dawn
past garbage trucks a-clatter with empty bottles, frilly flower-
topped females wolfing raw steak at El Prado, Very Important
People from very unimportant places waiting uncomplainingly
for tables at Trader Vic's, the wind toppling a geranium-filled
coffee can off an Eddy Street ledge and a sad, empty face peering
down from the window; Brooks Brother'd, Jay Briggs'd, Roger
Strobel'd, Robert Kirk'd commuters hurring up Third Street
past the Skid Rowgues, whose natural shoulders are slack, their
pleated pants uncreased, pockets filled with nothing but
clenched fists.

Post-midnight cars U-turning in an endless circle at Sutter
and Polk to reach the all-night newsboy at the Foster's-lighted
curb, the Van Ness auto salesman standing in the gutter kicking tires and knocking competitors, 450 Sutter's many nurses
streaming out to lunch with their white uniforms showing
like slips beneath their overcoats, the bulging bay-window'd

eyes of the Western Addition looking around fearfully as one
after another of their old neighbors disappears, to be replaced
by square newcomers that stare straight ahead and coldly;
booming silence of the ages in the cold market place of the
financial district at night, the millions in deep-vaulted sleep,
Corinthian pillars standing guard, row upon row—O Capitalism
My Captain.

Funny old town. The Ferry Building looking taller somehow
as it stands on tiptoe to peer over the freeway, cars parked all
day in alleys under signs reading "No Parking At Any Time"
and the cops on tricycles getting rider's cramp writing two-
dollar dejection slips, trees toppling and cliffs crumbling to
make room for houses that will then have a veiw of nothing
but each other, funny old February town of wind and rain beating at the huddled, mud-puddled hills, gray, but still strangely
gay through it all.

49. AMONG MY SOUVENIRS

I remember Mamma, I'll remember April—and I remember
Franklin Roosevelt sitting in his open car on Treasure Island
during the 1939 fair, gazing at the city's skyline and groping for
the proper word. At last he found it. Uptilting his cigarette
holder to a forty-five-degree angle, he smiled in that unforgettable voice: "Magnificent!" . . . Fiorello La Guardia on Telegraph Hill, looking at the view: "Fantastic." Lily Pons, same
place, same view: "*Fantastique*." Bruno Walter, ditto, ditto:
"*Fantastishe*" . . . Captain Fritz Wiedemann, the prewar nazi
consul here, deciding that his block-long Mercedes-Benz was

attracting too much attention, putting it in storage, and creeping around thereafter in a battered old Chevrolet . . . And Winston Churchill's son, Randolph, suddenly getting tired of It All at a party in Parkmerced and bouncing off into the midnight on a pogo stick he'd "borrowed" from the hosts' sleeping son.

I remember Pearl Harbor, I don't remember the *Maine*—and I'll never forget Konrad Bercovici, the noted author, making his first visit to North Beach and leaving his literate mark on the men's-room wall in the Black Cat: "Veni, vidi, Bercovici" . . . The old days of Sausalito, when nobody had an address because the streets had no names; you simply lived on the first, second, or third terrace . . . And a padlocked (by the police) house of joy on Columbus Avenue, with this neat little sign over its doorbell: "Belle Not Working."

I remember Cremo, the GOOD five-cent cigar, and the Jordan Playboy, out where the West begins—and I remember Fatty Arbuckle, the late great movie comedian, spending a night in the county jail, appalled at the conditions; when he got out next day, he sent a new mattress, with his compliments, to every prisoner . . . At Frank Norris's house, Vincent Sheean making an impassioned plea for financial aid to the Spanish Loyalists—and getting no response till Kathleen Norris (who disagrees, politically, with everything Sheean stands for) broke the ice with a large donation. "I couldn't stand the silence," she explained simply . . . And Tyrus Raymond Cobb, the baseball immortal, playing a friendly game of softball down the Peninsula, hitting a dinky roller to third base, and getting thrown out at first—until, as he reached the bag, he knocked the ball out of first-baseman Lewis Lapham's hand. "Cut it out, Ty," snapped Lapham. "This is just for fun, remember?" Cobb, his old eyes afire: "When I play, I play to win!"

I've forgotten the Alamo, Tippecanoe and Tyler, too—and

Al Jolson singing for fifty dollars a week in the National Theatre, a corrugated iron shed at Post and Steiner, after the earthquake; when he was raised to seventy-five the second week, he sighed happily, "I didn't know there was this much money in the whole world" . . . But I do remember Sally Stanford in 1936, handing out personal cards reading "Sally Stanford, Certified Bridge Instructor, 1926 Franklin St." . . . And Duncan Hines visiting San Quentin, where then Warden Clinton Duffy asked with a grin, "Are you going to recommend our place?" "No," answered Hines stiffly. "It's against my policy to recommend any place that caters to a restricted clientele."

I recall the crooked railway that climbed Tamalpais, Bill Wobber becoming a police commissioner to loud cries of "Cops and Wobbers," Mimi Imperato crying as he closed his restaurant forever—and the great Mary Garden singing free for nothing at Caesar's Cellar in North Beach, on the nights she wasn't appearing with the opera company . . . Dorothy Lamour and Lawyer Greg Bautzer curled up cozily in a Sir Francis Drake suite, listening to a Roosevelt fireside chat. And, down the hall, Lana Turner answering a knock on the door, sticking her head out, and screaming, "Go away, I'm naked!" She wasn't. But she'd shaved off her eyebrows for a movie role, and hadn't penciled new ones on yet. And two ladies from Boston, on their first visit to San Francisco, walking out of the Mark Hopkins on an unusually muggy day. "Goodness, it's warm," said the first Boston lady. "Naturally," remarked the second. "After all, we're three thousand miles from the ocean."

The memories: Olive Shumate—what girl has her dash today?—strolling down Grant Avenue with two white Russian wolfhounds on a leash. Dave Brubeck playing for peanuts to nobody in the Geary Cellar. Sally Rand's fabulous chorus girls at the Music Box, every one of whom (fairy tales do come true) married a rich man. And, in 1938, a well-known

San Francisco couple waking up fuzzily at noon in the old Del Monte Hotel, whereupon she yawned, "Y'know, darling, I s'pose we really SHOULD get married." He, turning over and going back to sleep: "Who'd have us?"

Memories, memories—but live for today, and live it well. Because ten years from now you'll want to look back on it and remember.

50. IN THE HUSH OF EVENING

San Francisco—city of magic hours. Dawn, and the sun rising out of the east with a sudden burst that dims the amber lights of the Bay Bridge. Noontime: The Ferry Building raising its siren's voice, stenographers grouped prim as schoolgirls around the base of the Mechanics Monument to eat their paper-bagged lunches, the day's first martini-on-the-rocks shimmering (and shivering) on a marble table in the Palace's Happy Valley. Midafternoon's gaggle of children heading home, a horseman cantering along the Great Highway, a golfer in Lincoln Park silhouetted against the Chinese red of the Gate Bridge. Magic hours, all.

But to me the hour that spells San Francisco most strongly comes at dusk, when the city hovers breathlessly between its two lives. For a timeless instant the day seems to stand still, as though putting off its plunge into darkness. The light becomes hazy and dreamlike, and wraiths of the past stir in the soft shadows cast by buildings that are suddenly indistinct, ageless.

Day's end, and the sun sinking to a glorious death in the West, touching fire to a hundred thousand windows. Russian Hill a black Stonehenge against the fading crimson sky. The first street lights coming on—pale, oh so pale under the extravagant heavens. Red taillights streaming homeward like so many luminous fish along the one-way rivers of traffic, and the great searchlight coming to life atop Alcatraz—beacon on a stone ship going nowhere.

Dusk: The great city slowly letting down at the end of the day. Skyscraper windows slamming shut. Bootblacks padlocking their stands. Sidewalk flower peddlers wrapping their leftovers in newspapers. Inspectors walking out of the Hall of Justice and heading home—once again, just people. At the employees' entrance to the Emporium, Macy's, the White House, City of Paris, Magnin's, hundreds of shopgirls standing all in a tired row, waiting for their men to pick them up. One by one they disappear into the oncoming cars. Some with a kiss. Some with a bone-weary "Where the hell have you been?"

A day dies in a dizzy burst of activity: Commuters trotting along Third Street (past Skid Rowgues ranged against pawnshop walls in a deep frieze), cars spewing out of garages as though shot from cannon, bundle-packing women chasing cabs that flee for their lives (they're Yellow, of course), cops standing like white-capped statues in a sea of cars, busses following each other elephantlike—each window framing a not so quietly desperate face that seems to cry out silently for rescue. In the soft light, the Eight Hundred Thousand being drawn home in invisible strings—home to the hearth, home to the thawing dinner; and in a thousand anonymous corridors in a thousand all-alike apartment houses the smell of cooking stealing slowly down the hallways.

Dusk: Hint of excitement in the air—the evening lies ahead,

full of promise. Maybe tonight will be the night: the secretaries, trim in their little black dresses that will go anywhere, going somewhere—the bar on Montgomery Street, or just around any corner. Buzzing over the bourbon, murmuring over the martinis, sly glances over the scotch, and the unquenchable excitement of the Oldest Game being played by a new team. It is all spelled out invisibly in the dusk that crawls out of the ocean and over the city: On to dinner with the perfumed girl, on to dancing, on to the intertwined fingers, the nuzzled neck, and let the hangovers fall where they may.

A city's past: It seems to sleep, well hidden under the hard light of day. It is only when the street lamps come on and the cables rattle past (dimly lit, as though by gaslight) that the long, dead nights fairly clamor to live again. Izzy Gomez, Poppa Coppo, Amelio Pacini, Halsey Mainwaring—you can see them all again, greeting you with the casual warmth of their casual nights. Behind drawn shades, shadowy figures move in the upstairs dining rooms at Jack's, at Blanco's, at the St. Germaine, where the duck is being pressed and the champagne iced as the laughter rises. Already the mysterious buzzers are beginning to ring at Tessie Wall's and Jessie Hayman's, for darkness is falling over the city where history, among other things, has always been made at night.

And suddenly, in the twinkling of a sigh, it is all over—for the dusk is a fragile thing, a precious moment to be snatched from reality. Now the sun is far below the rim of the sea, and the last lingering traces of red and gold, of malachite and purple incandescence, have faded from the western sky. The homeward-bound traffic has disappeared into 1001 garages; 1001 front doors have slammed shut for the night. Coit Tower stands stark white against the sky, the East Bay lights glitter against velvet, a ship steals across an inky Bay—and it is too late, too late. The magic moments of dusk have stolen away, the moments when you make or break your evening, your enchantment, your life. Or maybe you were one of the lucky ones who made your move before the spell was broken . . .

The hours of a metropolis: Silence and forgetfulness at midnight, peace at dawn (broken by the clatter of garbage cans), the morning's bright earnestness, and the fading (of spirits, energy, arches) of the afternoon. It is only at dusk, with the city turning all pink and gold and twinkling over ice cubes, that we all start from scratch—young and headstrong again, ready for anything in this best of all possible cities.

51. THAT WAS SAN FRANCISCO

The city was younger and gayer (weren't we all) and the four lines of streetcars rattled and crashed with a satisfying racket along Market Street. You could ride from the Ferry Building to the Cliff House for a nickel, and you could ferry across the Bay for twenty-one cents, and if a sea gull successfully made a target out of you, you were enrolled with great ceremony into the Sea Gull Club, complete with lapel insignia that made you look like a target all over again. The Sunset District was a vast expanse of sand, and nobody thought much about it except the members of the town's glider clubs, who went out there on weekends and sailed their gliders all over the place.

You could walk down the street and nod hello to almost everybody, because you knew almost everybody. It was that kind of a town. You knew that the teamsters' favorite hangout was a saloon at Fourteenth and Mission, where the beer mugs were so big they had two handles on them, and they held two quarts, and most of the teamsters could hold four. The taxi-cabs didn't have meters in those days, and you could haggle with the driver and sometimes win. "Twenty-five cents," he'd say, after driving you from Third and Market to Scott and Green, and when you'd say in an outraged voice, "Twenty-five cents for WHAT?" he'd be likely to shrug wearily "Okay, okay, so fifteen cents." That was more like it. After ALL.

Yesterday's San Francisco. Always a place where everybody knew what was going on. If they weren't yakking about the bootlegger barons who hid from the Prohis in a certain fashion-able midtown hospital (where they were stylishly "sick" in suites that were fancier than a hotel's), they were gabbing about the brilliant young lawyer who smashed his career by intro-ducing a banker—whose daughter was about to marry an im-poverished nobleman—as "that prince of bankers and that banker of princes." Yes, plenty to talk about. Remember "Is your girl married, or does she live on Bush Street?" Was that not a hot one?

A lot of things to do in the old town. You could go to the Orpheum, if you didn't mind parking around the corner. Some-times it was a little difficult to find a space across the street. The traffic problem was getting critical, even then, but chances are it wouldn't get much worse. Saturation point, you know. Or you could rent a hack at the Fashion Stable, on Ellis be-tween Mason and Taylor, and take your girl for a spin through the Park in fine, old-fashioned style. And on the way back you might clatter along Van Ness Avenue, the street of beautiful mansions. With such big wonderful trees on the center parkway, like Dolores Street. You couldn't imagine Van Ness without its trees—then.

Everybody loved San Francisco, and everybody loved Mayor "Sunny Jim" Rolph, too. He was this kind of a guy. One hot

August day, he was riding in his limousine down Mission Street, when suddenly he spotted an open manhole. "Hey, wait a minute," he yelled to his driver. Then he got out of his car, climbed down the manhole, and smiled, "Mind if I join you?" to the two mystified workers below. "Hot outside," explained Jim. He pulled a silver flask out of his rear pocket, handed it to the men, and said "Go on, have a drink. Good stuff." After a few minutes of chatting and sipping, "Sunny Jim" said good-by and "thanks for letting me cool off with you," and climbed back up the ladder to his waiting limousine. And as he drove off, the two workers stuck their heads out of the manhole and watched, amazed, until he disappeared from view.

The sand-lotters used to play baseball on Army Street near the viaduct—on a stretch of land called "the Hornpile," because the horns from recently deceased animals in Butchertown were stacked there. Ah yes, Butchertown. All you had to do was take a pillowcase out there, and the workers would fill it to the top with livers, brains and hearts, all for free, happy to have you haul it away. You were a real witty kid in those days if you called the P.G. & E. "Pigs, Goats, and Elephants," and hollered at your stool-pigeoned playmates, "Tattletale tit, your tongue shall be split, and every dog in Chinatown shall have a piece of it."

How far back do you want to go, old-timer? Remember when the Chinese cemetery was at Larkin and McAllister, now the site of the Public Library? You're right. Neither do I, friend. Remember when they removed the cemetery from Lincoln Park to make room for the golf course? A little hazy now, but I recall it. Sure, I went to the medicine shows in the vacant lot at Kearny and Bush—in a pig's eye and in my mind's eye. And I loved the races at the old Emeryville track, and the turkeys they used to give away on Thanksgiving to everybody, but EVERYbody. At least, I think I loved them. It was such

a long time ago. And I was so very much younger than I was
when I was born.

Ponder, for a moment, the old Balconades ballroom on
Market, where they used to have a charged electric rail in front
of the bandstand—to keep the people from crowding too close.
And how about the band they had for dancing at the Cliff
House in the long nights of yesteryear? A zither, a piano, and
a violin, and they sounded terrible in a wonderful sort of way,
and vice versa. You ask about the municipal brothel in the
600 block on Jackson? I merely heard about that, sir. Three
floors and hundreds of women, and the mayor himself was
president of the board of directors who ran the place for the
city. The directors were the supervisors. Being a supervisor was
a most interesting job in those days.

Well, pardon me for rambling. But before I go, do you remember Henry Beyer and his horse, Pilot? Sure you do. Henry
used to collect for a brewery, and he'd go from saloon to saloon
on Pilot—a horse who loved his beer. In fact, Pilot wouldn't
move on until he'd been fed his schooner. So one day Pilot
was arrested for being drunk on Market Street, and was duly
fined fifteen dollars, which Henry soberly paid. Yep, that was
San Francisco. And that Pilot—THAT was a horse!

52. WHAT IS CHRISTMAS?

Christmas is a small boy staring transfixed at an electric train
making its endless circles in the windows of Western Pacific;
a lighted Christmas tree atop a Yellow Cab, disappearing like
a will-o'-the-wisp into the dark depths of the Stockton Tun-

nel; a little girl sobbing on Santa's lap in a department-store window because she tugged on his white whiskers and they came off; the legless man who sells pencils on the cold sidewalk outside the Palace Hotel, waving a warm "Merry Christmas" to a passing customer in a long limousine . . . And the carillon at SS. Peter and Paul, filling the gray morning air with the timeless chimes of tradition.

Christmas is a cold-eyed store detective watching the nervous fumblings of a woman shopper as she paws her way along the glove counter; Bach chorales filtering through the evergreens under the awnings at Gump's and inspiring only a yawn from the sidewalk flower merchant out front; the strands of colored lights glowing from house to identical house in the outlying districts as the neighbors join forces in the universality of the holidays . . . And the warmhearted ones who troop out to Laguna Honda Home to remember the forgotten ones with gifts and good cheer.

Christmas is a gold star in the window of a Mission District home, hanging alongside the Christmas tree in memory of one who died in the cause of a dubious peace on earth; an Opera House full of chattering children watching *The Nutcracker* —between long looks at an even more fascinating show: each other; the Christmas cocktail parties, with the host dutifully making up a big batch of eggnog, which he hates, for his guests, who hate it too but are just as polite about it as he is . . . And the pale, dedicated faces of the Salvation Army musicians, marching from corner to corner with the eternal reminder that it is more blessed to give.

Christmas is the red and green of the traffic signals, changing back and forth in their well-appointed rounds while the traffic itself stands still in the Great Christmas Freeze; a small merchant on Chestnut Street, crying alone in his shop at 10 P.M. because he hasn't made a sale all day; a dazzlingly dressed woman in Laykin's, the jewelers, fingering a $50,000 pearl neck-lace with cold and avaricious lust and whispering to the sales-man, "If my husband comes in and asks, tell him that he must buy these for me, he simply must"; and a group of Peninsula businessmen, dressed as clowns, filing into the Shrine Hospital for Crippled Children to entertain the tiny patients—and walking out again with tears smearing their trag-ically hilarious make-up.

Christmas is a young mother in the county jail on a check charge, wondering whether her children will really miss her on the night that Santa (in the form of her good friends) comes down the chimney with their presents; the well-heeled groups, making their plans to "get away for the holidays" to Squaw Valley or Vegas or Mexico or Hawaii, as though Christ-mas were something to run away from . . . And the hungry, pinch-faced men who stand in line for a free meal at St. Anthony's Kitchen, and ask hopefully, "Ya think there'll be a little turkey, maybe, on Christmas Day?"

Christmas is a sprig of holly in the cap of a Muni conductor on the Geary Street line; the sour expression on the face of a Montgomery Street elevator operator who was counting on a Christmas bonus and didn't get it; a sightless couple on Post Street, singing their sad songs in thin voices and wearing little buttons reading "It Is Christmas and We Are Blind"; passers-by staring entranced at the wonderful animated figures in the White House window, women with their arms full of bundles and their hands full of children, and men in the swank salons pricing negligees and the models who are showing them . . . And the Christmas wreath at the entrance to a Howard Street flophouse, with a sign on the bottom reading "Please do not steal this."

Christmas is the A.P.L.'s *President Cleveland* sailing out the Golden Gate, a floating city that will celebrate its own holidays in magnificent aloneness, somewhere in the Pacific; Andy Bell, the good old cop at Post and Powell, saying, "Merry Christmas" as though he means it—and the rookie cops, saying it too while they slip a parking tag under your windshield wiper; the holiday lights on the boats in Yacht Harbor, bobbing back and forth with the steady beat of a metronome . . . And the men of the Muni Railway, passing the hat to provide a good Christmas for the children of two of their buddies, killed in an accident.

Christmas is a group of businessmen from the Kiwanis Club, putting on a downtown street-corner show to help the Salvation Army kettle tender—while a merchant tells them nervously (but futilely) that "you'll have to move along, you're scaring people away"; the young men with hands in empty pockets, looking longingly at the treasures in the windows of Shreve's and then shuffling on, their shoulders sighing; the season's greeting soaped on the back bars of dreary saloons in the Tenderloin, while the bartenders eye you as coldly as ever . . . And, shattering the silence of the night, a thousand jukeboxes blaring the cynical sentiments of "Santa, Baby."

Christmas is the feverish last-minute search for the right present that was snatched up days ago, the ever-growing antic- ipation in the young eyes that look at toys but can't read price tags, the Christmas cards that flutter across your desk on their way to the wastebasket—so fast that you hardly have time to read the names on them . . . And over the whole frenetic scene, as lofty as ever, the hope that still lives in the quiet dreams of everyone—the eternal hope of Christmas: peace on earth, good will to men—the hope that must never get lost in the crazy shuffle.

53. CLASS REUNION

Sacramento, the city I'm proud to call my birthplace—the feeling isn't mutual—has changed a lot in the last few years. It has broken out of its old boundaries and is spewing tract houses in all directions. The old town is now a big city, with traffic jams, one-way streets, freeways, streamlined glass buildings—and thousands of newcomers with Southern, Boston, and Midwest accents. When I was a kid, practically everybody who lived in Sacramento was born in Sacramento.

But there's one thing that hasn't changed. Sacramento, I'm gasping to report, is still hot. When I drove across the muddy Sacramento River one recent day, it felt like somebody had left the oven door open and the gas on. Pores that hadn't been open in years suddenly came to life.

The above is not written as criticism. A lot of the landmarks may be gone—M Street is now Capitol Avenue. Y Street is Broadway and the Sacramento Hotel has been torn down —but when I felt that first blast of hot air, I knew I was home.

However, I didn't make the perilous trek along Highway 40, past the Nut Tree and the sun-blanched hills, just to research the weather. Sacramento High, the oldest high school west of something-or-other and east of Lowell, was celebrating its hundredth anniversary, and I wanted to see how the old girl was holding up. Also the old girls and boys I went to school with.

The school looks better than ever. I could say the same about the old boys and girls, and I think I will. But only to be polite.

A lot of what I always assumed to be bum humor has been

written about class reunions—but I see now that it was merely painfully accurate reporting. Our class ('32) gathered in a classroom to register and have a look at one another, and everybody acted according to script. You'd have thought they'd all read the same stories about class reunions.

The men clustered in a corner and looked at each other's hairlines and waistlines. Then they counted the wrinkles (nobody looked anybody square in the eye). After that they compared notes on the number of wives and/or children they've had, lied a little about their jobs, and wound up with the biggest lie of all:

"Y'know, you haven't changed a bit?"

The girls went through the same routine, skipping the hairline check. They worked on one another from the bottom up, mentally pricing the shoes and the dresses, checking the jewelry, and throwing an imaginary tape measure around the other's waistline. Then they all cat-grinned at one another:

"Darling, you don't look a DAY older!"

Darling, we all look a lot older. But one cliché of the class reunion didn't turn out to be true. You know how the dumbest kid in the class is always supposed to wind up a millionaire? Not true. The dumbest kid is still dumb, and reduced to writing a column for a pitiful living. And you've read how the guy voted Most Likely to Succeed turns into a bum on Skid Row? This guy (Tommy MacBride) is now a state official, a lawyer, and bright as ever.

But boy, has HE lost a lot of hair. Looks a lot older, too. And skinny as a rail. But he hasn't changed a bit.

After the registration, we wandered through the halls of lower learning, smelling the familiar smells of chalk dust, paste, and disinfectant. I stopped in front of the principal's office and smoked a cigarette, something I've wanted to do for twenty-five years. But old fears die hard. I kept it cupped in my hand, so the principal wouldn't see it.

We looked out across the street at the little beanery where we ate so many nourishing lunches of jelly doughnuts, soda pop, and frozen Milky Ways. We stopped by the gymnasium and kidded our old instructor, Pop Brorsen, who used to make us duck-walk till we quacked. "Hey, Pop, weren't we the best class you ever had?" "No," he said, but we didn't believe him.

Out in the old football field, a program was going on, with that bright Tommy MacBride in charge, of course. The high-school band played, sounding as weak as it ever did. A group of children led a yell. The children turned out to be high-school seniors.

Herman Phleger, Class of '06, distinguished lawyer, legal adviser of John Foster Dulles, and an Under Secretary of State, arose to make a speech. He traced the history of the school, starting in 1856, but got no further than 1890 when he began to lose his audience. Poor Mr. Phleger, all the way from Washington and all dressed up in coat and tie. His speech was good, but not as hot as the Sacramento sun, and the bald heads were beginning to blister.

A girl (I suppose you'd call her a woman) from our class said, "See you next year for our twenty-fifth reunion," and I got back in the car and drove slowly through the streets of the baking city. The great shade trees met overhead and the kids wandered around in shorts. The old folks were rocking on their porches, and a little boy was sitting on a curb, eating watermelon and spitting seeds into the street. On K Street, a magnolia tree was in full bloom, and next to it, an orange tree heavy with fruit.

Sacramento hasn't changed much, at that. It's just a little older, like the Class of '32.

54. THE GLORIOUS FOURTH

America's most American holiday—except in San Francisco, where it's highly illegal to shoot a firecracker—started with a clashing of fenders and a banging of horns early one Wednesday evening. Despite the solemn warnings of press and radio against setting foot outside the doubtful safety of one's own home—after all, you can stay in bed and be misled too—the citizens wasted no time in heading for the highroad, and by dusk, you could see the jukebox array of tail fins swishing off in all directions. What it proved, if it proved anything, is that the fine American spirit of independence is not yet dead. Too bad so many motorists had to die proving it.

By Thursday morning, the traffic along Bayshore-101 had slowed to a snarl. The cars inched along, the drivers staring fiercely from behind their sunglasses. Kids poked their heads out of the windows, and you could see their lips moving in the timeless chant, dating back to the first oxcart: "How much farther, Daddy?" Every now and then, predictably, a car would drop out of line, and a mother and her moppet would disappear into the underbrush, while Papa slumped behind the wheel and glared at his wrist watch. Everybody was in a hurry to Get There, no matter Where.

It was hot on July Fourth—this is also traditional—and the endless mass of steel and chrome sweet chrome grew molten under the sun. You could tell it was the Fourth because you'd pass a firecracker stand, with its products looking ready to burst in the heat. Here and there a faded American flag drooped limply from its thumbtacks—and now and then an idiot would

throw a lighted firecracker from a car. Then pretty soon you'd
hear the wail of a siren and see a fire engine streak by. A great
day of firemen and fools, who are not soon parted. At Redwood
City, the girls in shorts were jaywalking across the highway toward a carnival that shimmered like a mirage, and the cops, in
their heavy black uniforms, were sweating. So were the kids in
the cars, already red-faced and tired and close to tears. But
this was Independence Day, and you go Fourth, no matter
what.

New paragraph, old thought. Ah, to be in chilly England,
now that July is here. South of Moffett Field, some of the
traffic turned off Highway One Oh Gad and headed through
the long hot valley toward the far-off sea. The fruit trees sim-
mered under their coats of gray dust. Los Gatos lay asleep
with its mouth open and its stores closed, and the only life
was on the main road as the cars pressed on, some inexorably,
others execrably. In the Santa Cruz Mountains, the older
models began boiling and stood in knots with their hoods up,
looking like prehistoric monsters having a conference. The kids
chased each other up and down the road, bang-bang, while Papa
trudged off in search of water. Mamma sat on a rock, with her
skirt above her knees, fanning herself with a newspaper that
had warned her to stay home.

Eventually the Pacific shone in the near distance, and another contingent of cars dropped out of the parade and headed
down the rocky road to Aptos, the beach that is divided against
itself just south of Santa Cruz. At one end, a public trailer
park, and already the trailers were in place, the clotheslines
strung, and the card tables set up outside for dinner. At the other
end of the beach, the clustered, sometimes elegant little houses
of the San Francisco fashionable who come to Aptos to get
away from each other together.

The people who don't have either trailers or houses parked

alongside the road tumbled out in amazing numbers, like the armies that emerged from Model T's in the Keystone Kop comedies. They hauled forth the wicker lunch baskets and stood around their cars, eating in identical groups: The kids stripped down to their trunks, the old man in his undershirt, the little woman in her damp flowered print, and Grandma looking oddly out of place in her black dress. They ate the food off their fenders, staring around as they chewed.

The stylish end of Aptos has sometimes been compared to the Cap d'Antibes. It is more accurately a Sportscap d'Antibes. The Jags, with buckles on the back, are parked outside the villas, and the barbecue fires are always ready to go. The men sit around, trimming the frayed edges off their rope-soled shoes. The women go calling up and down the beach, with highball glasses in their hands. The kids complain that it's all lousy because "you can only get one channel" on the TV.

Just offshore, the sea birds flock past by the thousands, driving the fish in toward shore, and the huge pelicans hover and then dive straight down, like the Stukas in an ancient war. It is beautiful at Aptos, if you live at the right end of the beach.

By Sunday afternoon, the task force on wheels was already beginning its exodus in reverse, leaving in its wake the usual spoils of peaceful war: The empty beer cans, the crumpled cellophane, the night-blooming Kleenex. Occasionally, the grim silence would be broken by a leftover firecracker to remind you that it had all been undergone for the most American of all possible reasons: Independence Day. Our forefathers had not fought, bled, and died in vain. The least we could do, in their honor, is suffer a little too.

55. AH, SAN FRANCISCO

Twin Peaks blooming in green freshness at the end of drab Market Street, the sun reflecting fiercely on the windshields of a thousand cars filing across the Bay Bridge, the East Bay hills softly golden at the end of a perfect spring day, Alcatraz looking suddenly like an enchanted isle as it sits and stares dreamily at its own perfect reflection in the still waters . . . Ah, San Francisco.

Harold Zellerbach riding democratically in the front seat with his chauffeur as his black limousine drones through the Broadway Tunnel, the Oriental sharpies with patent-leather shoes and hair to match enjoying the warm sun on the fringe of Portsmouth Square, the plain-clothes coppers cruising around in the overly plain sedans that shout, "Police!" louder than any sign, the good jazz of Cal Tjader filtering out of the Blackhawk and getting lost under the stars that shine down on Turk Street, too . . . Oh, San Francisco.

The red-and-blue stacks of an American President Liner shimmering in the sun as the great liner floats like a mirage past the Marina, the silhouette of the clipper ship *Balclutha* adding a touch of square-rigged glamour to the waterfront, an ancient trolley rattling past Lotta's Fountain exactly as it has done for forty long years, the red beacons atop the Clay-Jones and Bellaire apartments blinking back and forth from Nob Hill to Russian, like pulse beats in the night sky . . . Ah, Baghdad-by-the-Bay.

The big signs that invite you to the little joints along Broadway, the newsboy who was once a stockbroker hollering his headlines off in the ticker-taped heart of Montgomery Street, the motorists who drive the wrong way on one-way streets and answer your warning honk with a pickle-faced look, the dozens of mailboxes clustered at the entrances to the smelly tenements of Chinatown, jammed together like the people who live upstairs . . . Oh, cool gray city of love, hate, filth, beauty and incense and garlic in the air.

The people who take a Sunday drive through Golden Gate Park and gnash their ulcers in irritation because they can't drive through its beauties fast enough, the bobby-soxers and the grandmothers eying each other curiously as they wait at the Curran stage entrance for an autograph from Jack Benny, the withered little man who peddles his sacks of lavender on Grant Avenue near the entrance to flower-bowered Podesta Baldocchi, unemployed B-girls wandering along Mason Street in search of a guy who'll buy them a real drink for a change . . . Ah, Queen City of the West, with white, pennant-topped towers that reach to the sky and gutters that need cleaning and mansions with marble halls and streets that need sweeping.

A Powell Street cable waddling slowly across the Broadway Tunnel's concrete bridge as though it's not quite safe for cables to cross bridges, longshoremen playing catch like kids in the shadows of the great piers that have known so much strife, the thin-faced artists of Little Bohemia showing their wares on the sidewalks and trying not to look disappointed when passers-by keep passing by, the polo players and the soccer players in the Park and the yachtsmen in their self-conscious blues in Yacht Harbor and the near-nudes baking to a turn and turning to bake on the Marina Green . . . Oh, Pearl of the Pacific, treasure of the trade winds, mecca of the mariner, sanctuary of the screaming sea gull, port of call for half the world and beloved landmark for the other half.

The Post Street clerks who pause to stare appraisingly at the

$10,000 trifles in the windows of Shreve's and then move on with a silent shrug to indicate that they weren't quite satisfied with the quality, girls shrieking on the rides at the beach and sounding exactly like every girl who has ever shrieked on any ride anywhere, the old men who sit alone in side-street hotel lobbies and then walk alone to eat in cafeterias where they can be alone together and share their misery in unspoken understanding . . . Ah, city of sophistication and culture and hammer murders and shakedowns, and people who are overcrowded together and never speak to each other.

The Negro children of Sutter Street staring out of their cracked windows at the tennis players in their white-white shorts chasing a white-white-white ball across the courts of the California Tennis Club, a jet plane leaving a vapor trail smudged across the blue like a sky writer who started a message and then forgot it, springtime's young lovers parked at Land's End to enjoy the view of each other, the grown-up kids who hang around Earle Swenson's ice cream parlor at Union and Hyde and say, "Gee, thanks" (just like their children) when Earle rewards them with a free sample, the unemployed guys in their dirty non-working clothes clustered on Howard Street to discuss their last meal and wonder where the next one is coming from . . . Oh, big-little town of wide views from dark alleys.

An extravagant sunset fading so fast you can't fully enjoy all the work that must have gone into it, a long white sail fluttering home at dusk past the amber lights of the bridge that only a dreamer could have built, the ceaseless nighttime hum of life and tires and lights and horns in this worldly town that never quite finds time to go to sleep, and then—the moon rising fast out of the far-off east to beam whitely down on the hills and valleys and restless waters of the tiny city that has no boundaries . . . San Francisco. Ah, San Francisco.

56. SPRING COMES TO MARIN

Have you been over there lately? I mean, to the softly rolling
Marin country between Mill Valley and Stinson Beach, where
the sun beats down on the warm valleys, and the fog miraculously finds other places to go, and the trails lead you gently
across a countryside that seems a million miles from cities
and four-lane highways.

If you haven't taken this quick trip to faraway places this
year, it's time you had a look. For spring is there, bubbling in
the streams, billowing across the meadows in clouds of blue
and yellow, and singing in the trees, and we wouldn't want you
to miss it—this year, of all dark and horrendous years.

Don't get me wrong. I'm no Nature Boy. To me a bluejay
is still a corn plaster, and old crow is something 100 proof
that comes in bottles, and I wouldn't climb the highest mountain even to write a best-seller—but this annual miracle in Marin
is as easy to get as it's easy to take.

You merely drive toward Mill Valley, take the Stinson road,
turn off toward Muir Woods, find a place to stash your car,
and head for the hills. San Francisco is still only a few minutes
away—but lost forever behind the last bend in the road. To
the right, Tamalpa, the Indian maiden, sleeps her endless sleep
atop her mountain. In the far-off distance, the Pacific sparkles.
And all around, you can hear the busy silence of the open
spaces—the trees murmuring far overhead, a lizard scuttling into
a thicket, a chipmunk rattling through the underbrush.

You take a long look around, and then you know that spring
is everywhere—but especially here.

The hills are green in Marin at this time of year, green with clover, green with iris spikes, green with a damp freshness in the earth. And the hills are blue, blue with mountain lilac and wild iris and tiny forget-me-nots. And the hills are yellow with Scotch broom and white with daisies and trillium and orange and pink and purple with primrose.

You walk along the trails and rub elbows with the shiny manzanita, and wend your way through the deep calm cool of the redwoods. And all around the poison oak, still mainly green but turning to its familiar red in places, reaches out as though trying to touch you—yet all of a sudden, this seems a small risk to take.

What is a tiny rash when you are one with Pizarro, Magellan and Balboa, breaking new trails into the wilderness? For that is the feeling you get, the evergreen feeling of discovery.

Of all the last frontiers around San Francisco, only this stretch of Marin seems to have escaped the poisonous blessings of progress. On a long Saturday afternoon, the trails seem to be yours alone. Around the next bend, you know you will find no service station or cracker-box community. No Oh Henry wrappers or Coke bottles clutter the countryside. Here, and here alone, time seems to have stood still.

In the fragrant hush, you can almost hear the whistle and chug of the long-gone "Crookedest Railroad in the World" that once wound its way around Tamalpais, you can almost hear the rattle of the gravity cars that rattled down the hills into Muir Woods, you can almost hear the shouts of the hikers who took the ferries to Sausalito, rode the Northwestern Pacific to Mill Valley, and spread out along the Dipsea Trail.

And in Muir Woods, all is as it was—and should always be. The middle-aged tourists peering at the cross-section of redwood tree. The family group having its picture taken alongside the sign marking "The Largest Tree in Muir Woods," and the

Gray Line guide pointing to the river and grinning confidentially to his group, "Don't tell the Chamber of Commerce I told you, but this happens to be the Los Angeles River"—just as he's been saying it for thirty years.

And in Cathedral Grove, where the old men of the redwoods stand and sigh with their heads together, you stop and read the plaque dedicated in 1945 to Franklin Delano Roosevelt and the hope for peace—a hope as timeless and sturdy as the redwoods themselves.

The feeling of being lost in yesterday's magic persists even on a Saturday night at the Tourist House—for although a crowd is here it is a quiet crowd. People in Tyrolean hats, singing old German folk songs. Yawning young men in leather jackets and jeans, tired from a day of bicycling. A pretty girl named Elsa playing softly on a guitar, a man named Hans who yodels. Tony, the eighty-three-year-old gardener, who singlehandedly built the road down to the Tourist House. And the manager, Fritz Huttemann, who sings, plays the piano, blows a harmonica, and finds time to fill the huge steins, too.

And when darkness finally falls, out of the hills come the raccoons, to set comically on their fat haunches and beg for scraps of bread and meat. Still wild, these raccoons, although one of them, a one-eyed oldster named Mickey, has been coming down for his handout every night for fifteen years. And he takes the food out of your hand slowly and gently—and yet warily—ready to disappear into the forest gloom at the first unfriendly move.

Spring and peace—these beautiful words live in the warm hills of Marin, on the trails that lead from Mill Valley toward Stinson, and from today into the long yesterdays that now seem all sunny and golden. And somehow, you feel that there will always be spring and peace here—even though one slope of Tamalpais is now covered with radar equipment, and the jets from Hamilton Field swish overhead like supersonic vultures. The redwoods are so much older and wiser.

57. DEATH OF AN ATOMIC PIG

It is quite possible that San Franciscans, per capita, are more aware of bullfighting than the residents of any other city in the country. This is not because the local S.P.C.A. is any less vigilant than its counterparts elsewhere, but because San Francisco is the home of Barnaby Conrad, the most articulate and prolific chronicler of the *corrida* since Hemingway stopped acting like a human and became a legend. To the outraged annoyance of the mink-clad defenders of animals, Mr. Conrad writes exceedingly popular tracts on bullfighting, gives lectures on the subject, makes radio and TV appearances extolling the ancient ritual, and (when he isn't painting portraits of Manolete or carving fighting bulls out of Ivory soap) runs a thriving saloon called El Matador—which, local legend notwithstanding, does NOT serve Bloody Marys made with real blood.

Having seen one or two good bullfights and many bad ones, I have not fallen under the spell of *los toros*, and I find the self-conscious prattle of most *aficionados* a dreadful bore. Mr. Conrad, however, is different. He is also the first to admit that there is nothing worse than a bad bullfight. Hence, disarmed by his charm and honesty, I took his word for it one Sunday when he said a good bullfight was about to be enacted in Tijuana—and the report thereof follows:

Six bulls and four bees died slowly in the Mexican border town on Tijuana one sunny September Sunday. The bulls died in the Plaza de Toros. The bees died, in what must have been a state of high confusion, some eight thousand feet aloft—in a United Mainliner. But more about THEM later.

Tijuana was far from sleepy that day. True, a few Mexicans were dozing here and there under their sombreros—on orders from the Tijuana Chamber of Commerce, to keep things authentic—but elsewhere, things were definitely at fever pitch. About 101 degrees.

For on Sunday, Carlos Arruza, the greatest living matador, was launching a brand-new career in the bull ring—as a *rejoneador*. That is, he will now fight bulls on horseback, weakening them with *rejones* (long lances) and then dismounting to make the kill. You gather, of course, that it is Arruza who is on horseback. Not the bull. The bull walks to death, as always.

To observe this memorable event, the drybacks poured into Tijuana Sunday in near-record numbers. They came from San Diego, in their pedal pushers and sport shirts. From Hollywood, with their movie cameras and their low necklines. From Mexico City, with their knowing looks and flashy women.

And they even came from San Francisco, in their Ivy League suits and button-down shoes, led by the noblest *aficionado* of them all, Señor Barnaby Conrad, official biographer of Carlos Arruza and the man who has sold bullfighting to almost everyone except the S.P.C.A. And me.

On Tijuana's main drag—and I use the word advisedly—the carnival spirit was already approaching the bacchanalian. The sidewalks were jammed with tourists, inviting disaster by foundering themselves on stuffed tacos sold by sidewalk vendors. Little girls walked up and down selling "chewn gom." Hawkers implored you to have your picture taken in tiny carts drawn by burros painted with black stripes to make them look like zebras.

Everywhere the atmosphere of Old Mexico was heavy, even rancid, in the air. At the Waikiki Club. At the Alt Heidelberg, whose sign reads "Mex-German Dishes." And especially at Caesar's, where the bar was loaded with gringos getting loaded.

The talk was of nothing but Arruza and the fight. "Carlos has been sick all night," breathlessly exclaimed a ravishing blonde who turned out to be ex-San Franciscan Cynthia Baxter. "He only had two hours sleep."

We trooped up to the matador's quarters in Room 18 at the Foreign Club Hotel. The great man looked a little peaked, and the dramatic vertical wrinkles in his sunken cheeks stood out sharply. He chatted pleasantly, but a large bottle of Kaopectate on a nearby table spoke mutely of his woes.

You see? It doesn't happen only to tourists.

The fights began at 3 P.M. in Tijuana's then rickety, splintering old arena. Arruza, despite his inner grief, looked dashing on his Portuguese-trained stallion, and although the bull (a smallish eight-hundred-pounder) almost caught him twice on the far turn, he dispatched it with consummate grace, to the *"Olés!"* of the mob of eight thousand. As he strode around the ring, women threw their shoes at him. Also scarfs and handbags (all of which he threw back). And one girl tossed him her brassiere—an empty gesture if I ever saw one.

After the fights, we wandered along the main street, mingling with the exciting likes of screen star Ruth Roman, Robert Taylor and Ursula Theiss, and Orson Welles, who now weighs about three hundred and was smoking a cigar only slightly larger than the Goodyear Blimp.

In a little novelty shop, we found the perfect souvenir of our mad day in Alt Mexico. *Puercos Atómicos*—atomic pigs! These are pecan shells, artfully carved and decorated to look like tiny pigs. Their wooden ears, eyes, and tail move constantly and mysteriously—"because," said the salesgirl, "they have Mexican jumping beans inside." We bought out the shop, at fifty cents per atomic pig.

But alas. Once on the plane across the border, the atomic pigs became lifeless, immobile. The tiny ears no longer wiggled so intriguingly. The tiny tail was once more just a stick. The tiny eyes no longer jiggled around like Eddie Cantor's.

As the plane roared aloft, Señor Conrad pondered this problem. Then the man who has faced many a bull in the ring came to grips with the problem of the pig. "We'll have to break one open," he said gravely, "and see what's inside."

He broke off the wooden snout—and out of the pig crawled a bee. Then three other bees fell out and dropped to the floor of the Mainliner, quite dead. While Señor Conrad watched in awed disbelief, the first bee slowly spread its wings and buzzed through the ship, while passengers screamed, children cried, and the stewardess ran up and down the aisle, in cold pursuit.

The bee, like the bulls of a few hours earlier, struggled gallantly to keep going, and then suddenly fell lifeless to the floor. We saluted the brave bee, and then sat silent, contemplating the strange land of Mexico—where bulls die in the afternoon, and bees wiggle the ears of atomic pigs.

58. THE WAY IT WAS

"The Timeless City," "The never-changing city"—that's what we call it in sporadic fits and starts of nostalgia. But the city is always moving away from you, even as it surrounds you, and in your own short half-a-lifetime you have seen their faces, heard their voices, and stood by helplessly as they grew dimmer and dimmer, then vanished:

The mounted cops on the downtown streets, their horses standing with stately dignity while their rider clambered down to scribble a ticket for an illegally parked Chandler (or Chalmers, or Auburn, or Moon). Leathery-thin Maynard Dixon, great artist of the Old West, lounging gracefully against the Montgomery Block, his face shadowed under a cowboy hat, his sunken cheeks moving as he munches on a carrot. Izzy Gomez, the peerless saloonkeeper of Pacific Street, making a bet that he could smoke a cigar in a shower; he won, but his wide-brimmed black fedora, which was never seen to leave his head, didn't dry out for days. Novelist Gertrude Atherton posing for a snapshot in front of the vastly beautiful Silas Palmer mansion on Van Ness, turning to admire the house, and murmuring, "Nobody would ever be cruel enough to tear that down. It would be like tearing down San Francisco." But it is gone. And so is Gertrude. The snapshot remains, faded and curling up.

So much a part of our lives, but already beyond recall—the midnight whistle of a steam locomotive (blast the horn of a Diesel), the incomparable corned-beef hash on the Oakland ferry (on the way back after a night with Benny Goodman at McFadden's Ballroom), the strange gadget in the Ferry Building that dispensed collar buttons, the Sunday-night crowd at Roberts'-at-the-Beach (the old judges, the old politicos, the old roués) racing on wooden hobbyhorses for a bottle of champagne; days of innocence, days of honest graft, when everybody knew who was paying off whom and nobody cared because it was All in the Family—and the Family ran the town. It would always be that way, but the hobbyhorses gallop no longer, and neither do the benign old crooks who used to tumble off them, their fall well cushioned by the huge roll of bills they always carried.

Faint babble of voices in faraway places—but once they were here and now: Bill Saroyan booming his loud dreams in the Black Cat, and the tourists discovering a smoky Columbus Avenue basement called Mona's, where, my dear, the women dress like men, you wouldn't believe it, and you can't tell them APART, it's too AWful and wonderful. Everybody who was anybody gathered at 5:30 P.M. in the Mark's lower bar, or went tea-dancing to Tom Coakley at the Palace.

For ten whole years the population stood exactly at 640,000 and we thought the clock was standing still too. Meredith Willson led the NBC orchestra in a studio atop 111 Sutter (only it was the Hunter-Dulin Building then), there were iron arches over the Fillmore intersections, and "Cardinal Puff" was the big game at Joe's Wine Cellar on the Green Street hill. The kids frolicked in the sand dunes for forty blocks to the ocean, and who was this guy Doelger who was beginning to build little look-alike houses across this unlikely wasteland? Never mind—let's go ride the roller coaster at Playland, or see the big stage show (with Walt Roesner) at the Fox, or go to Blackjack Jerome's dog track in El Cerrito. They'd be there when those houses in the sand were long gone.

The echoing back, the blues and the booze in the night—and Jerry Lester telling his off-color jokes in the Greenwich Village on O'Farrell. Gunfire on the Embarcadero, gunfire on Alcatraz, with the Marines scaling the rocks, and Sausalito standing serene and unbridged, and with no street signs and no addresses and no traffic except the Northwestern's little trains rolling the hikers to Mill Valley. You could play roulette in the Marina and shake dice on O'Farrell and you could hear the rattle and whirr of slot machines all around Sutter and Powell at 3 A.M. Joe "Silver Fox" Bernstein and Eddie Sahati would play poker for three days and nights in the "Fox's" all-white apartment above Tiny's on Powell, with sometimes only $100,000 changing hands. And "New Joe's" was so new that "Original Joe's" hadn't even been invented.

Strange little world of innocence, with two-way traffic (moving) on every street and meterless parking spaces, restaurants offering "All You Can Eat" for a dollar, and, at the Orpheum, the Hallroom Boys singing "In Room One Hundred and Two, the Walls Talk Back to You."

The cables rolled up Sacramento Street because, thank heaven, no bus would ever be able to scale THAT hill, and, at the City Hall, Mayer Rossi sometimes signed documents without looking at them (until Controller Harold Boyd slipped Rossi's resignation into the pile, and Angelo signed it). Newspapers used the phrase "twenty-five-cent-cocktail route" to signify complete and utter swank, and Fisherman's Wharf was so sleepy you could drive up in your Marmon and get a crab cocktail via curb service.

All in half-a-lifetime, days of our years that stole in and out like the fog and stole away our youth. The changeless city changing, the familiar faces becoming faceless, and the memories, carefully stored for future reference, already beginning to blur.

59. THESE FOOLISH THINGS

San Franciscans like to laugh.

At themselves: "We are the city that knows how—but when?"

At Los Angeles: "How can a city go on growing out and out without ever growing up?"

At Oakland: The day after the 1906 earthquake, someone pointed out that the city across the Bay still looked intact. "Certainly," sniffed a cynic. "There are some things even the earth can't swallow."

The laughter goes on, by day and night, on the streets, in the skyscrapers, even in the courtrooms. I remember the day Lawyer Robert Partridge was questioning a juror in Judge Dan Shoemaker's court, to loud cries of protest from the opposing counsel, J. Francis Shirley.

"I object!" shouted Shirley. "The question is ambiguous, compound, and confusing."

"Overruled," snapped Judge Shoemaker. "Answer the question."

"I can't," complained the juror. "It's too confusing."

There was the day Lawyer Andrew Eyman took a client to the Hall of Justice for fingerprinting by an officer who directed, "First wash your hands."

"Both of them?" inquired the prisoner.

There was a glaring pause, and then the officer spoke.

"Nnnno," he drawled elaborately, "just wash one. I want to see how you do it."

I often hung around the courtroom of the late Judge Eustace Cullinan, Jr., for there, under his urbane and civilized auspices, defendants sometimes felt at ease to speak up.

One Rocky Chavez, on trial for burglary, was asked by the judge, "And how many children do you have?"

"Nine."

"Nine, eh?" mused the judge. "How divided?"

"Oh, you know, Judge," shrugged Rocky. "Boys and girls."

During the trial of Joe Modesto on a bookmaking charge, an officer who was in the raiding party testified, "We kept answering the phone in his place, and took over $800 in bets."

"That true, Joe?" asked Judge Cullinan.

"Mebbe so," admitted the defendant defensively, "but believe me, Judge, they took a lotta bets I woulda turned down."

Laughter, in the streets, on the cable cars—oh, especially on the cable cars.

Interested tourist to Powell Street gripman: "I see you use batteries to light the cars, but what keeps them warm?" Gripman, with a grunt: "Togetherness."

Shout of a Powell Street conductor, squeezing his way through the crowd: "Fares, fares! How come I gotta do fifty cents' worth of yellin' to get fifteen cents outta you people?"

One windy day, a tourist lady was standing on the back platform of a Powell cable when her hat blew off and rolled down the street. With a groan, the conductor signaled for a halt, turned to the hatless visitor and said in a weak, tired voice:

"Chase it yourself, lady. I'm sick of being quaint and colorful!"

And let us not forget the motorman on Market Street who grunted, "Seventh Street" at every intersection, to the fascination of Passenger Ken Ishizaki, who eventually asked why.

"So why should I memorize the streets?" yawned the motorman. "Who listens?"

Waiting for a bus at the intersection of Columbus, Green,

and Stockton, Eugene Jackson looked up and down the street in vain and then said to the Muni Railway starter, "Late again, eh?"

The starter looked hurt. "It isn't late now," he insisted, looking at his watch. "Of course," he added, putting the watch away, "it will be when it gets here."

Laughter in the restaurants:

Dr. Tom Ypsilantis, distinguished co-discoverer of the anti-proton at University of California's Radiation Laboratory, tried to cash a check at Larry Blake's restaurant in Berkeley, made out like this:

> *Pay to the order of thirty dollars,*
> *the sum of thirty dollars.*

"Sorry, Doctor," smiled Blake's Perry McIlvaine, returning the check. "That may equate in physics, but not in applied economics."

At Johnny Kan's restaurant in Chinatown, Mayor H. Roe Bartle of Kansas ordered chop suey, to the annoyance of Kan. "Chop suey," he pointed out, "is an imitation of Chinese food, and we wouldn't insult our customers by serving it."

"Wellll, okay then," grumbled Mayor Bartle, "I'll have something else—but it'd better be as good as chop suey!"

While Edmund Gerald "Pat" Brown was in the midst of his successful campaign for governor, he made a reservation for eight people at the Ondine in Sausalito, and showed up so late his table was given to another party that had been waiting a long time.

"You may have lost a table," greeted owner George Gutekunst when Pat finally showed up, "but you gained eight votes!"

Laughter in the saloons:

At the Brokers Club on Sutter Street, a customer asked bartender Gene Seadler for a "Lloyd's Special."

"Sorry," apologized Gene. "Never heard of it. How does it go?"

"Like this," instructed the customer. "Three parts vodka, one part sweet vermouth, tablespoon of olive juice, mix like a martini."

As the drinker was sipping away contentedly a few minutes later, Gene shook his head. "I thought I knew all the drinks," he sighed, "but a 'Lloyd's Special' is a new one on me. By the way, who's Lloyd?"

"I am," said the customer.

Scene: The Steeplechase bar. Cast of characters: bartender Ralph Chase, customer Dale Wights, and Unknown Customer, deep in his third drink.

The phone rings, and as Chase starts to answer, the Unknown Customer looks up suddenly and shouts, "Hey—I'm not here!" Chase nods, winks, and says into the phone:

"Hello. Hm? Nope, haven't seen him all day. No, no—he wasn't here yesterday, either. Yep—positive. What's that? Okay. G'by."

Chase to Unknown Customer as he hangs up the phone: "That was your wife. She says for you to come home as soon as you finish that drink."

Curtain.

Laughter—here, there and everywhere:

At Town Craft of California, manufacturers of women's clothes, the foreman phoned the owners, Mrs. Leila Alder and Al Simmonds, to complain: "You know that rush order we're trying to get out? Well, we'll never make it. Too many of the crew are taking time off for Good Friday."

"I see," said Simmonds. "How many?"

"The same bunch," hollered the foreman, "that took time off for Rosh Hashana!"

On Third Street, in the tacky heart of Skid Row, Howard Young was approached by an imaginative panhandler who announced, "Mister, I'm building a bridge from here to Madagascar, and I can't do it on coffee." Impressed by this new approach—a bridge approach—Howard tossed him a quarter.

"Thanks," said the Skidrowgue, walking away. "This'll handle one piling."

(This, perhaps, was the same gentleman who was seen to wave and holler enthusiastically on Third Street one day when Harry S. Truman sped past in a limousine, red lights flashing, sirens wailing. As the entourage disappeared, the Skid Roader beamed to a buddy, "I like old Harry. He's one of us!")

Voice on the telephone:

"These people, the Clarence Randles, they live at 2848 Twenty-third Street, well, they bought a new refrigerator. I mean a real nice one, too, except that it had the FUNniest squeak. Well, Mister Randle was absolutely perplexed, it being so new and all, so finally he turned it off and it kept squeaking away anyway. I mean it was really fanTAStic. So, being sort of mechanical, he took the motor apart—and guess what? Well, you'll NEVer. Out jumped a tarANtula! But HUGE! This spider just jumped out and began hopping all over the floor. I mean it was AWFUL! Mister Randle was beside himself and Missus Randle ran to the phone and called the cops. Well, YOU know cops. She said, 'What'll we do?' and that old cop said, 'Step on it, lady, step on it.' So who could step on it with it hopping all OVER like that? Mister Randle finally got it trapped under a broom but he didn't like the idea of stepping on it, being poisonous and all, so Missus Randle got a bottle of

Clorox and poured it on the tarantula, and y'know what? Killed it deader'n a doornail. Now what I'm calling about is you should tell the people to by all means keep a bottle of Clorox handy."

In case a tarantula jumps out of YOUR refrigerator.

Chingwah Lee, the noted art dealer of No. 9 Old Chinatown Lane, has two eighteenth-century Peking Imperial Palace jade bowls—price-tagged at $3000 the pair—and is hunting frantically for ten more. That's because during the American Petroleum Institute convention a Texas millionaire looked at them and drawled, "Not bad. If you can get ten more, I'll take the lot."

"Uh—why ten more?" wondered Chingwah.

"Why d'ya think?" snapped the Texan. "What good are finger bowls unless you have a dozen?"

Charles C. Chinn, who lived in the East before moving to San Francisco, is much happier with the way spring arrives in California. For example:

Don't have to: Take Mommy's mink to storage, take down storm windows, put up screens, disinter any plants, burn leftover leaves, unwrap water pipes, plant new lawn, take off snow tires, summerize car.

Have to: Clean out fireplace till it's needed again (in August!), see the blossoms around Japanese Tea Garden, make plans for that annual picnic you never go on in Marin, cut excess roses off vine so more can grow, phone Peninsula pals to see whether they've turned the heat on in their swimming pools, get liniment for sore back caused by patting same because you live in California.

Jean Finch, the Red Cross executive, was in a pixy mood that particular morning.

Leafing through the phone book, she ran across two telephone numbers for the Broadway Tunnel—one for the east end, one for the west. This fascinated her. She had no idea the tunnel had one phone, even.

So she called the west end. The phone rang and rang, and finally a voice answered breathlessly, "Hello, west end." Still feeling pixilated, she hung up immediately and dialed the east end. Again the phone rang and rang, and at last a voice answered with a painful gasp, "H-h-hello, east end."

Same voice.

The slightly daft mood was still upon her. She hung up and dialed the west end again. But this time the phone just rang and rang. Nobody answered, and with a back-to-earth sigh, Jean returned to her duties.

After all, a man can run back and forth just so many times. And a pixy mood doesn't last forever.

One of my favorite organizations, Clif Mayne's Let's Have Better Mottoes Association, stages an annual income-tax protest meeting, and although I never get there (not being a joiner, I protest alone), it is always a rousing success. At its last meeting, the members gathered under a large banner reading "If You Can't Understand It, Oppose It." George Earnshaw showed up with a rubber stamp reading "Allowance taken for annuities listed under fiduciary trust funds under special state tax except where falling under special deficit as previously noted." With a flourish, he stamped his own return with the foregoing and claimed an immediate $2000 refund. "It'll take 'em ten years to figure it out," he predicted confidently. Messrs. Lapp, Mitchell, Barnum, and Crump chanted, in four-part harmony, "'We're Honest, If You Know What We Mean.'" And H. Milton Chase handed out cards reading "Deduct It Today—Tomorrow It May Be Illegal."

Wonderful organization, the LHBMA. I'd join it myself, except that the dues aren't deductible.

When Maury Wolohan celebrated his tenth anniversary as a San Francisco band leader, a newspaper interviewer asked, "And what have you had the most requests for?" " 'Where's the men's room?' " answered the maestro.

Old-time inmates of San Quentin Prison tell me they can never eat a pork chop without thinking of the pig that gave up its life so that men may die more painlessly.

Back in 1938, when the prison's gas chamber was installed, a pig was strapped into the chair and killed with cyanide fumes as the final test. The innocent little porker died without a squeal and the authorities, figuring what's good enough for a pig is good enough for a man, thereupon announced the gas chamber fit for human consumption.

One thing for sure. The chamber might be efficient, but it isn't kosher.

You've no doubt seen (and heard) those alarm-clock wrist watches. Well, Al Fischer, the San Francisco manufacturers' agent, took one with him on a fishing trip to Montana—and it went off while he was standing on the edge of a forty-foot cliff. Thinking it was a rattlesnake, he jumped over the cliff, and rolled all the way down to the river. Got pretty banged up, too, but you can't beat those watches. At the end of his fall, it was still buzzing merrily away. So he drowned it.

As the ancient tale would have it, Robert Louis Stevenson was lunching with a friend at the Poodle Dog, and telling him that San Francisco waiters never admit they don't have everything that's on the menu. "Why," smiled Stevenson, "they'll take your order for a slice of the moon, come back and tell you they're just out of it. Look, I'll show you."

Turning to the waiter, he ordered, "A double order of broiled behemoth, please."

"Rare or well done?" dead-panned the waiter.

"Well done," said R.L.S. with a wink at his friend. A few minutes later the waiter returned to announce, "We are out of the behemoth." Then he leaned over confidentially. "To tell the truth," he whispered, "we DO have some, but I wouldn't want to serve it to YOU, Mr. Stevenson. It isn't fresh."

Nothing ever changes in San Francisco—and if you don't believe it, have a look one day at a framed political poster on the wall of Cookie Picetti's bar on Kearny Street.

The poster concerns the 1913 race for police judge, and declares in big, black type, "Honesty and Decency Vs. the Tenderloin!" It then goes on to point out that whereas one candidate, William P. Caubu, has the support of all the respectable, God-fearing elements in town, his opponent, J. J. Sullivan, "is supported by the Tenderloin and red light districts."

Under the poster, you can read the results of the election: Caubu, 18,526. Sullivan, 28,259. And I'm surprised, too.

I thought Sullivan would do better than THAT.

60. REMEMBRANCE OF FLINGS PAST

"You are a foolish man," writes a reader, not at all inaccurately. "You write reams about an Old San Francisco that none of us ever knew, including yourself, probably. Kindly bear in mind that there are hundreds of thousands of newcomers to this area who don't give a damn about the past you keep prattling about" . . .

Well now, there is something to be said for that attitude. It's hard, forthright, practical. And, for all I know, it's a realistic summing-up of the attitude of the New San Franciscans, who came here—and are still coming—for any number of unromantic reasons: job opportunities, fed up with the Eastern climates, looking for a bridge to jump from, or whatever. I confess that I know very little about these newcomers and their tastes—and if their ladies like to come downtown in slacks and if their gentlemen prefer to wear sport shirts to restaurants, I'm sure only a hopeless fuddy-duddy could object. For this is the way things are in the age of the split-level barbecue-pitted mind, and I agree it makes precious little difference to them that the Pacific Union Club was once "Bonanza Jim" Flood's mansion, or that the White House Department Store was founded by a Frenchman who invented a chicken dish acclaimed from here to the classic eating places of Paris.

However, I'm a hopeless fuddy-duddy (see above). I am also a hopeless nostalcoholic—a disease that afflicts all San Franciscans sooner or later, and will strike the newcomers eventually. It comes from drinking of the past, and there is no escaping it in this city where it is always present. Damn and doom me for a reactionary if you will, but I still find a cable car a more cunning piece of design than a freeway built across the graves of houses that once knew laughter and tears.

It is true, Newcomer, that I remember things I never saw, but then, all San Franciscans are born with memories. I never attended the Midwinter Fair of '94, but when I pass the glassily

Victorian conservatory in Golden Gate Park, I can imagine the way it was, and see the bicycles coming in many-legged clusters down the Main Drive, and the ladies in their plumed hats, wasp-waisted and shy. I never saw the 1915 exposition, but when I stand below the Palace of Fine Arts, I can visualize its sister buildings ranged across the Marina, and the tiny mirrors of the Tower of Jewels aglow with a thousand fires, and Al Jolson and Sid Grauman and Harry Richman entertaining along the Midway. And can you pause alongside Lotta's Fountain at Third and Market without remembering exactly the way it was—even if you weren't there—on the night in 1910 when Tetrazzini sang "Last Rose of Summer" for the assembled 100,000? Of course you can't, if you're really a San Franciscan, for all this has been woven somehow into your fiber.

You are looking bored, Newcomer. You are worrying about the mortgage on your tract house, the tax rate, the next payment on your flip-wing car, where to go on Fourth of July weekend. These are nothing. You can worry about them ANYwhere. As a San Franciscan, you should have more important things to worry about.

For a start, worry about all the old buildings that are disappearing. You won't miss the Montgomery Block, felled for a garage? You should, for it was part of San Francisco from its earliest days, and without it, the city will never be the same again. Do not ask for whom the wall falls; it falls eventually on thee, Newcomer. A group of totally undistinguished buildings has been razed at Sutter and Stockton, likewise for a garage, and I will miss them, too—even the Philadelphia Coffee Shop, with its hamburgers forever sizzling and curling up in the front window. There is something eternally and infernally sad about a fallen building—especially one that has stood so long and housed so many and become such a familiar part of the scenery.

It disappears so fast, with hardly a whimper, under the relentless blows of the steel ball.

You won't miss the gingerbread monstrosities of the Western Addition? But they, too, were part of the warped roof of San Francisco: bulging bay windows glinting in the sun, wooden stairs leading to the past, peaked roofs totally unsuited for a TV aerial. They weren't good for much, agreed, except that they made a city look like San Francisco. When the gentle old buildings go, to be replaced by hard cubicles, the city changes and becomes harder, too—and this is not good for any of us, Newcomer.

The past: Does it really mean so much? Does it matter, now, that the Ferry Building was once the most important building in town; it will disappear, too, one of these days, and then a fresh batch of newcomers will wonder why YOU'RE so upset, Newcomer turned Old-timer. Is the city any the less because all the renowned characters have gone forever—from Emperor Norton and Oofty-Goofty on through Barney Ferguson and Tiny Armstrong? I think so. I think it's too bad that the city has grown so big and impersonal that nobody has time for the care and feeding of characters, be they bearded poets in search of the truth—whatever that is—or hopeless lunatics with a pathetic willingness to be laughed at. But then, as I said earlier, I'm a fuddy-duddy. When I hear a Chinese and a Texan in conversation, it's the Texan who sounds foreign to me.

"You are a foolish man," the reader wrote, and I plead guilty. People in love—especially people in love with a city's will-o'-the-wispish spirit—can't help looking foolish.

INDEX